# Black Elk

# FAITH AND CULTURES SERIES
An Orbis Series on Contextualizing Gospel and Church
General Editor: Robert J. Schreiter, C.PP.S.

The *Faith and Cultures Series* deals with questions that arise as Christian faith attempts to respond to its new global reality. For centuries Christianity and the church were identified with European cultures. Although the roots of Christian tradition lie deep in Semitic cultures and Africa, and although Asian influences on it are well documented, that original diversity was widely forgotten as the church took shape in the West.

Today, as the churches of the Americas, Asia, and Africa take their place alongside older churches of Mediterranean and North Atlantic cultures, they claim the right to express Christian faith in their own idioms, thought patterns, and cultures. To provide a forum for better understanding this process, the Orbis *Faith and Cultures Series* publishes books that illuminate the range of questions that arise from this global challenge.

Orbis and the *Faith and Cultures Series* General Editor invite the submission of manuscripts on relevant topics.

*FAITH AND CULTURES SERIES*

# Black Elk

## Colonialism and Lakota Catholicism

*Damian Costello*

ORBIS BOOKS

**Maryknoll, New York 10545**

Copyright © 2005 by Damian Costello.

Published by Orbis Books, Maryknoll, New York 10545-0308.
Manufactured in the United States of America.
Manuscript editing and typesetting by Joan Weber Laflamme.

**Library of Congress Cataloging-in-Publication Data**

Costello, Damian.
  Black Elk : colonialism and Lakota Catholicism / Damian Costello.
     p. cm. — (Faith and cultures series)
  Includes bibliographical references and index.
  ISBN 1-57075-580-9 (pbk.)
  1. Black Elk, 1863-1950. 2. Oglala Indians—Biography. 3. Oglala Indians—Religion.
4. Indian Catholics—Biography. I. Title.
  E99.O3B5353 2005
  978.004'975244'0092—dc22

                                                              2004023733

# Contents

# Acknowledgments

Many people have helped with this book. Without Jan Ullrich and his assistance with the Lakota language this book would not have been possible. William Portier, Sandra Yocum Mize, Anthony Smith, M. Therese Lysaught, Cecilia Moore, Brad Kallenberg, Katherine Whalen, and Christal Costello all read various stages of this project and provided invaluable advice.

I am grateful to Sr. Marie Therese Archambault, O.S.F, for her insightful comments and Michael F. Steltenkamp, S.J., for his comments and encouragement. Thanks especially to Susan Perry for her close attention to my many mistakes.

# Introduction

This story, the story of Black Elk (1863–1950), could have taken place almost anywhere on earth because it is a small part of a much greater story. By 1930, the story of colonialism had encompassed the entire world. This story began even before Columbus arrived in the Americas in 1492, as the nascent European nations had already extended their reach to other lands. But it was not until the beginning of the twentieth century that their grip tightened around the world. A few decades earlier the European nations had set their sights on Africa and, in a matter of years, had carved up the entire continent among themselves. The United States completed its quest to rule over the American West, completing the conquest of the Americas. The British Empire was so great that, indeed, the sun never set on it. And the last nations untouched by the Western powers, the highland peoples of Papua New Guinea, were discovered by plane and soon conquered. In the end, the colonial powers were everywhere.

In an eerily similar fashion, colonialism reordered the peoples of the world. The conquerors arrived and asserted their control by military force. Some nations were able to resist for years, even decades. But in the end the military power of the colonizers proved too great. Colonized peoples found themselves vassals of new political and economic systems with little or no control over their future. Colonial expansion disrupted or destroyed traditional economies as indigenous peoples were pushed to marginal land and robbed of their natural resources. Disease and poverty often followed such disruptions. The massive reordering of power and the destruction of traditional economics initiated complex cultural changes. Often the nations rebelled to overthrow their conquerors and drive them back across the sea, far enough away that even memories of the "New World" would fade. But the rebellions were futile in comparison, and defeat usually meant greater suffering. Often the only thing left was a battle site, a memorial to a rebellion, another permanent symbol among the peoples of the world of their final defeat at the hands of what became the Western powers. And in the midst of this, those who reordered the nations with violence brought news of the Messiah, the Prince of Peace.

There are countless stories within this large story. One story that could have taken place anywhere throughout the world of the nineteenth century occurred on a small tract of land in South Dakota, one of the small islands of land that remained of the Lakota nation. In Pre-Columbian times the Lakota inhabited the woodlands of middle America, bordered by the Missouri River to the west and the Great Lakes to the east.

Even before the Lakota encountered the American military, they had been touched by the wake of colonialism. In the sixteenth century the Iroquois in the New York area had obtained European weapons and begun an expansion westward. The Iroquois displaced the tribes of the Great Lakes regions, such as the Ojibwa, who in turn gradually pushed against the territory of the Dakota.[1] European and subsequent American colonial expansion exacerbated this ripple effect. Over the course of two centuries the Dakota people migrated west from the woodlands to the plains of the Midwest and became the Lakota. They separated into seven main bands: Oglala, Brule, Hunkpapa, Minneconjou, Blackfoot, Two Kettle, and Sans Arcs.[2] The Lakota acquired horses in 1750 and crossed the Missouri River in 1775. Through armed conflict, the Lakota pushed the Kiowa and Crow tribes out of the Black Hills of South Dakota, which then became the sacred center of the Lakota world.[3]

In response to the changes initiated by colonialism, the Lakota transformed their semi-sedentary woodland economy to a nomadic culture to match their new environment. This new economy was based on the buffalo, which provided all the necessities of life that were not obtained through trade. The buffalo hides themselves provided the currency for trade goods. The Lakota spent the summers in nomadic fashion, following the buffalo herds across the Plains, and wintered in the sheltered valleys of the Black Hills.

In the mid-nineteenth century Western expansionism arrived in full force. The forerunners of the American economy—colonists, prospectors, and traders—arrived in increasing numbers. They brought epidemics and liquor while they annexed Lakota land and undermined the Lakota economy. Their presence provoked armed conflict and the U.S. government waged intermittent war against the Lakota from 1855 to 1890, pursuing a policy of reservation confinement. Though the Lakota won great victories, such as the Battle of Little Bighorn, Western expansionism prevailed. Through coercion, deception, and the complete destruction of the buffalo herds, the U.S. government finally forced the Lakota to settle on seven separate reservations in the present-day states of North and South Dakota. The final blow came in 1890 at the small creek of Wounded Knee, where hundreds of Lakota were massacred by the U.S. army.

This story within the story of Western colonialism began in a small government office. It could have been almost any colonial administrative office in

---

[1] Guy Gibbon, *The Dakota and Lakota Nations* (Malden, Mass.: Blackwell, 2003), 3, 86-89; and Michael F. Steltenkamp, *Black Elk: Holy Man of the Oglala* (Norman: University of Oklahoma Press, 1993), 9-10. The Lakota subdivisions are the English names commonly found in historical sources. The Lakota names in the same order are Oglalas, Sicangus, Hunkpapas, Minneconjous, Sihasapas, Oohenunpas, Itzipcos. See Jeffrey Ostler, *The Plains Sioux and U.S. Colonialism from Lewis and Clark to Wounded Knee* (Cambridge: Cambridge University Press, 2004), 23.

[2] Clyde Holler, *Black Elk's Religion: The Sun Dance and Lakota Catholicism* (Syracuse, N.Y.: Syracuse University Press, 1995), xxv.

[3] Steltenkamp, *Black Elk*, 9–10.

Africa, Asia, the Pacific, or the Americas. The world was full of places like that, offices that administered the policies of Western governments that controlled the now colonized peoples. These offices were the places where the colonized had to go to receive permission to engage in what were previously seen as normal activities. Idle young males and old-timers also gathered there to fill the time once occupied by traditional cultural practices and economic activity, waiting for something to happen and looking for new opportunities for survival.

One such agency was in Pine Ridge, South Dakota, and the group gathered there was Lakota. One day in early 1930 an unfamiliar car approached the agency. A white man and his son exited the car and entered the agency. The man, who identified himself as John G. Neihardt, said he was looking for a Lakota elder to interview about the defeat of the Lakota at Wounded Knee. Neihardt, a poet, was writing an epic about America's westward expansion, a story that would culminate with the massacre of Wounded Knee, "symbolizing the completion of the white men's conquest of the New World."[4] When the agent could not immediately think of someone, he turned to the group of Lakota. After talking among themselves in their language, the men directed Neihardt to Nicholas Black Elk, who agreed to tell them his story.

So a year later, in the early summer of 1931, John Neihardt and his two daughters made the long drive from Branson, Missouri, to the Pine Ridge Reservation. Like most land that was left for colonized peoples, it was poor land. The land was locked in the beginning of a great drought. The rain had stopped, the crops and wild foods failed, and a plague of insects swarmed over the dusty Plains. The Great Depression had just begun, reducing the struggling reservation economy to ruins and the Lakota to poverty. In the words of Fools Crow:

> There was no rain at all, and nothing grew—not the gardens, not the wild fruits, not the crops in the fields. Every year it got worse. The grasshoppers came in swarms, the grass didn't grow, and tumbleweeds were everywhere. Always the wind blew, and the air was thick with dust. It got through everything, sifting into our homes and even our clothing. Most of our horses and cattle starved to death, and the poultry and the pigs shriveled up and died too.[5]

On the way, the Neihardts passed Wounded Knee Creek, site of the massacre that marked the end of the Lakota armed resistance and the final dominance of American colonialism. The massacre and the mass graves of forty years ago were present, although unmarked.

The car finally arrived at the barren, treeless hillside where the small, weathered cabin that housed the Black Elk family sat in the middle of brown grass.

---

[4] Raymond J. DeMallie, ed., *The Sixth Grandfather: Black Elk's Teachings Given to John G. Neihardt* (Lincoln: University of Nebraska Press, 1984), 26.

[5] Thomas E. Mails, *Fools Crow*, with Dallas Chief Eagle (Garden City, N.Y.: Doubleday, 1979), 145.

The family hosted the Neihardts for three weeks. The Neihardts were foreigners in this land. They did not speak the language or have any idea of how the people lived their lives in the new world of colonialism. Neihardt arrived, seeking the old world that had existed more than forty years before. Through an interpreter, Ben, who was Black Elk's son, Neihardt heard Black Elk's story.

Neihardt did find the end to his epic about the Western expansion. In his *Black Elk Speaks,* a beautiful story of a young holy man and the defeat of the Lakota, the outside world learned of Black Elk and the Lakota people, who had fought a tragic battle to stop the West, but in the end it was futile.[6]

But what Neihardt didn't realize was that this story didn't end with the final battle. Although the West had reordered the world, the Lakota and colonized nations across the world had survived. In their survival and struggle to face the future, the Lakota were different from the romanticized Plains warriors that Neihardt described. And this hidden part of the story, the survival of the Lakota and the message of the Messiah, holds the most important lesson for a world still ordered by Western colonialism.

    [6] John G. Neihardt, *Black Elk Speaks: Being the Life Story of a Holy Man of the Oglala Sioux / as Told to John G. Neihardt (Flaming Rainbow),* illustrated by Standing Bear (1932; repr., Lincoln: University of Nebraska Press, 2000).

# 1

# The Story of Black Elk

Black Elk's life spans the Lakota change from a Plains culture into a reservation culture. Black Elk was born into the Oglala Lakota in December of 1863, on the Powder River, probably within the borders of present-day Wyoming.[1] His father was a medicine man, a cousin of Crazy Horse. When he was nine years old, he had a great vision. One night, while settling down for camp, Black Elk heard a voice saying, "It is time, now they are calling you." The next day, while starting out on horseback, he collapsed with a great sickness. While lying in a tipi, he saw two men coming from the sky saying, "Hurry up, your grandfather is calling you." He was taken up to the clouds, where he visited the spirit world where his "grandfathers [were] having a council."[2]

During the course of his visit, the six grandfathers brought Black Elk to the different regions of the spirit world: the four directions, the cloud tipi of the six grandfathers, the black sacred road from west to east, the red sacred road from south to north, and the center of the earth. At the center of the nation's hoop the sacred tree was established. The six grandfathers also gave Black Elk two specific powers: the power to heal and the power to destroy.

> I remember that the grandfather of the west had given me a wooden cup of water and a bow and arrow and with this bow and arrow I was going to destroy the enemy with the power of the fearful road. With the wooden cup of water I was to save mankind.
>
> This water was clear and with it I was to raise a nation (like medicine).[3]

---

[1] Michael Steltenkamp argues that Neihardt records an incorrect birth date. The Holy Rosary Mission archives give the year 1866 as the year of Black Elk's birth, and his daughter Lucy corroborates this. In addition, Lucy claims that Black Elk was born in July and that December was the month of his baptism, or spiritual birthday (see Michael F. Steltenkamp, *Black Elk: Holy Man of the Oglala* [Norman: University of Oklahoma Press, 1993], 131, 136).

[2] Raymond J. DeMallie, ed., *The Sixth Grandfather: Black Elk's Teachings Given to John G. Neihardt* (Lincoln: University of Nebraska Press, 1984), 4, 111, 114, 115.

[3] Ibid., 119.

**"BLACK ELK AT THE CENTER OF THE WORLD," PAINTING BY STANDING BEAR,**
*JOHN G. NEIHARDT, PAPERS, c. 1858–1974, WESTERN HISTORICAL MANUSCRIPT*
*COLLECTION—COLUMBIA, MISSOURI.*

The vision of the six grandfathers changed Black Elk's life. The vision was a call to become a *wicasa wakan*, a "holy man."[4] This made Black Elk responsible for the survival and prosperity of his people on earth, for "a nation [Black Elk] shall create." Black Elk believed that he was "appointed by [his] vision to be an intercessor of [his] people with the spirit powers."[5] Black Elk was called to create a nation, bring his people on the sacred road into the sacred hoop, and make the sacred tree bloom by using the power he received from the six grand-fathers. Black Elk interpreted his life based on this message and continually tried to find the way that best corresponded to his vision.[6]

Black Elk grew up during the Lakota Wars. He witnessed the Battle of Little Bighorn and killed an American soldier at the age of thirteen. He was among the last of the Lakota to surrender, living for three years with Sitting Bull's band in Canada. After Sitting Bull surrendered in 1881, Black Elk settled on the Pine Ridge Indian Reservation, which became his home for the remainder of his life.

In 1886 Black Elk took the opportunity to travel with Buffalo Bill's Wild West Show with a two-year contract as a dancer. The show traveled to New York City in the winter of 1886 and then to London in the spring of 1887. Black Elk also visited France, Germany, and Italy with a show run by Mexican Joe. He had

---

[4] There are various spellings of Lakota words. I have tried to follow the pattern of the most recent scholarship, but some quotations will have variant spellings.

[5] DeMallie, *The Sixth Grandfather,* 293.

[6] Ibid., 126, 293.

gone to explore "the ways of the white men," and if any of these ways were better, he "would like to see my people live that way."[7]

In 1889 Black Elk returned to Pine Ridge. That fall, messengers brought the Lakota news of Wovoka the Messiah. Wovoka was a Paiute from Nevada who taught that by practicing the Ghost Dance the whites would disappear, the buffalo would return, and all would be like the olden times.[8] After a long period of cautious investigation, Black Elk joined the ghost dancers due to the strong connection between the imagery of his vision and the Ghost Dance. The Ghost Dance culminated in the Wounded Knee Massacre, in which American troops killed around 260 Lakota. In the days that followed, Black Elk participated in battles against the U.S. army. It became clear that military resistance was futile, and the Lakota finally surrendered to the U.S. government.[9]

Neihardt ended *Black Elk Speaks* with the image of an old Black Elk, broken and defeated, remembering Wounded Knee:

> I did not know then how much was ended. When I look back now from this high hill of my old age, I can still see the butchered women and children lying heaped and scattered all along the crooked gulch as plain as when I saw them with eyes still young. And I can see that something else died there in the bloody mud, and was buried in the blizzard. A people's dream died there. It was a beautiful dream.
>
> And I, to whom so great a vision was given in my youth—you see me now a pitiful old man who has done nothing, for the nation's hoop is broken and scattered. There is no center any longer, and the sacred tree is dead.[10]

This "death of a dream" passage became the most quoted passage and the enduring image of Black Elk.[11] Although originally published in 1932, it was not until the late 1960s and early 1970s that *Black Elk Speaks* gained national attention. The book's portrayal of Black Elk was uncritically accepted as America's archetypal Indian.[12] The growing counter-cultural movement adopted Black Elk as a figure of environmental concerns and New Age spirituality. The book also profoundly influenced the growing Pan Indian movement. The Native American intellectual Vine Deloria Jr. called *Black Elk Speaks* a "North American

---

[7] Ibid., 245.

[8] DeMallie, *The Sixth Grandfather*, 256–57.

[9] Laurie Collier Hillstrom, "Lakota," in *Gale Encyclopedia of Native American Tribes*, vol. 3, ed. Sharon Malinowski, Anna Sheets, Jeffrey Lehmer, and Melissa Walsh Day (Detroit: Gale, 1998), 291.

[10] John G. Neihardt, *Black Elk Speaks: Being the Life Story of a Holy Man of the Oglala Sioux / as Told to John G. Neihardt (Flaming Rainbow)*, illustrated by Standing Bear (1932; reprint, Lincoln: University of Nebraska Press, 2000), 276.

[11] DeMallie, *The Sixth Grandfather*, 55.

[12] Dale Stover, "A Post Colonial Reading of Black Elk," in *The Black Elk Reader*, ed. Clyde Holler (Syracuse, N.Y.: Syracuse University Press, 2000), 137.

bible of all tribes" in the introduction of the 1979 edition.[13] Native American activists, many of whom were raised in urban settings and knew little of their religious traditions, turned to *Black Elk Speaks* and *The Sacred Pipe*[14] as sources of cultural renewal.[15] And most significant for this study, *Black Elk Speaks* created the "essentialist Black Elk," which became the starting point for the academic study of Black Elk and Native American studies in general.

## UNCOVERING THE HISTORICAL BLACK ELK

In the 1980s two developments occurred in Black Elk scholarship that challenged Neihardt's portrayal of Black Elk. The first was the publication of Neihardt's interview transcripts by Raymond DeMallie in 1984. Neihardt's role in shaping the text came to the forefront. Scholars demonstrated that *Black Elk Speaks* was not an unbiased biography but an artistic interpretation of the interviews shaped by Neihardt's assumptions.[16] Social Darwinism shaped Neihardt's work, as he emphasized a tragic reading of Lakota history by addressing only pre-reservation life and the finality of Wounded Knee.[17] In addition, the narrative was shaped to emphasize the mythic nature of Black Elk's life and the otherworldly spiritual nature of his vision and life. The final aspect demonstrated Neihardt's cultural illiteracy: he misinterpreted the ritual despair of Lakota prayer and made Black Elk's concluding supplication the dominant theme of the book and the narrator's basis for self-understanding.[18]

In other words, Neihardt already had a story, the modern Western story of colonialism. According to DeMallie, Neihardt interpreted Black Elk through the lens of his great epic work, *A Cycle of the West*.[19] Neihardt wrote that the purpose was "to preserve the great race-mood of courage that was developed west of the Missouri River in the 19th century." DeMallie writes that "the corollary to the

---

[13]  Vine Deloria Jr., "Introduction," in *Black Elk Speaks*, ed. John G. Neihardt (Lincoln: University of Nebraska Press, 1979), xiii.

[14]  Joseph Epes Brown, *The Sacred Pipe: Black Elk's Account of the Seven Rites of the Oglala Sioux* (1953; repr., Norman: University of Oklahoma Press, 1989).

[15]  Amanda Porterfield, "Black Elk's Significance in American Culture," in *The Black Elk Reader*, ed. Clyde Holler (Syracuse, N.Y.: Syracuse University Press, 2000), 42.

[16]  DeMallie, *The Sixth Grandfather*, 62. DeMallie says that there was a fundamental misunderstanding concerning the purpose of the interview; Neihardt conceived the project to be the story of Black Elk's life, while Black Elk understood it to be a record of Lakota religion.

[17]  Stover, "A Post Colonial Reading of Black Elk," 131–35. Social Darwinism believed that the "European race" was most evolutionary advanced, and that non-Europeans, especially the "Vanishing Americans," would inevitably decline to extinction.

[18]  See Stover, "A Post-Colonial Reading of Black Elk."

[19]  John G. Neihardt, *A Cycle of the West: The Song of Three Friends, the Song of Hugh Glass, the Song of Jed Smith, the Song of the Indian Wars, the Song of the Messiah*, fiftieth anniv. ed. (Lincoln: University of Nebraska Press, 2002).

triumph of the 'westering white men' was the inevitable defeat of the Plains Indians. It is not that Neihardt misunderstood Black Elk, but that he perceived his life as embodying the whole tragic history of defeat whose emotional tone he was trying to convey in verse in *A Cycle*."[20] The most famous passage, the death of a dream quoted above, was not even spoken by Black Elk. Rather, it was a literary device composed by Neihardt.

The second development from 1980s scholarship focused on the omission from *Black Elk Speaks* of Black Elk's life after Wounded Knee. While working in Pine Ridge, Michael F. Steltenkamp, S.J., met and interviewed Black Elk's daughter Lucy Looks Twice. Lucy—along with the testimony of Lakota elders, including Frank Fools Crow, the noted Lakota holy man and ceremonial chief of the Lakota nation and also a nephew of Black Elk, and Jesuit records—filled in Black Elk's missing years. Unlike the defeated old man in *Black Elk Speaks*, an active, positive Black Elk emerged. During his reservation life he became a participant in the new economy and by reservation standards was successful. DeMallie calls him "one of the most successful old-time, uneducated Indians in adapting to the exigencies of life in the Pine Ridge Reservation."[21] Most surprising, Black Elk lived as a practicing Catholic for forty-six years, many of which he worked as a catechist.

Black Elk first encountered Christianity with the Wild West Show. While in Europe, Black Elk wrote a letter to the *Iapi Oaye* (the "Word Carrier"), a monthly newspaper, dated February 15, 1888, in Lakota, under the Indian Mission of the Presbyterian and Congregational Churches. He wrote of his trip and what he had learned of the white man's customs. "One custom is very good. Whoever believes in God will find good ways—that is what I mean."[22]

After Wounded Knee, Black Elk settled down and married Katie War Bonnet in 1892. For the next fourteen years Black Elk worked as a store clerk and a *yuwipi* healer.[23] It is likely that his wife became Catholic during this period. Also, his three sons were baptized: William and John in 1895, and Ben in 1899.[24] His role as a *yuwipi* man brought him into conflict with the Catholic presence on the reservation. John Lone Goose, who worked with Black Elk as a catechist, states:

I first met Nick around 1900—when I was a young boy and he was not a Catholic. I don't know what they call him in English, but in Indian they call him *yuwipi* man. Sam Kills Brave, he's a Catholic, lived close to him.

---

[20] DeMallie, *The Sixth Grandfather*, 56.

[21] Ibid., 57.

[22] Black Elk, letter to *Iapi Oaye* (Santee Agency, Nebraska), 17/3 (March 1888), 9, trans. Raymond J. DeMallie in collaboration with Vine V. Deloria Sr., cited in DeMallie, *The Sixth Grandfather*, 8.

[23] The fact that Black Elk earned part of his living as a *Yuwipi* healer is evidence that the government ban on Native religion was not completely effective.

[24] DeMallie, *The Sixth Grandfather*, 13.

And before Nick converted, Kills Brave would say, "Why don't you give up your *yuwipi* and join the Catholic church? You may think it's best, but the way I look at it, it isn't right for you to do the *yuwipi*." Kills Brave kept talking to him that way, and I guess Nick got those words in his mind. He said that after Kills Brave spoke to him, he wanted to change.[25]

Through family involvement and the urging of his friends, the context for Black Elk's conversion was set.

While the evidence indicates that Black Elk had been exposed to Christianity for some time, and even had reacted favorably to it, he did not feel the need to convert. In 1904 he went to administer the *yuwipi* to a small boy in a neighboring community. After being confronted by a Jesuit, Black Elk changed his life. His daughter Lucy Looks Twice tells the story:

> When he got there, he found the sick boy lying in a tent. So right away, he prepared to doctor him. My father took his shirt off, put tobacco offerings in the sacred place, and started pounding on his drum. He called on the spirits to heal the boy in a very strong action. Dogs were there and they were barking. My father was really singing away, beating his drum and using his rattle when along came one of the Blackrobes, Father Lindebner, Ate Ptecela (short father). At that same time the priests usually traveled by team and buggy throughout the reservation. That's what Ate Ptecela was driving.
>
> So he went into the tent and saw what my father was doing. Father Lindebner had already baptized the boy and had come to give him the last rites. Anyway, he took whatever my father had prepared on the ground and threw it all into the stove. He took the drum and rattle and threw them outside the tent. Then he took my father by the neck and said: "Satan, get out!" My father had been in the IOI [Wild West] show and knew a little English so he walked out. Ate Ptecela then administered the boy communion and the last rites. He also cleaned up the tent and prayed with the boy.
>
> After he got through, he came out and saw my father sitting there downhearted and lonely, as though he lost all his powers. Next thing Father Lindebner said was "come on and get in the buggy with me." My father was willing to go along and so he got in and the two of them went back to Holy Rosary Mission. . . . My father never talked [i.e., normally] about the incident but he felt it was Our Lord that appointed or selected him to do the work of the Blackrobes. You might think he was angry, but he wasn't bitter at all.
>
> He stayed at Holy Rosary two weeks preparing for baptism and at the end of those two weeks he wanted to be baptized. He gladly accepted the

---

[25] Steltenkamp, *Black Elk*, 32.

faith on December 6, 1904, which was the feast of St. Nicholas. So they called him Nicholas Black Elk.[26]

Whether coercion, a moving emotional experience, the culmination of inquiry, or a combination of all three was at the root of Black Elk's conversion, he dedicated himself to the communal life of Lakota Catholicism. He joined the St. Joseph Society, a Catholic men's society, and quickly impressed the Jesuits. Raymond DeMallie writes: "In recognition of his zeal and of his excellent memory for Scripture and the teachings of the church, the priests soon appointed him to the position of catechist, an office that usually paid a stipend of $5 per month."[27] In the vast expanses of the reservation, priests were able to celebrate mass in isolated communities only about once a month, and catechists fulfilled the role of contemporary permanent deacons. They held Sunday services, led the prayers and hymns, read the epistle and the gospel, baptized, prayed for the sick in the absence of a priest, and preached in the Lakota language.

During the early period of his work as a catechist, Black Elk wrote letters to the *Sinasapa Wocekiye Taeyanpaha*, or "Catholic Herald," a Lakota-language newspaper that started on the Devil's Lake Sioux Reservation in 1892. According to DeMallie, in these letters "Black Elk reported news from Manderson, told of his church activities, and exhorted his people to be faithful to the church."[28] These letters are also a record of Black Elk's understanding of the Catholic tradition.

The transition from a *yuwipi* man to a Catholic catechist was not without consequences. Black Elk lost an important source of income during the early reservation period. There were social ramifications as well. Lucy Looks Twice recalls the difficult time he had at the beginning of his conversion.

Once, after he retired, my father told me about the years when he first became a catechist. He said the people would scourge him with vicious

---

[26] Ibid., 33–35. Steltenkamp reports that Lucy "regarded [Black Elk's] conversion story as rather amusing and understood the event to be a great occurrence in her father's life. Moreover, she had difficulty understanding why [Steltenkamp] did not join with the others present, who laughed and smiled in hearing the incident." Steltenkamp also gives a compelling argument that this story was an oral construct designed to express the meaning of the conversion, rather than present actual occurrences. On page 36 Steltenkamp states: "In the opinion of several Manderson residents who heard Lucy's account of the story, liberties were taken in telling what probably transpired. Although no one claimed to speak with certitude, it was commonly assumed that medicine men such as Black Elk would not allow themselves to be pushed around in that fashion. Similarly, the priest had a reputation for being very kind and gentle and could hardly have been the ruffian portrayed" (36). Steltenkamp also cites Lucy as comparing her father's experience with Paul's conversion. It is possible that Lakota oral tradition embellished the story to emphasize the radical change in Black Elk's life.

[27] DeMallie, *The Sixth Grandfather*, 16.

[28] Ibid., 17

words and make fun of him, since he had been a *yuwipi* medicine man. The people made a lot of vicious talk concerning him, but he held on and did not go back to his old ways.[29]

According to Looks Twice, Black Elk adhered to his Catholic life despite social pressure.

Black Elk became a prominent evangelist. He used this skill to bring people into the Catholic church. One Jesuit attributed at least four hundred conversions to Black Elk's work as a catechist.[30] He was godfather for 113 people.

He went to other Native American tribes to preach and witness to the gospel. Black Elk spent a month on the Winnebago Reservation in Nebraska in 1908 and went on a short mission to the Sisseton Reservation in 1910. He also spent two months among the Arapaho on the Wind River Reservation. Black Elk had originally planned on staying a year but deemed the missions successful. In the July 1908 issue of the *Catholic Herald* Black Elk wrote: "Last February 20 we went to the Arapahoe tribe in Wyoming and preached the gospel. . . . We asked them to join the holy church of God. . . . With all our might we taught them about church work and now about half of the people believe."[31]

In 1926 the Jesuits built a catechist's house next to the church in Oglala, a community north of Holy Rosary Mission. Father Eugene Buechel asked Black Elk to live there and assume a pastor-like role. Black Elk's house became "a kind of mission center, with neighbors often gathering to pray and sing hymns."[32] He instructed the children, conducted services on Sundays when the priest was absent, visited the sick, and brought new people into the church with his preaching. Pat Red Elk, a young man when Black Elk was a catechist, remembers Black Elk's oratory skills: "Nick was a catechist, and when he got up he really preached. People sat there and just listened to him. They could picture what he was talking about."[33]

As he grew older, his official catechist duties waned, but he remained active in the Lakota Catholic community. Pat Red Elk remembers seeing him walking the two to three miles to Manderson to go to mass:

> In wintertime he didn't hardly come—too cold. But summertime, spring, and fall, he'd be walking. He was so old, so he got an early start and wouldn't catch a ride. And every Sunday, he'd join up with John Lone Goose right around where the store is now, and they'd say the rosary together. . . . By the time they got to church, they had said the whole thing.[34]

---

[29] Steltenkamp, *Black Elk*, 89.
[30] Ibid.
[31] DeMallie, *The Sixth Grandfather*, 18.
[32] Ibid., 26.
[33] Steltenkamp, *Black Elk*, 121.
[34] Ibid., 122.

On August 19, 1950, Black Elk received last rites for the fourth time and died at his home in Manderson, South Dakota. Shortly before his death Black Elk told his daughter Lucy: "I have a feeling when I die, some sign will be seen. Maybe God will show something. He will be merciful to me and have something shown which will tell of his mercy."[35] Both Lakota and Jesuits observed strange lights in sky the night of his wake.

William Siehr, a Jesuit brother at Holy Rosary Mission since 1938 remembers: The sky was just one bright illumination. I never saw anything so magnificent. I've seen a number of flashes of the northern lights here in the early days, but I never saw anything quite so intense as it was that night. . . . It was sort of a celebration. Old Nick had gone to his reward and left some sort of sign to the rest of us.

John Lone Goose remembers: Yes, I remember that night very well, and those bright stars. Everything looked miracle-like. I'm not the only one who saw it. Lots of people did. They were kind of afraid, and I was scared a little bit—but I knew it was God's will. I know God sent those beautiful objects to shine on that old missionary. Maybe the Holy Spirit shined upon him because he was such a holy man.[36]

## THE ESSENTIALIST BLACK ELK OR THE CATHOLIC BLACK ELK?

As a result of the new scholarship outsiders are left with two seemingly contradictory Black Elks. On the one hand, there is Neihardt's literary creation of the essentialist Black Elk: the proud, defiant, yet vanquished warrior embodying the Lakota defeat. On the other hand, there is the Black Elk described by the Lakota community and historical record: the Catholic agent actively and successfully participating in the new reservation economy. These two new themes created a dissonance in Black Elk studies that has yet to be overcome. In academic circles the image of the proud yet defeated warrior is incompatible with participation in a missionary church. The hotly contested issue became how to provide a consistent Black Elk who seems to outsiders to act very inconsistently. How can modern interpreters make sense of Black Elk's Catholicism?

The first group of academics accepts the historical validity of Neihardt's Black Elk and tries to reconcile the contradictory Catholic Black Elk with it. Raymond J. DeMallie was the first to provide an account of this problem. In his introduction to *The Sixth Grandfather*, DeMallie describes a Black Elk whose reservation years were divided into two stages. During the years after his conversion to Catholicism he lived as a sincere Catholic, repressing his involvement in Lakota

---

[35]  Ibid., 131–32.
[36]  Ibid., 134–35.

tradition. The second stage starts with his encounter with Neihardt. The interviews inspired Black Elk to return to a more active participation in Lakota ceremonial life, with a waning of interest in Catholicism.

Julian Rice offered the second interpretation of Black Elk in *Black Elk's Story: Distinguishing Its Lakota Purpose*. Rice portrays Black Elk as primarily committed to Lakota tradition. Black Elk may have participated in Catholicism as a means of survival but was not affected on the level of belief.

The third interpretation in this group is *Black Elk's Religion: The Sun Dance and Lakota Catholicism* by Clyde Holler. Holler describes Black Elk as a "dual participant." Black Elk participated in both Lakota tradition and Catholicism at the same time. Black Elk did not need to deny either one but could accept both as true, if distinct, ways of life.

All of the previous accounts accept Neihardt's Black Elk as normative and assume that Black Elk's Catholicism needs to be explained. In other words, the essentialist Black Elk is the real Black Elk and the Catholic Black Elk is the anomaly. They tend to assume that participation in Catholicism is an assault on Lakota identity. As a result, all of the previous attempts are unable to resolve the dissonance and provide a unified Black Elk. They describe a Black Elk who must (1) be insincere in his conversion to Catholicism, (2) deny Lakota tradition and identity, or (3) live two disparate lives at the same time. In other words, the pieces that the scholars are trying to put together do not fit; at some point they all contradict the Black Elk described by the Lakota sources.

Two other interpretations take the opposite perspective. *Black Elk: Holy Man of the Oglala* by Michael F. Steltenkamp and *Pipe, Bible, and Peyote among the Oglala Lakota* by Paul B. Steinmetz start with Lakota testimony as normative. Steltenkamp and Steinmetz—both Jesuit priests and trained anthropologists who worked on Pine Ridge Reservation—describe Black Elk as a primarily committed Catholic. According to both authors he did not deny Lakota tradition but reinterpreted it in light of Catholicism. Put more simply, the Catholic Black Elk is normative, and the essentialist Black Elk needs to be explained. This position has the advantage of starting with Lakota testimony. Moreover, starting with the Catholic Black Elk gives priority to the totality of Black Elk's life as opposed to three weeks in 1931.

Despite these advantages, Steltenkamp's and Steinmetz's interpretations face a number of problems. While starting with Lakota testimony and the historical fact of Black Elk's Catholicism, they have not given a conceptual account that satisfies modern academic categories. Modern Western assumptions about Native Americans and Christianity that strike most Americans as common sense make it impossible for Black Elk's conversion to be sincere. Christianity represents colonialism and a sell-out for Native Americans; missionaries are ruthless colonialists. As a result, those who argue for Black Elk's Catholicism are often dismissed as Catholic apologists who reflect a substantial bias.

As a result, Neihardt's image of the essentialist Black Elk remains normative in most areas of the academic world and popular culture. Those who are aware of Black Elk's life as a Catholic often dismiss it as unimportant or simply as an instrumental means of survival. The *Encyclopedia of North American Indians* provides a paradigmatic description of Black Elk:

> During Black Elk's young adulthood, missionaries attempted to convert the Oglala Lakotas to Christianity, and not many escaped the intense measures inflicted upon those who resisted. Black Elk was no exception. He attempted to understand Christianity after he was subjugated to it, and was baptized Nicholas Black Elk on December 6, 1904, at the Holy Rosary Mission near present-day Pine Ridge, South Dakota. Although the role of staunch Catholic was forced upon him, he played it well to appease his oppressors.[37]

The quotation makes clear that despite the new sources the essentialist Black Elk is still normative. But to invalidate the new sources the encyclopedia needed to make a number of assumptions. First, missionaries were oppressors who inflicted Christianity on the Lakota. Second, the Lakota resisted Christianity but were powerless to stop their subjugation. Finally, the Christian life of the Lakota was not sincere, but "played" or performed only to appease the oppressors. Christian life made no substantial impact on Black Elk or the Lakota. These three assumptions drive the Black Elk debate and make it possible to discard the Catholic Black Elk and protect the essentialist Black Elk's normative status.

## POSTCOLONIALISM AND POST-WESTERN CHRISTIANITY

Since Neihardt left Pine Ridge to write *Black Elk Speaks*, the powers of the world have changed. While the colonial system still dominates the world, colonized people have won a voice and written a new story of colonialism that challenges the assumptions that drive the Black Elk debate. These take the form of two different movements. First, colonized people have now entered the academy on their own terms, creating postcolonialism. Second, the majority of Christians now come from colonized nations, creating what Gambian theologian Lamin Sanneh calls post-Western Christianity. Both of these movements are making claims outrageous to modern Western academic ears, claims that completely undermine the assumptions made in the Black Elk debate. The five most important claims are the rejection of the noble savage, rejection of the binary cultural system, the focus on native agency, the anti-colonial uses of Christianity, and the formation of indigenous Christianity.

As we have already seen, Neihardt's portrayal of Black Elk is largely a literary creation. According to postcolonialism, Neihardt's essentialist Black Elk is not unique to interpreters of the Lakota or even Native American studies. The defiant warrior and his imagined cultural purity is a colonial phenomenon

---

[37] Frederick E. Hoxie, ed., "Black Elk," *Encyclopedia of North American Indians* (New York: Houghton Mifflin, 1996), 73.

created by Western outsiders. In 1978 Edward Said described this search for the pure native as Orientalism. In essence, the West creates the pure native by viewing only those cultural traits that differ from the West and essentializing them into the authentic native. R. S. Sugirtharajah describes the Orientalism that the essentialist Black Elk demonstrates:

> Behind the hunt for the authentic Indian or African lies the notion that, in spite of the long history of Western colonization, non-Western cultural productions should remain pure, original, truly indigenous and totally untainted by the impact of older and newer forms of colonialism.[38]

According to Sugirtharajah, characterizations of the authentic native like the essentialist Black Elk depend on an a priori assumption that despite long histories of colonialism, natives should not change.

The noble savage is a product of the broader Western phenomenon that Sugirtharajah calls the binary Western colonial paradigm. In this paradigm all members of a particular culture share similar traits by nature. Colonizers are universally and equally oppressors, while colonized people are universally and equally noble and just. In contrast, he describes the new postcolonial enterprise that emphasizes the complexity and agency of both colonists and colonizers in "critical exchanges and mutual transformation between the two."[39] Sugirtharajah explains:

> Postcolonialism does not mean that the colonized are innocent, generous and principled, whereas the former colonizers, and now the new colonizers, are all innately culpable, greedy and responsible for all social evils. Not only is such a notion an inverted form of colonialism but it also absolves the Third World elite from their patriarchal and vassalizing tendencies. The current postcolonialism tries to emphasize that this relationship between the ruler and the ruled is complex, full of cross-trading and mutual appropriation and confrontation.[40]

In this complex relationship competing groups existed within particular cultures during colonialism. For example, Hernando Cortés found many allies among the vassal tribes of the Aztecs during his conquest of Mexico. On the other side, Bartolomé de las Casas sided with Native Americans against the colonial practices of the Spanish.

Because of postcolonial writers' emphasis on complex relationships of mutual appropriation and confrontation, the history of Christianity in colonialism occupies a much more ambiguous—and often positive—role. Christianity is no

---

[38] R. S. Sugirtharajah, *The Bible and the Third World: Precolonial, Colonial and Postcolonial Encounters* (Cambridge: University of Cambridge Press, 2001), 279–80.
[39] Ibid., 250.
[40] Ibid.

longer interpreted as an exclusively destructive force but an area where both the colonized and the colonizer challenged the unmitigated forces of colonialism through the exercise of their agency.

Sugirtharajah describes how missionaries often occupied an ambivalent social location in a colonial situation. They participated in colonial practice and often shared the Western view of the essentialized native. However, missionary work put them into close communal contact with the colonized. This contact often influenced or required missionaries to engage in native cultural practices and language, which allowed them to see the colonized as human beings. Despite their inability to extract themselves completely from colonial practices, this contact also led missionaries to critique colonialism explicitly. Sugirtharajah calls this phenomenon "dissidence," where the Christian narrative is used by missionaries to challenge colonialism from within the system. As noted above, Las Casas challenged colonialism because of the Christian narrative and used the structures of the Catholic church to mitigate the destruction of Spanish colonialism.

Lamin Sanneh develops this point further in what I will call implicit dissidence. He claims that mission work not only led missionaries to critique colonialism explicitly, but that the very nature of Christian practices implicitly challenged Western colonialism. An example is the use of vernacular languages to translate Christian scripture.

That some missionaries wanted to dismantle the older indigenous cultural dispensation, to subvert the native genius, is without question, but employing mother tongues in their Scriptural translation is a tacit surrender to indigenous primacy, and complicates the arguments of Western cultural superiority.[41]

According to Sanneh, use of vernacular language to translate the biblical text ran counter to the colonial claim that Western culture is inherently superior. The missionary use of vernacular language, whether intentional or not, made the counter claim that indigenous culture is of equal value and able to carry a message of eternal significance.

We have seen how Western colonial narratives tend to portray colonized peoples solely as powerless victims. Whether they portray the spread of Christianity among colonized peoples as a positive or negative process, the primary agents are Westerners. Perhaps the most important aspect of postcolonialism and post-Western Christianity is their emphasis on the role of the colonized. Lamin Sanneh claims that the indigenous had the primary agency in the spread of Christianity. In his story of post-Western Christianity he gives priority to the response of indigenous people and local appropriation over missionary transmission. In essence, Sanneh reverses the story: post-Western Christianity is the

---

[41] Lamin Sanneh, *Encountering the West: Christianity and the Global Cultural Process* (Maryknoll, N.Y.: Orbis Books, 1993), 16–17.

story of *"indigenous discovery of Christianity* rather than the *Christian discovery of indigenous societies."*[42]

Postcolonial writers stress the importance that the indigenous discovery and appropriation of Christianity had for confronting colonialism. According to postcolonialists, colonized peoples are active agents that created the means to their survival. Natives appropriated new colonial cultural practices and transformed them to confront colonialism. Natives used this process in their encounter with the Christian narrative.

Irene S. Vernon demonstrates that this is not an isolated example by providing five examples of Native American postcolonial use of the Christian narrative.[43] She states: "In Native Christian writings, and through the lens of postcoloniality, Christianity is presented as a means of survival and as a vehicle of adaptation, reflecting considerable choices which do not necessarily imply rejection of Native spirituality or 'Indianness.'"[44] Viewed from postcolonialism, the use of the Christian narrative does not compromise identity but can be an exercise of Native Americans' agency in confronting colonialism.

The final theme from post-Western Christianity that challenges the assumptions of the Black Elk debate is what Sanneh calls "indigenous Christianity." The West, both Christian and non-Christian, has tended to assume that in order to be sincere Christians, colonized peoples must mimic uncritically the forms of Western Christianity. Any difference from modern Western Christianity is a deviation and delegitimates Native Christianity. Sanneh emphasizes that new cultural forms of Christianity do not negate the validity of indigenous Christianity. But even more important, he presses the claim that indigenous Christianity can be *more* faithful to the Christian narrative than the West and presents a lesson for the church and the "Western evasion of the Gospel." According to Sanneh, "the Modern West has demanded a retreat from any real and meaningful adherence to the central claims of historic Christianity."[45] Unlike the West, the newly evangelized do not have the culturally conditioned caveats that exempt them from the transformative demands of the gospel. As a result, they apply the gospel to the entirety of their culture. Thus, the evangelized preach the newly incarnated Christ to a church that has forgotten his message.

## RELOCATING THE BLACK ELK DEBATE

The claims of postcolonial and post-Western Christian writers undercut the assumptions that maintain the essentialist Black Elk and drive the Black Elk

---

[42] Lamin Sanneh, *Whose Religion Is Christianity? The Gospel beyond the West* (Grand Rapids, Mich.: Eerdmans, 2003), 10.

[43] Irene S. Vernon, "The Claiming of Christ: Native American Postcolonial Discourses," *Melus* (Summer 1999), 1–13. Available online.

[44] Ibid., 2.

[45] Lamin Sanneh, "Vincent Donovan's Discovery of Post-Western Christianity," in Vincent J. Donovan, *Christianity Rediscovered,* twenty-fifth anniv. ed. (Maryknoll, N.Y.: Orbis Books, 2003), 155.

debate. They show that the images of unambiguously evil missionaries, oppressive Christianity, essentialist natives, and insincere native Christians who falsely replicate Western Christianity are Western colonial assumptions. In contrast, postcolonial and post-Western writers replace these images with a Christianity that produces implicit and explicit dissidence, ambiguous missionaries, active native agents, and indigenous Christians who lived unique Christian forms arguably more faithful than Western forms of Christianity.

The previous postcolonial and post-Western Christian claims are not contradictory or even foreign to the Lakota. First, the very formation of Lakota Plains culture is a creative adaptation to the changes initiated by Western colonialism. The Lakota actively transformed their culture with the adoption of two Western innovations, the horse and the gun, in response to the demographic pressure that pushed the Lakota onto the Plains.

Second, as argued by Michael Steltenkamp, the holy man was one of the main agents in this cultural transformation. The adoption of new traditions, such as the Sun Dance, was a means of gaining new power to survive in new circumstances.

Third, the historical record demonstrates that the Lakota acted in ways described by postcolonial and post-Western writers such as Sugirtharajah and Sanneh. There were implicit and explicit dissidence, ambiguous missionaries, and active Lakota agents who appropriated Western technology and Christianity and formed them anew in unique and faithful ways.

Thus, the question of Black Elk is a question of stories of Western colonialism. To understand Black Elk properly, we must place his story within the story of Western colonialism as told by the colonized. Thus, the thesis of this book is that Black Elk's Catholicism as described by the Lakota community and historical record is normative and more easily understood by relocating it within the framework of postcolonialism and post-Western Christianity. These movements give outsiders the conceptual tools to understand the historical fact of Black Elk's Catholicism.

This book also argues that Neihardt's work is understandable in the context of postcolonialism and post-Western Christianity. Neihardt's biography of Black Elk is essentially accurate but problematic because of its location within the story of Western colonialism as told by modern America: the triumph of Manifest Destiny. While well intentioned, Neihardt was similar to most Europeans who interacted with colonized peoples during this time. He looked for what was different, what made the natives "other," pure creatures in juxtaposition with the Western world. While Neihardt's perspective is understandable, given his cultural context, it is not tenable in a contemporary academic context.

My project has two simultaneous thrusts. First, I will deconstruct the particular assumptions used to maintain the essentialist Black Elk. Using the categories of postcolonialism and post-Western Christianity, I will show that each particular assumption is in fact a product of the Western colonial narratives in the form of modern Western philosophical and secular American assumptions that scholars import into the sources. I demonstrate that they are foreign to Black Elk and the Lakota of his generation. Second, using the new story of colonialism, I will provide the conceptual categories that will allow for a unified understanding of Black Elk as a Lakota Catholic agent.

Chapter 2 challenges the unequivocal equation of missionaries and Christianity with colonialism. While agreeing that Catholic missionaries to the Lakota did not escape complicity with colonialism, I argue that they initiated dissident practices, the most important being the use of the Lakota language. The use of the Lakota language allowed the Lakota converts to discover Catholicism within the Lakota tradition, a process described by Sanneh that I will refer to as "the internal dynamic." Lakota language, along with the Catholic missionaries' commitments to the Christian narrative and the church, led the missionaries to challenge colonial practices implicitly and explicitly. As a result, the Lakota of Black Elk's generation would not directly equate Catholicism with colonialism or discover Catholicism in radical opposition to Lakota tradition.

In Chapter 3 I further examine the assumption that the essentialist native is the standard for Lakota identity. The main emphasis of the essentialist native is that Christianity is a sell-out of Lakota "identity." In order to make this claim, scholars often view Christianity as the primary—or only—source of the loss of Lakota culture and language. In addition, they assume that this is a critique universally voiced by Lakota people and a reason for insincere participation in Christian life. However, the voices of Lakota from Black Elk's generation formed in their own language show no indication that they share this assumption. Rather, they demonstrate Sanneh's internal dynamic: they remain secure in their Lakota identity while sincerely participating in Christianity. After examining the few historical sources that dismiss Black Elk's Catholic life in favor of the essentialist Black Elk, I argue that in light of the internal dynamic, there is no reason to doubt the Lakota community's description of the Lakota Catholic Black Elk.

Chapter 4 turns to the implications of the internal dynamic. Most scholars describe Lakota tradition and Christianity as two separate religious systems that do not influence each other. The Lakota must either erase one system or participate in one without "believing" in it. And, of course, Christianity is the system that is not believed. Thus, Black Elk can participate in Catholicism without compromising the essentialist Black Elk. Using the categories of Sanneh's internal dynamic, I show that Black Elk lived in one Lakota Catholic world by refashioning Lakota tradition in light of the Christian narrative. In addition, I argue that this process is a result of the natural dynamics of Lakota tradition and the role of the holy man.

Chapter 5 addresses the assumption that Black Elk's vision is separate from, or even directly opposed to, his Catholic life and conversion. This is maintained in direct contradiction to Black Elk's daughter, who claims that Black Elk's vision is in fact a Christian narrative. I hope to validate her claim using Lakota biblical texts to demonstrate that his vision directly correlates with and cannot be separated from Christian tradition. Going further, I hope to show that Black Elk's vision is, in fact, a Lakota version of Catholic salvation history. I am indebted to Lakota linguist Jan Ullrich for his assistance in the Lakota language.

If the previous chapters focused on the accuracy of the Lakota Catholic Black Elk, Chapter 6 explains the two reasons why Neihardt's essentialist Black Elk was an incorrect interpretation. First, Neihardt had a number of cultural limitations that prevented him from accurately interpreting Black Elk's discourse. Second, the economic context encouraged a process of cultural essentialization similar to the dynamics that create the third-world tourist industry today. I hope to show that while Black Elk spoke truthfully and Neihardt interpreted sincerely, the dynamics prevented Neihardt's accurate interpretation of his discourse, allowing for the creation of the essentialist Black Elk.

In the final chapter I offer an interpretation of the purpose and meaning of Black Elk's conversion. By understanding Black Elk's Catholicism in terms of the new story of colonialism, I argue that Catholicism offered the Lakota a new power to confront the new world initiated by Western colonialism. Following Steltenkamp, I demonstrate that Black Elk's conversion is in continuity with the role of the holy man. In response to the West's massive re-ordering of the world, Black Elk, like the Ras Tafari and William Apess, re-orders the West with the Christian story. In the end the tables are turned. The ultimate question of the Black Elk debate is not about Black Elk. Rather, it is Black Elk's question for America, the Christian nation set on a hill: why is America not Christian?

Regardless of the answer, the resulting Black Elk resolves the previous tensions. Black Elk is at once a sincere Catholic, a Lakota holy man, and an active agent fighting for survival in a colonial world. Most important, Black Elk is consistent with the testimony given by the Lakota community and the historical record.

# 2

# Missionaries, Colonialism, and the Internal Dynamic

*My people, the Sioux nation, want a Catholic missionary. They are good men. They are the best servants of the Great Spirit. They know our people well. Let them be agents of the Great Father. They will serve him as well as they serve the Great Spirit.*

—SITTING BULL, HUNKPAPA

The Black Elk debate is underwritten by the assumption that equates Christianity with colonial military force. Russell Means quotes fellow American Indian Movement (AIM) activist Clyde Bellecourt, who stated in a 1970 rally that "the missionaries came with the Bible in one hand and the sword in the other. They had the book and we had the land. Now we've got the book—and they've got the land."[1] Popular imagination and much scholarship conflate Christian missionaries with the forces of colonialism into one unrelenting, destructive force bent solely on the eradication of Native Americans and their culture. Gordon MacGregor writes in 1946 that missionaries tried to "eradicate all the native religion instead of using it as a frame of reference in which to introduce Christianity. . . . They tried to drive out indiscriminately Indian ways which had no relation to religion in the Indian mind."[2] Julian Rice continues this theme in 1991:

Black Elk's power at Pine Ridge was quickly being supplanted by Jesuit missionaries who were changing Lakota land from a visionary matrix to

---

[1] Russell Means, with Marvin J. Wolf, *Where White Men Fear to Tread: The Autobiography of Russell Means* (New York: St. Martin's Press, 1995), 160. (The quotation originated in Africa and often has been cited by Desmond Tutu and other African theologians.)

[2] Gordon MacGregor, *Warriors without Weapons* (Chicago: University of Chicago Press, 1946), 92.

an earthly training ground. During the fourteen year period after his return from Europe, the Jesuits had largely overwhelmed Lakota resistance so that most of the traditional healers like Black Elk had been converted or discredited.[3]

These portrayals often leave the impression that Christianity and missionaries are a major or primary source of colonialism.

However, this view of the rampaging missionary does not accurately describe early Catholic missionaries to the Lakota. In *Missionary Conquest*, Osage/Cherokee theologian George Tinker offers a better model for the Black Elk debate. In his thematic critique of missionary activity in general, missionaries are not the primary source of colonialism. Rather, Tinker argues that all missionaries were people of a cultural heritage of "pronounced cultural and intellectual superiority."[4] That is to say, missionaries may not have created colonialism, but all missionaries participated in colonial practices that contributed to the conquest of Native America. For Tinker, the result was that

> Christian missionaries—of all denominations working among American Indian nations—were partners in genocide. Unwittingly no doubt, and always with the best of intentions, nevertheless the missionaries were guilty of complicity in the destruction of Indian cultures and tribal structures—complicity in the devastating impoverishment and death of the people to whom they preached.[5]

Tinker defines cultural genocide as "the effective destruction of a people by systematically or systemically (intentionally or unintentionally in order to achieve other goals) destroying, eroding, or undermining the integrity of the culture and system of values that defines a people and gives them life."[6] According to Tinker, cultural genocide consists of four major interrelated vehicles: political, economic, religious, and social. The first aspect, political, is perhaps most obvious:

> The *political* aspects of cultural genocide involve the use of political means and political power, always with the threat of military or police intervention, by a more powerful political entity in order to control and subdue a weaker, culturally discrete entity. This constitutes genocide because it

---

[3] Julian Rice, *Black Elk's Story: Distinguishing Its Lakota Purpose* (Albuquerque: University of New Mexico Press, 1991), 1–2. This portrayal of missionaries is a corrective to some of the older romanticized missionary saints of Catholic hagiography. While this hagiography is not adequate to describe the Catholic missionaries to the Lakota, it has not been an influential assumption in the Black Elk debate.

[4] George E. Tinker, *Missionary Conquest: The Gospel and Native American Cultural Genocide* (Minneapolis: Fortress Press, 1993), 8.

[5] Ibid.

[6] Ibid., 6.

results in the loss not only of a people's political viability but also their cultural viability.[7]

The second theme, economic, is closely related to the political theme. Tinker writes that "the *economic* aspects of genocide involve using or allowing the economic systems, always with political and even military support, to manipulate and exploit another culturally discrete entity that is both politically and economically weaker."[8] Political groups often undermined Native American economic systems in the process of colonization, such as the destruction of the buffalo or the appropriation of land used for hunting and gathering.

Tinker describes the third aspect, religious, as "the overt attempt to destroy the spiritual solidarity of a people."[9] Tinker refers to the outlawing of Native American ceremonial forms and the use of military suppression. Most often, missionaries accepted claims of European superiority and belittled Native American religious traditions.

The fourth aspect of cultural genocide is social. Tinker writes, "The *social* aspects of cultural genocide involve a wide variety of social changes that have been imposed on Indian nations with disruptive consequences."[10] Tinker uses the example of the emphasis on the nuclear family and the displacement and destruction of larger social groupings.

While Tinker does not refer to the Black Elk debate, his model offers a good framework to assess the Catholic presence among the Lakota. In my examination of the Catholic missionaries to the Lakota, I adopt both Tinker's thematic model for cultural genocide and his conclusion that the missionaries ultimately failed to oppose colonialism unequivocally. The Catholic missionaries to the Lakota could not escape the accepted European attitudes toward colonized peoples in general and Native Americans in particular.

However, Tinker's conclusion is not the last word. The history of Lakota Catholicism indicates that Catholic missionaries were more than just complicit in colonialism. The following story from Fools Crow's autobiography makes this clear. Fools Crow, a nephew of Black Elk, recalls a vision quest that he undertook during the 1930s in order to discover the source of Lakota social and economic problems. Before Fools Crow left to pray, he visited an unnamed Jesuit:

> I decided to go again to Bear Butte to fast and pray. I would pray for an end to the liquor problem, for a change in the attitudes of the youth, for crops, wild fruits, and for the grass. . . . For some reason I couldn't pin down, I felt that before leaving I should go and talk to one of the Jesuit Black Robes I had gotten to know well. He was a fine man who seemed to understand the problems of our people. I did so, and when I told him what

---

[7]  Ibid.
[8]  Ibid., 7.
[9]  Ibid.
[10]  Ibid.

I had decided to do, the priest replied that he would pray for me while I was on the butte, but in his own way, according to the way of the Roman Catholic Church. I really appreciated this, and it gave me added comfort to know that one white man at least would be joining in sincere concern for a just and lasting change for the Sioux.[11]

In a sea of white apathy and hostility, the Jesuit understood the problems of the Lakota and wanted to see justice and change. In other words, Fools Crow does not present the Jesuit as someone complicit in colonialism. Rather, the Jesuit is someone who understands colonialism and at least partially separates himself from the colonial practices of other whites.

Fools Crow's story suggests that instead of analyzing the missionaries with the advantage of a modern perspective, they should be measured from the perspective of the Lakota from the early reservation period. During this period there was a whole spectrum of Anglo responses to Native Americans from government officials, traders, colonists, prospectors, and the military. According to Ross Alexander Enochs, the Lakota themselves made these distinctions, distinguishing among different "tribes" among the whites, such as the "Longknives" (U.S. military) and "Blackrobes" (Jesuits).[12] Consequently, a proper perspective for historical analysis should examine how missionaries differentiated themselves from these other groups of whites and how the Lakota would have perceived these differences.

The early Lakota reservation perspective converges with the postcolonial perspective described by Sugirtharajah and Sanneh's post-Western Christian perspective (outlined in the previous chapter). According to both Sugirtharajah and Sanneh, the West was not one undifferentiated body. Rather, the West was composed of many groups with competing interests. The two groups with the greatest colonial interest, government and business, had long been working to reorder the Lakota world both economically and politically.

Economically, Westward expansion was fueled by the pursuit of financial gain, whether through the fur trade, agriculture, or mineral wealth. In the case of the Lakota, the Black Hills were annexed for their gold deposits, and the Dawes Act was enacted to provide more reservation land for the colonists. In addition, the government and colonists consciously destroyed Lakota economic practices such as the buffalo hunt in order to undermine the ability of the Lakota to resist colonization.

Politically, the American government ceased to consider the Lakota an independent nation. Lakota autonomy was replaced with American political authority. This dependency was exacerbated by the lack of effective representation. Both diplomatic deception and military force were acceptable means to achieving American political domination. The pacification of the Lakota may have

---

[11] Thomas E. Mails, *Fools Crow: Wisdom and Power* (Tulsa, Okla.: Council Oak Books, 1991), 149.

[12] Ross Alexander Enochs, *The Jesuit Mission to the Lakota Sioux: Pastoral Theology and Ministry, 1886–1945* (Kansas City, Mo.: Sheed & Ward, 1996), 20.

been noble or tragic for competing American groups, but most agreed that it was necessary in order to colonize the American frontier.

Thus, the two main forces of Manifest Destiny encouraged further reordering of Lakota society and religion. To accommodate the new economy and political arrangement, Lakota social organizations needed to be broken into the smaller units of American society. Lakota bands and societies were now reduced to nuclear families composed of autonomous individuals.

This reordering required the destruction of the religious practices that reinforced the Lakota economic, political, and social order. The government repressed Lakota religious practices, such as the Sun Dance, *yuwipi,* and the Ghost Dance, with military force. Conversion to Christianity was seen as a method of "killing the Indian and saving the man." This policy promoted active destruction of all aspects of Lakota culture, including language, as a means of eliminating the "Indian problem."

Of course, there were individuals who worked in the government or colonists who deviated from the American state's Indian policy. However, American policy advocated cultural genocide (see Tinker's definition above) to accomplish an economic conquest of the American continent.

While Catholic missionaries to the Lakota may have participated in the vehicles of cultural genocide pursued by the American government and business groups, they were not the primary source of colonialism. Rather, the missionaries inherited a westward American expansion based on the colonial ideology of Manifest Destiny. Despite their failure to separate themselves completely from colonial ideology, missionaries to the Lakota were both implicitly and explicitly postcolonial dissident voices. First, even in their complicity, missionaries worked to mitigate the violence of the colonial project. Second, missionaries initiated cultural practices that by their very nature challenged colonial practices and claims; in the previous chapter this was termed implicit dissidence. Third, their social location and participation in implicit dissident practices often led them to explicit dissidence: the conscious critique of colonialism.

Missionaries did not differ from the standard colonial approach because they were a collection of better or nicer individuals.[13] Rather, their opposition appears to have stemmed from their commitment to the claims of the Christian narrative and Catholic political structure embodied in their vows of poverty, obedience, and nonviolence.[14] These commitments led to a different vision of

---

[13] Even though I will not argue that what distinguished missionaries from the standard colonial ideology stemmed from their being good individuals, there is evidence that they were. William K. Powers, an anthropologist who could never be accused of Christian bias, states that "it cannot be overemphasized that the Oglala have always maintained that the missionaries are basically good people" (William K. Powers, *Beyond the Vision: Essays on American Indian Culture* [Norman: University of Oklahoma Press, 1987], 104).

[14] Nonviolence is not an explicit vow that Jesuits take, but it is implicit in their commitment to imitate Christ. Jesuits also take a vow of chastity, which benefited the mission work. Enochs argues that "the Catholic priests' celibacy was one of the characteristics

both their presence among the Lakota and the future of the Lakota. As a result, this vision encouraged radically different practices in all of the four areas given by Tinker: political, economic, religious, and social. These practices were embodied in a hybrid manner that in many ways worked to counter the practices of colonialism. As a result, the Catholic missionaries to the Lakota occupied an ambiguous location—neither native nor white, neither colonizers nor colonized, neither completely guilty nor innocent. Black Elk's generation, as well as the American colonists, recognized this ambiguity.

My purpose here is not to provide an apology for Catholic missionaries. Rather, first, it is to show that because of their dissident missionary practices, the Lakota would not see Catholicism as radically opposed to Lakota tradition. This missionary approach allowed the Lakota to have an integral encounter with Catholicism in at least partial continuity with the Lakota tradition.

My second purpose has greater import for the question of Black Elk's conversion. I maintain that the Lakota Catholic Church during the early reservation period represented a hybrid "third way": neither American colonialism with a commitment to the complete destruction of the Lakota nor a Lakota separatist movement with a commitment to gain complete Lakota autonomy and an unchanging Lakota tradition. Rather, the Lakota Catholic Church was an area where both Lakota and Europeans worked to create a future that challenged colonialism and retained Lakota tradition. I maintain that this "third way" is a reason for Black Elk's conversion, a standard to which Black Elk's Christian discourse holds the colonial West, and a critique of missionary practices themselves.

I do not claim to offer a comprehensive history of Catholic missionaries; Ross Enochs has already provided that in *The Jesuit Mission to the Lakota Sioux*, and I am heavily indebted to his work. Rather, this chapter is designed to demonstrate the ways in which Catholic missionaries thematically differed from the colonial project.[15]

## LAKOTA LANGUAGE AND THE JESUIT MISSIONARIES

The history of Catholicism among the Lakota begins with the appearance of the Jesuit Father De Smet (1801–73), who traveled and evangelized among many tribes of the Plains and Rocky Mountains. He first encountered the Lakota at the Great Council at Ft. Laramie in 1851. At this gathering of over ten thousand

---

that distinguished the Blackrobes from other whites. Since they were unmarried, Catholic priests had the ability to travel far and fast without having to worry about the safety or prosperity of their families. Thus, celibacy was an ideal state for a missionary who had to travel with nomads" (Enochs, *The Jesuit Mission to the Lakota Sioux*, 20).

[15] This chapter may seem overly sympathetic or idealistic, but the reader must remember that I am emphasizing the differences between Catholic missionaries and other colonial groups. The more negative aspects of the Catholic missions are accounted for, if briefly, at the end of this chapter and the beginning of Chapter 4.

Native Americans, he baptized 239 Oglalas and 280 Brules.[16] Father De Smet, along with other wandering missionaries, made favorable impressions on many different groups of Native Americans. When the Yanktonnais Sioux, under Two Bears, were forced to settle on a reservation, Two Bears requested that Father De Smet settle with them and "bring other Black-robes."[17] After the U.S. government gave the Episcopalians the exclusive right to evangelize the Oglalas and Brules in 1876, many different chiefs, including Red Cloud, successfully lobbied for a Jesuit presence on the reservations.[18] As a result, St. Francis Mission was founded in 1886 on the Rosebud Reservation in South Dakota. A year later the Jesuits established the Holy Rosary Mission on the Pine Ridge Reservation.

From the outset the Jesuits adopted a number of practices that differed from the standard colonial ideology. The first practice had the most important and perhaps most unseen effect, because it encompassed aspects of all of Tinker's categories. The early Jesuits learned Lakota and made it the standard for Catholic life. Lakota language was used in preaching, prayer books, and scripture.[19]

By retaining the indigenous language for mission activity, the Jesuits asserted (perhaps unknowingly) a claim in opposition to colonial ideology. According to Sanneh, even if missionaries arrived with the intention of destroying indigenous culture, "employing mother tongues in their Scriptural translation is a tacit surrender to indigenous primacy, and complicates the arguments of Western cultural superiority."[20] In other words, the use of vernacular language to translate the biblical text ran counter to the colonial claim that Western culture is inherently superior. Sanneh expands on this counter-colonial aspect of mission activity:

> Missionaries accepted, or at any rate conceded implicitly, that mission was not the instrument for sifting the world into an identity of cultural likeness, with our diversities being pressed into a single mold in preparation for some millennial reckoning. So obedience to the gospel was distinguished from loyalty to a universal cultural paradigm. It seems to this

---

[16] Enochs, *The Jesuit Mission to the Lakota Sioux*, 10.

[17] Ibid., 19.

[18] Ibid. See also Clyde Holler, *Black Elk's Religion: The Sun Dance and Lakota Catholicism* (Syracuse, N.Y.: Syracuse University Press, 1995), 113. While not every Catholic missionary was a Jesuit, the majority were. They had the most influence during the early reservation period and were responsible for the approach to evangelization. The Jesuits were also the Catholic missionaries that Black Elk knew and worked with. For convenience, I use "Jesuits" to refer to the Catholic missionaries in this study.

[19] Ibid., 153. This is a marked difference from Protestant missionaries, who tended to view Native American religion as contrary to Christianity. Although Holler does not make the distinction between Catholics and Protestants, it is evident in the chapter "Sun Dance under Ban" (see Holler, *Black Elk's Religion*, 110–38).

[20] Lamin Sanneh, *Encountering the West: Christianity and the Global Cultural Process* (Maryknoll, N.Y.: Orbis Books, 1993), 16–17.

writer that everyone concerned with the religious motive of mission agreed that each people must be afforded the opportunity of discovering Christ in its own idiom, and against this view the advocates of universal Westernization were in necessary conflict.[21]

For Sanneh, even if missionaries saw their work only as a transmission of new thought and practices to indigenous peoples, their use of indigenous language implicitly legitimated the indigenous cultural framework as an idiom of equal value. By legitimating the indigenous idiom, missionaries committed themselves to much more than just a mode of verbal communication. Sanneh describes the totality of life that language encompasses:

> Indigenous cultures rely on language as a living resource of the whole system of life—social, economic, political, and personal. Without its language a society is certain not to survive, except perhaps as a client culture. The nonverbal systems of ritual and aesthetics are imaginative extensions of the verbal form. It is in language that we find a rich storehouse of the people's wisdom as proverbs, axioms, precepts, and sayings.[22]

According to Sanneh, the retention of language inherently preserves aspects of the very vehicles of cultural genocide used by Tinker: political, economic, social, and religious.

The Jesuits reinforced the use of indigenous language. This tended to legitimate the totality of indigenous culture and was reinforced by a second missionary practice that the Jesuits adopted: the use of the Lakota name for God, *Wakan Tanka*. Sanneh argues that the indigenous name for God had the same implications as language for the retention of indigenous culture:

> The name of God is basic to the structure of traditional societies. It forms and regulates agricultural rituals, territorial cults, agrarian festivals, the solar calendar, fertility ceremonies, mortuary observance, anniversary customs, units of generational measurement, naming rules, ethics, rank and status, gender relations, filial obligation, gift making, sacrificial offering, and so on. It's therefore hard to think of viable social systems without the name of God, but easy to envision societies that have become vulnerable because they lost the name or the sense of the transcendent. . . . The name of God contained ideas of personhood, economic life, and social/cultural identity; the name of God represented the indigenous theological advantage vis-à-vis missionary initiative. In that respect African religions as conveyers of the names of God were in relevant aspects anticipations of

---

[21] Lamin Sanneh, *Translating the Message: The Missionary Impact on Culture* (Maryknoll, N.Y.: Orbis Books, 1989), 170.
[22] Lamin Sanneh, *Whose Religion Is Christianity? The Gospel beyond the West* (Grand Rapids, Mich.: Eerdmans, 2003), 112.

Christianity; in the relevant cases Christian expansion and revival were limited to those societies that preserved the indigenous name for God. It suggests that theologically God had preceded the missionary in Africa, a fact that Bible translation clinched with decisive authority.[23]

According to Sanneh, the adoption of the indigenous name for God had wide-reaching effects. It legitimated previous religious practices and beliefs. But the name of God not only ordered a society's religious practices, it also contained a society's social and economic practices.

Because language and the name for God encompassed the entirety of indigenous culture, Sanneh argues that it encouraged indigenous conversions to operate in continuity with indigenous culture. Sanneh writes that "with the shift into native languages, the logic of religious conversion assumed an internal dynamic, with a sharp turn away from external direction and control."[24] Despite any missionary desire to control the direction of new converts (for example, their interpretation of Christian practices and their relation to indigenous culture), the indigenous have the advantage because they are masters of their own language. "Assuming that [the missionaries] do wish to control you, your best defense is the weapon they have as yet learned to grasp only imperfectly, namely, your language and all that goes with it."[25] Because missionaries rarely gain native fluency, the indigenous usually have the defense of their language.

In the Jesuit missions to the Lakota, the use of the Lakota language and the retention of the Lakota name for God affirmed Lakota culture in the new Catholic context. Regardless of intention, the Jesuits partially countered colonial ideology's program of cultural genocide in the four areas identified by Tinker. In addition, the use of Lakota language and the Lakota name for God prevented conversion from being a radical separation from Lakota tradition. In other words, these practices planted the seeds of Christianity *within* the Lakota tradition.

Ben Black Bear, a Lakota Catholic raised in the Lakota language, lends support to Sanneh's argument for the internal dynamic that indigenous language allows for conversion. In discussing the relation between Lakota tradition and Catholicism, Black Bear states that "one of the biggest blending points for me . . . [is] the Lakota language."[26] Because the traditional Lakota religious worldview is contained in the language, Catholic teachings done in Lakota inherently meld with that worldview.

So the sense of spirituality that I had—sort of meshed traditional Lakota spirituality with Christian/Catholic spirituality—was done in Lakota. . . . It helped me to see Catholicism in Lakota and then a lot of the traditional

---

[23]  Ibid., 31–32.

[24]  Ibid., 24.

[25]  Sanneh, *Translating the Message*, 173. Henceforth I will refer to this process as Sanneh's internal dynamic.

[26]  Marie Therese Archambault, O.S.F., ed., "Ben Black Bear, Jr.: A Lakota Deacon and a 'Radical Catholic' Tells His Own Story," *U.S. Catholic Historian* 16/2: 98.

teachings and beliefs that I learned in Lakota became a part of me. These were brought together by myself into my whole concept of how things ought to be. . . . There is a sense of [a] Catholic . . . sort of life style that meshes with traditional Lakota ways.[27]

According to Black Bear, Catholic and Lakota tradition compose one coherent worldview because they share the same language. Black Bear saw them together in one vision of how the world is.

Consequently, whether consciously or not, Jesuit missionaries made a radical commitment to Lakota tradition that was directly opposed to colonial ideology. The use of Lakota language had important implications not only for Lakota agency and tradition, but also for its important effects on the missionaries. First, it led some missionaries to study the Lakota language more formally, going beyond the typical need to learn Lakota and publish academic works. In 1939 Jesuit Father Eugene Buechel completed *A Grammar of Lakota*. He stated in the preface:

The Indians have again become race-conscious and want to speak the language of their forefathers. But who was to help them? In order to assist them, the author has prepared this book which may aid to preserve their speech for posterity.[28]

Buechel's work was not solely for missionary purposes but also intended to assist the Lakota in retaining their culture. Buechel collected tens of thousands of Lakota words and phrases. He was unable to finish a dictionary in his lifetime, but his work was collected and published by Paul Manhart, S.J., in 1970 as *A Dictionary of the Teton Dakota Sioux Language*.[29]

But more important for this study is the transformative effect that Lakota language use had on the missionaries' identity. Learning a new language is a long-term, time-consuming, messy process that, as Sanneh argues, requires a connection to the indigenous community: "If people are trying to learn your language, then they can hardly avoid striking up a relationship with you however much they might wish to dominate you."[30] According to Sanneh, learning language inherently challenges colonial assumptions of Western superiority, the intention to dominate, and promotes a relationship of equality.

At this point it becomes clear that by their use of the Lakota language Catholic missionaries deviated from colonial ideology. Missionary use of Lakota had a dual effect. The first effect was on the Lakota. The processes that Sanneh describes are an implicit acceptance of the Lakota tradition and worldview. This

---

[27] Ibid., 94.

[28] Ibid., 92. Missionaries, however, also collaborated with government language policies in schools that worked to promote English and denigrate native languages.

[29] Eugene Buechel, S.J., *A Dictionary of the Teton Sioux Language,*" ed. Paul Manhart, S.J. (Pine Ridge, S.D.: Red Cloud Indian School, 1970).

[30] Sanneh, *Translating the Message*, 173.

created the possibility that Christianity was not radically opposed to the Lakota tradition but had the opportunity to grow from within it. It also encouraged a leveling of the playing field, which limited missionary power and enhanced Lakota agency. The second effect was on the Jesuits. The use of the Lakota language initiated the Jesuits who learned it into the Lakota world and community. Sanneh argues that this initiation allowed a much more positive reading of indigenous tradition than the dominant colonial ideology.[31]

## RELIGIOUS CONFLICT AND CORRELATION

Government policy and the Jesuit missionary outlook converged in two areas: the Sun Dance and the *yuwipi* ceremony.[32] While the Jesuits were establishing their missions, the U.S. government banned the Sun Dance and native medicine practices such as the *yuwipi* from 1883 to 1934, arguing that the practice of native religion increased unrest and hostility.[33] Medicinal ceremonies were generally harder to control due to their private nature, but there was no official Sun Dance during this time period.[34] Violations to these policies resulted in the withholding of government rations or possible prison sentences.[35]

---

[31]  Ibid., 165.

[32]  Holler, *Black Elk's Religion*, 13; Arlene Hirschfelder and Paulette Mouline, eds., *Encyclopedia of Native American Religions* (New York: Facts on File, Inc., 2000), 289–92. The Sun Dance was the most important communal Lakota ritual. It was held annually in June or July, over the course of four days. A pole made from cottonwood was erected. Male dancers pierced their chest or back and tied the skewers to the pole with a long piece of leather. While dancing and staring at the sun, they strained against the ropes until they broke free. The dancers fasted from both food and water for the duration of the Sun Dance. The ceremony was conducted to pray for the renewal of the people and the earth, to give thanks, to protect the people, and for other religious purposes. The *yuwipi* was a ceremony in which spirits were said to be conjured and to give messages through lights, explosions, or animal noises. The *yuwipi* man combined psychological techniques with medicinal plants to produce an effective result. Some Lakota say that one of Black Elk's techniques was to create small explosions by placing small charges of gunpowder in a fire. This once backfired and caused an explosion that left him with permanent damage to his eyesight.

[33]  Colonial religious policy came about as an alternative to the earlier policy of eradication. These policies, called peace-policies, were the outcome of lobbying efforts by American Protestant reformers. They sought to mitigate the army's "war policy" of extermination, which had culminated in many unprovoked massacres, such as the Sand Creek Massacre of 1864 in Colorado. Through Christianization and acculturation, they "proposed to solve the Indian problem not by eliminating Indians . . . but by eliminating Indianness" (Holler, *Black Elk's Religion*, 113).

[34]  While there was no official Sun Dance, numerous sources attest to the continuation of hidden Sun Dance ceremonies.

[35]  Holler, *Black Elk's Religion*, 120. Sentences were ten days for the first offense and up to six months for the second offense.

The Jesuit critique of the two ceremonies was theological. They opposed the Sun Dance because of the severity of the piercing. This suffering was unnecessary because Christ suffered once for all and no further sacrifice was necessary for salvation.[36] The Jesuits also opposed the *yuwipi* for theological reasons. First, they considered it the conjuring of demonic spirits. Second, the Jesuits believed that the ceremony was deceptive. According to Enochs, they believed that the *yuwipi* men (who made up a small percentage of the Lakota population) "were deceptive charlatans who conspired to cheat the Lakotas out of their money and possessions."[37]

Despite agreement with the government on the Sun Dance and *yuwipi*, the Jesuits demonstrated a much more accepting view of Lakota religious traditions. Enochs argues that the Jesuits did not see Lakota culture as radically opposed to Catholicism. As a result, they saw their work as not trying to replace Lakota culture but rather "building on what was good in Lakota culture."[38]

This great openness to Lakota tradition allowed for a more positive view of the Sun Dance. In 1941 an American Jesuit, John Scott, who taught at Holy Rosary Mission School from 1939 to 1941, attended a Sun Dance and wrote about it in the *Jesuit Bulletin*. The government had lifted the ban on the Sun Dance but did not allow piercing. In the conclusion of the article Scott wrote:

Once more the brother Sioux could lift his head and walk erect, for he was a brother of Christ. Again he could dance and sing, but no longer would he have to scarify his body and subject himself to the long fast of the Sun Dance. This time it was a dance of joy for *wanka tanka* was his father.[39]

The missionary approach even allowed for what appears to be some opposition to government policy. One of the first priests to the Lakota, Francis Craft, who was of Mohawk descent,[40] may have participated in the Sun Dance. Clyde

---

[36]  Ibid., 123. There is some ambiguity as to what degree all Jesuits agreed with the theological critique of the Sun Dance (see the subsequent section on Father Francis Craft).

[37]  Enochs, *The Jesuit Mission to the Lakota Sioux,* 104. Jesuits did not restrict the use of traditional medicine. Father Dingmann wrote c. 1888: "We did not forbid them to use their herbs and roots and natural medicines but forbade them the use of all superstitious practices accompanying their conjuration" (ibid., 105).

[38]  Ibid., 104.

[39]  Ibid., 136.

[40]  Craft was born in 1852 in New York City to an Episcopal family. His paternal great-grandmother was a full-blooded daughter of a Mohawk chief. After studying to be a surgeon and fighting in three wars, he converted to Catholicism in the 1870s. After studying for the Jesuit order, he became a priest for the Diocese of Omaha, Nebraska, on March 24, 1883. Craft was an imposing figure, whom sculptor James Kelley described as "over six feet tall, and as keen, sinewy and powerful as a stag. . . . His voice was clear and cultivated, and his complexion weather-beaten" (Thomas W. Foley, *Father Francis M. Craft: Missionary to the Sioux* [Lincoln: University of Nebraska Press, 2002], 16).

Holler quotes a letter dated November 25, 1883, from R. H. Pratt, the superintendent of the Carlisle Indian School:

> I had it from a halfbreed [*sic*] at Rosebud who claimed to be an eyewitness that Father Craft solicited the privilege from the Indians of opening the ceremonies of the Sun Dance last summer with prayer, and from many sources, that he wore eagle feathers in his cap throughout these ceremonies, and entered into them to the full extent allowed by the Indians.[41]

In contrast to open hostility or mild indifference, Craft participated in the Sun Dance. Craft later compared the Sun Dance to the Eucharist.[42] In addition, he called the government-banned Ghost Dance "quite Catholic and even edifying."[43]

Thus, it appears that in contrast to the standard colonial ideology, the Jesuits were explicitly conscious of the importance of conserving and respecting Lakota tradition. Joseph Zimmerman, S.J., whom Lakota holy man Pete Catches calls "a saint who [*sic*] I pray to,"[44] worked among the Lakota from 1922 to 1954. Writing about the Jesuit tradition of adaptation Zimmerman states:

> The work of the missionary is spiritual. But in order to labor with the maximum efficiency, the missionary must know the customs of the people with whom he works. He must be acquainted with their background, their environment, and heritage. The Church has always emphasized that the missionary should adapt himself to the ways of thinking of his converts, should take what is good and noble in their way of life and preserve it not destroy it.[45]

According to Zimmerman, the missionary should adapt to the culture of the converts and work to preserve it. William Moore, a Jesuit scholastic at St. Francis Mission, wrote for *The Indian Sentinel* in 1939, echoing this approach to missionary work:

> The missionaries of St. Francis Mission on the Rosebud reservation, South Dakota, try to adapt their work to the Indian spirit. They are concerned

---

[41]    Holler, *Black Elk's Religion*, 123 ([*sic*] in Holler).

[42]    Foley, *Father Francis M. Craft*, 49. Craft saw numerous correlations between Lakota tradition and Catholicism, equating the seven Catholic sacraments with seven Lakota rites. This correlation is very similar to Black Elk's presentation of Lakota tradition in *The Sacred Pipe*, which we will examine in Chapter 4.

[43]    Ibid., 85.

[44]    Michael F. Steltenkamp, *Black Elk: Holy Man of the Oglala* (Norman: University of Oklahoma Press, 1993), 84 ([*sic*] in Steltenkamp).

[45]    Enochs, *The Jesuit Mission to the Lakota Sioux*, 148. The document has no recorded date. Enochs dates it to either the 1930s or 1940s.

about instilling the life of grace into the souls of their people, not about imposing alien customs upon a race which clings to its traditional ways.[46]

Moore makes clear that while laboring to spread the Christian message the Jesuits did not want to impose American culture or values.

Because of these perspectives and despite their criticism of the Sun Dance and *yuwipi*, the Jesuits maintained a more positive view of other aspects of Lakota religious ceremonies. Although not officially incorporated into the Catholic liturgy, the use of the Sacred Pipe was accepted and even participated in by Jesuits. At Standing Rock, Father Jerome Hunt permitted the Lakota to come to the altar to light their pipes from the candles during mass.[47] Weasel Bear, a Standing Rock Lakota, remembers the first masses at Fort Yates:

> I recall clearly how we old-time Indians acted when we first attended mass. It was our custom, while assembled in council, to sit on the ground in a circle and pass the pipe. To us, at the time, attendance at Mass was but another council where we came to hear a message for our benefit. So we came into the church and sat down on the floor, while one of the party filled a large, red-stoned pipe, lit it, and sent it around the circle.[48]

Jesuits also participated in the Lakota naming ceremony and the *hunka lowampi* ceremony, the ceremony in which people are made relatives of the Lakota. Concerning funeral rites, the Jesuits accepted the Lakota custom of wailing and also allowed the custom of placing the body on a raised platform. In addition, many Jesuits did anthropological work, such as recording Lakota stories.[49]

The Jesuit approach even translated into the explicit comparison of Lakota and Catholic tradition. Craft initiated an approach that viewed Lakota traditions as remarkably similar to and in continuity with Catholicism. Father Buechel[50] often worked with Black Elk, and Lucy Looks Twice remembers that they "would talk . . . about my father's visions . . . and the Sun Dance, and all the Indian

---

[46] Ibid., 149.

[47] Ibid., 138.

[48] Ibid., 138–39. The Sacred Pipe is a religious ceremony in which prayers of supplication and communion are combined in a ritual smoking of tobacco. It often precedes other Lakota ceremonies.

[49] Ibid., 137–40, 143, 113, 135–36. See also Ross Alexander Enochs, "Black Elk and the Jesuits," in *The Black Elk Reader*, ed. Clyde Holler (Syracuse, N.Y.: Syracuse University Press, 2000), 285.

[50] Eugene Buechel was born in Germany and spent most of his life working at the St. Francis Holy Rosary Missions. The Lakota named him Wanbli Sepa, or Black Eagle (Enochs, *The Jesuit Mission to the Lakota Sioux*, 91, 141). Buechel became an expert in the Lakota language; an aged informant described him as "the only man who ever spoke [Lakota] perfect" (Steltenkamp, *Black Elk*, 64).

ceremonies that my father said were connected to Christianity."[51] She also states that Buechel "accepted the Blessed Virgin as the same one who brought the pipe [White Buffalo Woman], and that was what we always thought."[52] In summary, Lakota tradition was explicitly connected to Catholicism.

## SOCIAL ORGANIZATION AND CATHOLICISM

The use of Lakota language and greater openness to Lakota traditions led the missionaries to commitments to Lakota societal organization. Rather than breaking Lakota society into autonomous individuals and nuclear families, the Jesuits initiated practices that preserved Lakota societal structures in the form of Catholic organizations. The most important were the St. Joseph and St. Mary's societies. Both Catholic men's and women's societies were founded around 1887. They became a strong part of Lakota life precisely because they were built upon the already existent Lakota organization of *okolakiciye*. These were smaller "voluntary" social groups within tribal bands during the pre-reservation era. The societies had specific roles and were of two basis types: dream societies and military or war societies.[53] Ben Black Bear says that because of communal practices, "Catholicism grew from within the Lakota way of life among my people."[54]

Within the *okolakiciye*, Christian holidays and feast days were celebrated. Like Lakota ceremonies, these feast days encouraged the traditional activities of gathering in a circle, communal meals, and communal religious ritual (now the mass). Christmas traditions of present-giving coincided with the Lakota *give-away*. Black Bear remembers that

> there were a lot of rules attached to these gatherings which were very traditional Lakota. As a child *I didn't make any distinction* . . . rules were rules and it didn't matter if they were Catholic or Indian or what. Later I began to realize that a lot of the rules were traditional practices carried into the Catholic practices.[55]

Again, Ben Black Bear exemplifies Sanneh's internal dynamic. Black Bear emphasizes that the communal Lakota Catholic practices created a world in which it was not natural to distinguish between Catholic and Lakota tradition. Catholicism and the Lakota world began to lose their distinct boundaries.

---

[51]    Steltenkamp, *Black Elk*, 102.

[52]    Ibid., 107.

[53]    Archambault, "Ben Black Bear, Jr.," 104. Archambault notes: "The strategy of societies in the Lakota world served many purposes: organizational and economic and most importantly, they provide a sense a belonging, individual achievement and recognition. . . . The societies open a stage of individual achievement which was not at the expense of the whole *toshpiya*, kinship group, band or lager tribal gathering" (104).

[54]    Enochs, *The Jesuit Mission to the Lakota Sioux*, 91.

[55]    Archambault, "Ben Black Bear, Jr.," 92.

The effect of the Jesuit use of Lakota societies was not strictly limited to religious factors. Marie Therese Archambault argues that this "shrewd missionary tactic" not only promoted an integral Lakota Catholicism, but it also challenged government colonial policy.[56] Government policy attempted to reduce the Lakota to individual families with private property, what it described as "civilizing" the Lakota. In contrast to this policy, the Jesuits "encountered and related to the people through the familiar structure of the societies, used their language, and did all this within the social framework and setting of 'meeting.'"[57] In other words, the Jesuits' religious work legitimated the traditional Lakota social framework, the very structure that government policy explicitly worked to deconstruct.

Unlike other colonial groups, the Jesuits attempted to develop Lakota leadership within the church. The most successful was the catechist system in which Black Elk participated. According to Enochs, from 1900 to 1940 each mission maintained a staff of about ten Lakota catechists.[58] There was limited success with Lakota nuns. Although they tried to develop a native clergy, the Jesuits were largely unsuccessful.

As a result, Jesuit activity in the social aspect of culture had two important characteristics. First, it resisted colonial ideology's attempt to reduce the Lakota to autonomous individuals and nuclear families. Second, as Black Bear demonstrates, this continuity with traditional Lakota social organization provided an opportunity for Catholic ideas and practices to grow within Lakota tradition.

## HUMANITY OF THE LAKOTA
## AND THE "LAKOTIZATION" OF THE MISSIONARIES

The very decision to go to the Lakota was based on at least a partial commitment to the humanity of the Lakota, an idea, based on the gospel, that ran contrary to the racism of colonial ideology. The Jesuit involvement in the Lakota community, traditions, and language reinforced this commitment and even encouraged two unique phenomena. First, missionaries began to voice the idea that Native American culture and faculties were superior to those of whites. Second, the Jesuits began to reassess their social location and embrace a kind of Lakota identity.

The earliest missionary, De Smet, challenged the accepted portrayal of Native Americans as savages. In describing the mission to the Flathead, he stated, "I have often asked myself: 'Is it these people whom the civilized nations dare to call by the name of savages?'"[59] In a letter to his provincial written in 1866, he further challenged the standard stereotype of unintelligent, blood-thirsty, debased savages:

---

[56] Ibid., 103.

[57] Ibid., 105.

[58] Enochs, *The Jesuit Mission to the Lakota Sioux*, 74.

[59] Ibid., 9.

[Native Americans] show order in their national government, order and dignity in the management of their domestic affairs, zeal in what they believe to be their religious duties, sagacity and shrewdness in their dealings and often a display of reasoning powers far above the medium of uneducated white men or Europeans. Their religion, as a system, is far superior to that of the inhabitants of Hindostan or Japan. . . . All these Indians believe in the existence of a Great Spirit, the creator of all things, and this appears to be an inherent inborn idea.[60]

According to De Smet, Native American religion and politics were well-developed cultural institutions. More important, De Smet claims that their intelligence was "far above the medium of uneducated white men." In a clear deviation from colonial ideology, De Smet asserted the superiority of Native American faculties. Father Craft makes a similar claim of superiority in speaking of Native American sisters:

Indian faith is pretty solid. I wish I had more of it. Perhaps only full-bloods can have it in its fullness. The fact is Indians are logical. "God has said it: therefore it is so," they say, and they can't understand why the white man won't see it in the same light.[61]

Craft asserts that the faith of Native Americans is deeper and stronger than that of Anglos and those of mixed Native American ancestry, which Craft considers himself to be. In the course of his work, Craft has not only ascribed equal status to Native Americans but attributed them with possessing greater virtue than Anglos.

It may be tempting to dismiss these portrayals of the Lakota as another manifestation of the idea of the "noble savage" held at the time by many Europeans. This comparison is inaccurate because the image of the noble savage originated with people who had no contact with Native Americans. The Jesuit views come from years of close communal contact and involvement with the Lakota.

A contemporary example from a "nonreligious" perspective may shed some light on this point. Jared Diamond, a professor of physiology at UCLA and a Pulitzer Prize–winning author, voices an almost identical view of the intelligence of "indigenous" peoples. Diamond has spent over three decades researching bird evolution in Papua New Guinea. While recognizing that New Guineans tend to perform poorly at tasks that Westerners have been trained to perform since childhood and thus look less intelligent when they enter Western environments, Diamond counters the theory that non-Western peoples naturally have lower IQs:

My perspective on this controversy comes from 33 years of working with New Guineans in their own intact societies. From the very beginning of

---

[60]   Ibid., 18.
[61]   Foley, *Father Francis M. Craft*, 104.

my work with New Guineans, they impressed me as being on the average more intelligent, more alert, more expressive, and more interested in things and people around them than the average European or American is.[62]

While Diamond theorizes why New Guineans might tend to be more intelligent,[63] he recognizes that the source of his opinion is over three decades of immersion into New Guinea society: "I am constantly aware of how stupid I look to New Guineans when I'm with them in the jungle, displaying my incompetence at simple tasks (such as following a jungle trail or erecting a shelter) at which New Guineans have been trained since childhood and I have not."[64] Attempting to live like New Guineans emphasizes to Diamond both their skill at difficult tasks and his own limitations.

Diamond indicates that the determining issue is which individuals are in what world. In dominant colonial structures, indigenous individuals are incorporated into the Western world and consequently seem stupid or inferior. However, the missionary and scientific projects incorporate Western individuals into indigenous worlds. As a result, Western individuals are forced to recognize the complexity of the indigenous worlds, the intelligence of indigenous people, and their own limited ability to learn and function in the indigenous world.

Like Diamond, the issue for the Jesuits was not only the intelligence of Lakota individuals; it was about the nature of the whole Lakota world. In addition to arguing for the superiority of Lakota intelligence and virtue, they argued that the Lakota cultural world was *at least* equal to the American cultural world. Cursing, alcohol abuse, and divorce were practices that the Jesuits attributed to the influence of American culture.[65] In a sermon he gave in 1912, Buechel said,

---

[62] Jared Diamond, *Guns, Germs, and Steel: The Fates of Human Societies* (New York: W. W. Norton, 1999, 1997), 20.

[63] The second reason that Diamond gives—the passive nature of contemporary Western entertainment and its large role in Western culture—is not relevant to our study. However, the first reason is relevant to the Lakota situation. Diamond asserts that mortality in European populations was largely due to epidemic diseases. As a result, natural selection was based on the development of resistance to disease, a process primarily based on chance and having little to do with intelligence. In contrast, hunter-gatherers' mortality stemmed largely from murder, tribal warfare, accidents, and problems in procuring food. According to Diamond, more intelligent people would be more likely to survive these sources of mortality and reproduce (see ibid., 20–22).

[64] Ibid., 20. This realization led Diamond to challenge the lingering colonial assumptions of European racial superiority used to explain greater Western technology and to answer his question, "Why did New Guineans wind up technologically primitive, despite what I believe to be their superior intelligence?" His one sentence answer, and summary of *Guns, Germs, and Steel: The Fates of Human Societies*, reads as follows: "History followed different courses for different peoples because of differences among peoples' environments, not because of biological differences among peoples themselves" (22, 23).

[65] Enochs, *The Jesuit Mission to the Lakota Sioux*, 126.

"Although I know that the Indians have no word for cursing, they will learn it from the wicked white people."[66] Father Charles Weisenhorn, S.J., wrote to his provincial in 1920:

> No people is more generous than the Indian. . . . Reference to good courtesy and good breeding may seem strange in speaking of these so-called savages. Yet I oftentimes feel that the white man may learn a lesson from them in this respect. For the Indians have a rigid etiquette of their own, which is carefully observed, especially among the older generation, who have not been spoiled by too much contact with Protestantism and the van of white civilization. There is no such thing as a curse in the Indian language; the Red man will never take the name of God in vain, unless he has heard the expression from such as are civilized.[67]

This generosity, from which the white man could learn, was equated with holiness. Father Sialm continued this theme in a *Sentinel* article from 1938:

> It is an old Indian custom for the more prosperous to share with the needy. "We Indians," they say, "are not like the white people. We feed our visitors when we have something to eat in our house." Back of this I seem to hear One who says "give and it shall be given to you."[68]

According to the Jesuits, Lakota tradition was not just neutral or equal to Anglo American culture but in many ways *superior* to Anglo American culture. Missionary work was not just the addition of the gospel but the retention of Lakota virtue. John Scott, S.J., wrote in 1940 that "thanks to the untiring efforts of the Black robe, the faith of the Sioux in *Wakan Tanka*, the Great Spirit, was not crushed under the wheels of the invading *Wasichu* [white people]."[69] Despite the missionaries' connection to colonial practices, missionary work was often done in conscious opposition to the destructive forces of colonialism.

This immersion in Lakota life and culture led not only to a generally more positive portrayal of the humanity of the Lakota and the value of the Lakota cultural world, but it also caused the Jesuits to modify their identity and blurred their social location. Jesuits were obviously not Lakota, but they were also not like the other white men who lived on the reservation. Most of the early Jesuits learned to speak Lakota. Just as they gave the Lakota Christian names at baptism, the Lakota gave most Jesuits Lakota names in formal ceremonies.[70] They were often made relatives of Lakota families and the tribe, and they also served as intermediaries between the Lakota and the government, especially in times of war.

---

66   Ibid.
67   Ibid., 126–27.
68   Ibid., 127.
69   Ibid., 99.
70   Ibid., 141.

Father De Smet exhibited this tendency. General Stanley wrote in 1868 that De Smet was "the only man for whom I have ever seen Indians evince a real affection. They say in their simple tongue and open language, that he is the only white man who has not a forked tongue."[71] J. A. Hearns, the government agent at the Grand River Agency in South Dakota, stated in a report to the Commissioner of Indian Affairs in 1870 that "Rev. Father De Smet visited the [Sioux] in July, they were all very well pleased to see him. . . . The Indians think he is the one white man that does not lie to them."[72]

Later, Father Craft also embodied this approach. When he arrived, he was viewed as the "fulfillment of their fallen patriarch's [Chief Spotted Tail] prophetic request."[73] Spotted Tail's family made Craft a relative in the *hunkapi* rite and gave him the name Wabli chica aglahpaya (The Eagle Covers Its Young, or Hovering Eagle). Craft wrote about his adoption:

> When the Sicangus [Brules] adopted me into their nation & into the family of their head chief, & made me their chief in his place, it seemed to be the will of God that I should be a savage among the savages to win the savages to Christ. . . . The Son of God made Himself to save man, & bore the consequences to the death, & still does not desert them. I have become an Indian to save the Indians, & I should stand by the consequences of my act to the end.[74]

For Craft, being a missionary required a change in identity. This shift of identity was even recognized in Lakota memory. Daniel Madlon, O.S.B., recorded Bull Man's description of Craft in a speech at the Catholic Sioux Congress of 1936:

> One day [fifty years ago, the Lakotas] had a visitor, Father Craft. He looked like an Indian. He was riding a horse and he had a feather in his hat. He came during the [sun] dance. Afterwards he spoke to the big chief, Spotted Tail, and told him he had respect for the Indians because they worshipped the Great Spirit.[75]

This blurring of ethnic division and social location was recognized by the Jesuits. In describing Father Buechel after his death, Joseph Karol said:

> Through his missionary work, his language study, and his artifact collection, Father Buechel gradually so identified himself with the Sioux that he unconsciously got into the habit of saying, "We Indians would say or do that this way."[76]

---

[71]  Ibid., 19–20.

[72]  Ibid., 20.

[73]  Foley, *Father Francis M. Craft*, 17.

[74]  Enochs, *The Jesuit Mission to the Lakota Sioux*, 28.

[75]  Ibid., 100.

[76]  Ibid., 124.

Thus, the missionary practices described by Sanneh not only pushed the Jesuits to recognize the humanity of the Lakota and the value of the Lakota world, but they also began to push the very identity of the Jesuits into the Lakota world over and against the white world. And apparently the Lakota also made a conscious distinction between the Jesuits and other whites. In 1940 Father Goll wrote that "up to this day the Indians refrain from calling a Catholic priest a white man."[77]

There is evidence that other whites noticed this. While the government and business institutions attempted to use missionaries for their own ends, it was recognized that the missionaries did not share their goals. An anonymous contributor to the *Daily Inter-Ocean* in 1891 stated:

> I have a ranch in this country [Dakotas], and go a good deal among them, and have been at Pine Ridge a good many times this winter, and know that the Catholic priests are worse enemies to the Government than old Sitting Bull was. . . . Father Jutz . . . doesn't believe in the Government or anything else, except to increase the power and influence of his Church. . . . The priests hate the Government, and we who live out here have good reason to believe that they put up the Indians to make war so as to get the commissioners and every one else in trouble, and then say that the Catholics are the only ones who have any influence and are the only friends of the Indian.[78]

According to the editorial, the missionaries' primary allegiance was to the church, and as a result they were enemies of the state. While this may be hyperbole, this observation indicates that allegiance to the church was inherently at odds with the colonial commitments of the settlers and the American government.

## ECONOMIC FACTORS

We have already seen how the government and business groups worked to convert the Lakota into a sedentary society based on an agricultural economy.

---

[77] Ibid., 124.

[78] Foley, *Father Francis M. Craft*, 96. Ironically, history remembers Father Jutz for his care for the wounded and his work for peace. In the aftermath of Wounded Knee the Lakota burned government buildings and the homes of white settlers in retaliation for the massacre. Despite the threat of violence, Father Jutz and the nuns stayed in Holy Rosary Mission and cared for their students, fed the refugees that arrived, and tended to the wounded (Sister Mary Claudia Duratschek, O.S.B., *Crusading along Sioux Trails* [St. Meinrad, Ind.: The Grail Press, 1947], 204). The next day the Lakota sought to continue the battle. According to Mails, "close to 5,000 alarmed and angry Sioux had left Pine Ridge and gathered at a place 15 miles away. For an instant they were ready to fight once more and die in an effort to drive out the detested white man. Thanks though to one white man they trusted, the Jesuit priest named Father Jutz, they were talked into returning to Pine Ridge, and on January 1, 1891, the threat of Sioux armed resistance came to an end" (Mails, *Fools Crow* [1979], 24).

In *Missionary Conquest*, George Tinker uses the figure of the Jesuit missionary De Smet to argue that the missionaries were complicit in this program in two ways. First, missionaries saw this economic conversion as necessary or at least beneficial for any Native American conversion to Christianity.[79] Second, traders and colonists often used the missionaries as tools to facilitate the economic conversion of the Native Americans in order to benefit colonial financial interests.

In Tinker's perspective, then, missionaries were complicit in colonialism. While this is true, missionaries' involvement in economics differed from that of other colonial groups in important ways. Missionary involvement in the Lakota community and the blurring of identity, along with their vow of poverty, meant that the Jesuits did not work among the Lakota for financial gain. Rather, their view of economics was based on the survival of the Lakota. Enochs describes how the early Jesuits made the new economy a priority in Catholic life. In response to the trauma of adapting to a new economy, "the Jesuits sought to integrate the Lakotas into the South Dakota economy, and help them find a new religious significance."[80] Elizabeth Grobsmith indicates this in her study of the Lakota on the Rosebud Reservation. She states that Christian churches in general were

> the only group continuously offering aid and hope during a period of rapid economic change. . . . The Indian people recognized that those missionaries were not themselves to blame for the changes; on the contrary, their sympathetic assistance was deeply appreciated and still is to this day.[81]

Even if the massive disruption of the Lakota economy was coming about because of the economic interests of the American government and the financial gain of business groups, missionaries did work to mitigate the ensuing Lakota poverty.

A particular example is the Jesuit response to alcohol. Historically, the alcohol trade had a dual benefit for traders: an immediate profit from the trade and the added benefit of addiction with the addicts' impaired ability to negotiate and trade. Missionaries gained no benefit at all from the liquor trade. De Smet attributed many of the problems in native society to Anglos, "whites who, guided by the insatiable thirst for sordid gain, endeavor to corrupt [the Native Americans] and encourage them by their example."[82] According to De Smet, the Anglos consciously manipulated and corrupted Native American society through the liquor trade.

This hostility to the liquor trade and its negative effect on the Lakota became an embodied part of Lakota Catholic life. At the Catholic Sioux congresses the Lakota established temperance societies and made pledges to abstain from

---

[79]   Tinker, *Missionary Conquest*, 76.
[80]   Enochs, *The Jesuit Mission to the Lakota Sioux*, 36.
[81]   Elizabeth S. Grobsmith, *Lakota of the Rosebud: A Contemporary Ethnography* (New York: Holt, Rinehart & Winston, 1981), 82.
[82]   Enochs, *The Jesuit Mission to the Lakota Sioux*, 9.

drinking any alcohol.[83] The earliest known written rules for the St. Joseph Society required that members abstain from the use of intoxicants.[84]

Another example came from the Dawes Sioux Bill of 1888. This bill established a commission to purchase eleven million acres of Sioux land at fifty cents an acre.[85] While the commission urged Father Craft to induce the Lakota to support the deal, he responded that his orders were to stay away from government business "unless in special cases where they could do great good for the Indians."[86] He later participated, after it was apparent that Cheyenne River and Pine Ridge were already signing the agreement, and "the best they could hope for was to hold off for better terms."[87] According to Craft, his involvement was not to facilitate government interests but to benefit the Lakota.

Consequently, the differences between the Jesuits and other colonial groups in economic involvement with the Lakota were not insignificant. The denial of personal economic gain and their location within the Lakota community encouraged the Jesuits to work for the economic survival of the Lakota. While other groups—traders, colonists, and the government—continued to pursue policies that made it more difficult for the Lakota to participate in the American economy, the Jesuits worked to involve the Lakota in the American economy and survive the poverty caused by colonial policies. Jesuit economic involvement continued even after the Lakota's economic usefulness (for the fur trade and further appropriation of their land) was spent.

## POLITICAL AMBIGUITY

Of equal if not more significance was the Jesuits' political activity. As noted above, the U.S. government commonly used violence to assert its sovereignty over the Native American tribes. Catholic missionaries to the Lakota never personally used violence and usually worked for peace between the government and the tribes. However, using De Smet as an example, Tinker argues that the missionary work for peace at least partially facilitated American westward expansion. Tinker quotes a letter from De Smet to a German prince who was interested in establishing a German settlement in the territory of modern Wyoming:

A colony established in such a neighborhood, and against the will of the numerous warlike tribes in the vicinity of those mountains, would run

---

[83]   Ibid., 64.

[84]   "St. Joseph Society, Organization Rules, January 1917," transcribed by Paul I. Manhart, S.J., in *The Crossing of Two Roads: Being Catholic and Native in the United States*, ed. Marie Therese Archambault, Mark G. Thiel, and Christopher Vecsey (Maryknoll, N.Y.: Orbis Books, 2003), 123.

[85]   Foley, *Father Francis M. Craft*, 67.

[86]   Ibid., 67.

[87]   Ibid., 69.

great dangers and meet heavy obstacles. The influence of religion alone can prepare these parts for such a transformation. The threats and promises of colonists, their guns and sabres, would never effect what can be accomplished by the peaceful word of the Blackgown and the sight of the humanizing sign of cross.[88]

Tinker interprets De Smet's missionary work as a means of effecting a more peaceful expansion of the American population. In other words, the political motivation of the Jesuits was the same as that of other colonial groups.

While one aspect of De Smet's work for peace may have been to facilitate American expansion, there is clear evidence that his work for peace was primarily for the survival of Native Americans. According to John J. Killoren, S.J., De Smet feared that armed rebellion would lead to the total destruction of Native America.[89] De Smet wrote in 1857 to the Flathead Confederation:

I know the case of the Indians is a hard one indeed. Many injustices and cruelties are committed against them; in many instances they are deprived of their just rights. But war, on their part can be no remedy in their favor, as the whole Indian history of this country fully shows. I daily beseech at the altar of God His holy protection over them—to guard them against bad counselors and advisors who may drag them along in wars against the whites. For these will end, at last, in the total destruction and ruin of the unhappy warring tribes.[90]

Here De Smet stakes out a position very different from that of most colonial groups who accepted the extermination of Native Americans as a necessary or the easiest means of conquering the American continent. Instead, De Smet was committed to rejecting violence to gain the survival of the Native American tribes. De Smet's Jesuit vow and its implicit rejection of violence in his own life reinforces this pragmatic decision.

This rejection of violence translated into numerous attempts at great personal risk to find nonviolent solutions to conflict and effect peace. In 1868 Sitting Bull, a chief of the Hunkpapa, then at war with the U.S. government, declared that he would no longer negotiate with whites. De Smet sent a scout to Sitting Bull with a gift of tobacco, and he allowed De Smet to enter the camp. According to Enochs, "the scouts told De Smet that Sitting Bull would have killed any other white man who tried to enter their camp at that time."[91]

De Smet did not work for peace only in negotiations between the U.S. military and the Native Americans; rather, peace was a universal standard that he

---

[88]   Tinker, *Missionary Conquest*, 86–87.

[89]   John J. Killoren, S.J., *"Come Blackrobe": De Smet and the Indian Tragedy* (Norman: University of Oklahoma Press, 1994), 222.

[90]   Cited in ibid.

[91]   Enochs, *The Jesuit Mission to the Lakota Sioux*, 16.

held for all peoples. According to Enochs, De Smet critiqued the tendency in Native American culture to see revenge as a virtue. He denounced a "battle" where the Sioux waited for the Omaha men to go hunting and then slaughtered the women and children and performed a scalp dance.[92] De Smet embodied this criticism by working for peace among tribes, and he often initiated negotiations between traditional enemies. In 1839 he worked a peace deal between the Yankton Sioux and the Potawatomi.[93] De Smet also berated the Sioux for attacking the Crow in 1849.[94] Peace was not just a colonial tool but an outcome of his commitment to the gospel and his view of Native Americans as children of God and potential members of the church.

As a result, the commitment of De Smet and the other Jesuits to nonviolence and the humanity of the Lakota moved them to challenge the violence of American colonial expansion. While not absolving the missionaries of their involvement in colonialism, their work for peace and for the survival of the Lakota was morally superior to the extermination policy of the Western expansionists. And most important for this study, from an early Lakota reservation perspective, those who worked for peace, like De Smet, were viewed more positively than those who killed.

## EXPLICIT DISSIDENCE

All of these implicit dissident practices—use of Lakota language, involvement in Lakota culture and community, differing economic motivation and political commitments, recognition of the humanity of the Lakota—contributed to explicit dissidence. In other words, despite the Jesuits' inability to extract themselves completely from colonial practices, they nonetheless explicitly critiqued colonialism. In a letter from Fort Benton, Montana, dated June 10, 1866, De Smet identified American colonialism as the source of the Lakota Wars:

> The grievances of the [Lakota] Indians against the whites are very numerous, and the vengeances which they on their side provoke are often most cruel and frightful. Nevertheless, one is compelled to admit that they are less guilty than the whites.
>
> The payment of their annuities, for the millions of acres of land that they have ceded to the Government, [is] often overlooked or deferred, though they are the Indian's only means of support. . . . The terms of the treaties are often transgressed, and the Indians overwhelmed with injuries and insults. Woe to them, if they resist the unjust and wicked aggressors, for then they are driven out or massacred like wild beasts, without pity, or

---

[92]  Ibid., 17.
[93]  Ibid., 5–6.
[94]  Ibid., 10.

the least remorse, or any thought that the killing of a savage comes under the head of murder.[95]

According to De Smet, even though the Sioux were not innocent of violence, it was the Americans who were responsible for initiating the conflict through deception and theft. For De Smet, the resulting massacre was nothing less than murder.

Over twenty years later, Father Craft repeated the same theme. Father Craft wrote in 1888 that "every single trouble I had was started, not by Indians, but by whites of the Agency."[96] In a letter to *Irish World* in August of 1890, he described this in harsher terms:

> These numerous tribes have almost entirely disappeared. In the territory claimed by the United States less than three hundred thousand now remain. What has become of them? Europeans, ignorant of the former and our later policy toward the Indians, very naturally suppose that, like the former barbarians of Europe, they still exist, no longer as savages, but as a civilized people, or have mingled with the white settlers of the country. We know too well that this is not the case. Though we might well desire to forget facts disgraceful to us, history, with cold, truthful, merciless justice, brings them before us, and makes us see that all "Indian Policy" has always been a policy of extermination, and it remains so today. Government civilization of the remnant of the tribes is merely an excuse for the existence of the Indian Department, with its officials and salaries, that politicians and not Indians may live.[97]

Though the United States may wish to ignore the truth, Craft argues that the U.S. Indian policy was genocidal and unjust. In writing about the cause of Wounded Knee, he stated:

> Just as the tree can be traced from its smallest branches to its root, just so all this Indian trouble can be traced through its phases to its true cause, *starvation, abject misery, and despair*, the cause of which is the outrageous conduct of the Indian Department for many years.[98]

Far from being the fault of the Lakota, the cause of rebellion was the suffering brought about by the injustice of U.S. government policy.

---

[95] Killoren, *"Come Blackrobe,"* 277–78. Enochs provides the date and a continuation of the quotation: "Nine times out of ten, the provocations come from the latter [white colonists]—that is to say, from the scum of civilization, who bring to them the lowest and grossest vices, and none of the virtues, of civilized men" (Enochs, *The Jesuit Mission to the Lakota Sioux*, 17).

[96] Foley, *Father Francis M. Craft*, 18.

[97] Ibid., 83.

[98] Ibid., 86.

While certainly not the equivalent of the extensive dissidence of the Spanish Dominican Bartolomé de Las Casas to the practices of the Latin American colonizers in the sixteenth century, these examples demonstrate that the implicit dissident practices the Jesuits adopted encouraged them to reject explicitly the dominant American colonial story. However limited, they were able to adopt the perspective of the Lakota.

## EVALUATION: FORGING A THIRD WAY

While Tinker makes a convincing case that missionaries are not beyond critique for participating in colonialism, the evidence examined in this chapter demonstrates that the Jesuits did deviate from the standard colonial ideology. Compared to military, government, political, and colonist interactions with the Lakota, the Jesuits demonstrated the most radically open responses to the Lakota people and traditions. Sitting Bull, the famous Hunkpapa leader and one of the last Lakota to surrender to the U.S. government, makes this clear:

> My people, the Sioux nation, want a Catholic missionary. They are good men. They are the best servants of the Great Spirit. They know our people well. Let them be agents of the Great Father. They will serve him as well as they serve the Great Spirit.[99]

Given the choice, the Lakota of the late 1800s would have preferred never to have encountered the white world or to be affected by American colonialism. However, given the reality, Sitting Bull stated that the Catholic missionaries were the best people from among the non-Lakota.

The evidence presented above indicates that the Catholic missionaries were more than "better people." Something about what Sitting Bull calls "serving the Great Spirit" is inherently anti-colonial. The Jesuit vows of poverty, obedience, and nonviolence came out of the Christian narrative and produced different practices than the commitments of colonial ideology. Nonviolence encouraged the Jesuits to work against government violence and for peace. Their rejection of economic gain led to at least a partial rejection of colonial economic manipulation of the Lakota. Their commitment to the equality of all humanity led to at least a partial acceptance of Lakota culture and social structure. All of these principles contributed to the "Lakotization" of the Jesuits. In other words, even if the Jesuits encountered the Lakota with the same prejudices of other colonial groups, their commitments to the gospel and the church—the servanthood of the Great Spirit—limited and reshaped their colonial prejudices and practices.

The evidence also indicates that the commitment to "serve God" described more than just the character of the Jesuits; it described something about the whole body of the church. Unlike colonial America, racism was not the final

---

[99]    Duratschek, *Crusading along Sioux Trails*, 26–27.

answer. Catholicism was a universal faith for "people of all nations." Father Buechel said in a sermon given in 1907: "Again we see not only old and young people in heaven but also different nations. The color of the face and the strange language do not make a difference with God, if they only love God and serve him."[100]

Even MacGregor, cited in the beginning of the chapter for his anti-Christian bias, admits that the Lakota "accepted Christianity because it was the one part of the white man's life in which the Indian was accepted as equal."[101] While true equality remained elusive, Christianity was a means for challenging the racism of colonial ideology.

As a result, the early Lakota Catholic Church is something of a "third way," similar to a third way advocated by the postcolonial writer Edouard Glissant from Martinique:

> We must return to the point from which we started. Diversion is not a useful ploy unless it is nourished by reversion: not a return to the longing for origins, to some immutable state of Being, but a return to the point of entanglement, from which we were forcefully turned away; that is where we must ultimately put to work the forces of creolization, or perish.[102]

According to Glissant, a return to precolonial cultural purity was not possible. In the face of colonialism, engagement, and appropriation, creolization was the only option for survival. Father Craft, the first Catholic missionary to the Rosebud Reservation, described his work in similar terms:

> The time surely has come when they must decide between giving up Indian ways, & adopting civilized habits, or perishing miserably. The Church does not condemn what is either good or indifferent, & when at Rosebud I told them that, though their customs required for their integrity the freedom of the old life, & must necessarily deteriorate when brought into contact, with civilizations, still I would not condemn them in toto, but would encourage what was good, as long as it remained so.[103]

According to Craft, colonialism is a reality that the Lakota cannot escape. However, this does not mean a total abandonment of Lakota culture. The work of the church is to forge this third way that allows the Lakota people to survive and to retain their Lakota world.

This is not to suggest that the Jesuits were consciously or even unconsciously postcolonial theorists. There are important distinctions between the positions of

---

[100]   Enochs, *The Jesuit Mission to the Lakota Sioux*, 121.

[101]   MacGregor, *Warriors without Weapons*, 92.

[102]   Edouard Glissant, "The Known, the Uncertain," in *Caribbean Discourse: Selected Essays*, trans. with an introduction by J. Michael Dash (Charlottesville: University of Virginia Press, 1989), 26.

[103]   Enochs, *The Jesuit Mission to the Lakota Sioux*, 28.

Glissant and Craft, particularly on control of the process of creolization. As we will see in Chapter 4, the Jesuits never fully relinquished control or allowed for full Lakota agency. Despite these Jesuit failings, I am suggesting that the Jesuits' commitments to the Christian story and the church forced them into positions that resembled Glissant's postcolonial emphasis on creolization. These positions allowed the Lakota Catholic Church to become something of a hybrid body in which both Lakota and Europeans worked to create a future that challenged colonialism and retained Lakota tradition.

Certainly, the Jesuit approach will strike many contemporary commentators as imperialistic, and they are not without justification. The fact remains that missionaries could not separate themselves from colonial practices. Even worse, the more radical approach of the early Jesuits was lost in later generations. By the 1930s most Jesuits no longer learned Lakota.[104] Mission schools enforced government repression of the Lakota language. An indigenous clergy did not develop. The window for developing a true third way closed.

But this window was open for people of Black Elk's generation. Given the context of the early reservation period, the Lakota would not have had reason to dismiss Catholicism as radically evil or the primary source of colonialism. Rather, the third way that emerged during the early reservation period would have allowed for what Sanneh describes as the "indigenous discovery of Christianity." That the third way allowed the Lakota to discover Christianity is not surprising, since the Lakota had already been discovering it in the Ghost Dance.[105]

As a result, it is possible to conclude that Catholic missionaries to the Lakota were not the primary source of colonialism. Because Catholicism offered a different vision than colonial ideology, the Jesuits worked at least partially to mitigate the "devastating impoverishment and death" that Tinker says was the result of cultural genocide. This Catholic vision encouraged missionaries to initiate alternative practices embodied in community that challenged colonial practices. This vision is also a standard against which to judge missionaries' failings and the church's part in closing the window to an integral Lakota Catholicism.

---

[104]  Ibid., 95.

[105]  Steltenkamp argues that "the Ghost Dance can essentially be regarded as a transitional doctrine that gave way to the different forms of mainstream Christianity" (Steltenkamp, "A Retrospective on Black Elk: Holy Man of the Oglala," in Holler, *The Black Elk Reader*, 119). In a slightly negative assessment, Kaye writes: "The Ghost Dance religion works as a bridge between the two systems, not only because the Ghost Dance has unmistakable Christian elements but also because Christianity is an overgrown 'Messiah craze' that started among a small sect of Jews, severely threatened, like the Lakotas and Paiutes, by an encroaching and technologically superior imperial culture" (Frances W. Kaye, "Just What Is Cultural Appropriation, Anyway?" in Holler, *The Black Elk Reader*, 157; see also Chapter 7 herein). Red Cloud told General Miles that although he had not participated in the Ghost Dance, he had seen it and what the dancers were doing "is the teaching of the [Catholic] Church" and that their "doctrines and belief and practice is what is taught in scriptures" (quoted from Jeffrey Ostler, *The Plains Sioux and U.S. Colonialism from Lewis and Clark to Wounded Knee* [Cambridge: Cambridge University Press, 2004], 273).

# 3

# Traditionals and Christian Conversion

*Ms. [Grace] Roderick does not attribute the falling away of Catholic Passamaquoddies to patterns of abuse or an overbearing emphasis on human sinfulness in the Church. To the contrary, she suggests that the Indians avoid institutional Catholicism because "people here have learned the white man's ways." Many residents of Pleasant Point have lived in mainstream America and have become "streetwise." They have picked up secular values of an America in spiritual breakdown.*
—CHRISTOPHER VECSEY, *THE PATHS OF KATERI'S KIN*

More than fifty years after Nicholas Black Elk's death modern academics struggle to understand Black Elk's conversion to Catholicism and its relationship to Lakota tradition. DeMallie wrote in 1984 that "Black Elk's Catholicism represents the biggest gap in our understanding of him as a whole human being."[1] This "gap" assumes that there is a division between Christianity and Native American identity. However, this scholarly assumption has a number of philosophical roots that are foreign to traditional Lakota culture. I maintain that this gap was born of American secular culture and nourished by modern Western assumptions, and that these assumptions have been thrust on Black Elk in an effort to keep him "pure" from what many academics consider the "contamination" of Christianity.

First and foremost, the separation between Native American culture and Christianity is based on the method of the Boasian school of anthropology. Born in Germany and trained as a physicist, Franz Boas became interested in ethnology.

---

[1] Raymond J. DeMallie, "John G. Neihardt's Lakota Legacy," in *A Sender of Words: Essays in Memory of John G. Neihardt*, ed. Vine Deloria Jr. (Salt Lake City, Utah: Howe Brothers, 1984), 124.

He began his ethnological career among the Kwakwaka'wakw communities of British Columbia. According to Charles Briggs and Richard Bauman, Boas characterized Native Americans as people who were "necessarily" falling victim to modernization.[2] They suggest that Boas's work filtered out aspects of the colonial context in both photographs and texts in order to present a pure traditional culture. This mode of inquiry "rested on a principal effort to construct history as a pre-contact, romanticized past."[3]

Boas went on to teach at Columbia University, where he trained most of the important anthropologists of the first half of the twentieth century.[4] His approach became the standard perspective in anthropology. The Boasian school conducted its work believing that indigenous traditions were inevitably disappearing. The anthropological task was to record the remnants of a dying culture. This data was then formulated into a system in order to re-create a pure native worldview. According to Richard Handler, any cultural or religious change was ignored, because it "was precisely this change that was destroying the all-important data."[5] One of the biggest changes anthropologists filtered out was the influence of Christianity.

This approach to anthropology of salvage and systemization was combined with a stereotype of the destructive missionary, whose main intent was the destruction of native culture and who served as a pawn of colonizing European and American forces.[6] Consequently, Christianity could function only as a corrupting force in Native societies.

This anthropological perspective is still alive today. Julian Rice asserts the Boasian method today when he states:

> The present study . . . makes no pretense of presenting purely objective information. . . . The following chapters present previously unpublished manuscript material, ethnographic texts little known to the general reader, as well as new interpretations of well-known writings, *to try and help the Sioux people remember who they were* and what they can be.[7]

Rice makes clear that in 1998 his role as an ethnographer is to remove cultural change. After filtering, he intends to re-create the Lakota world as it was, before

---

[2] Charles L. Briggs and Richard Bauman, "'The Foundation of All Future Researches': Franz Boas, George Hunt, Native American Texts, and the Construction of Modernity," *American Quarterly* 51/3 (September 1999): 515.

[3] Ibid., 516.

[4] Richard Handler, "Boasian Anthropology and the Critique of American Culture," *American Quarterly* 42/2 (June 1990): 252.

[5] Clyde Holler, "Black Elk's Relationship to Christianity," *The American Indian Quarterly* 8/1 (1984): 37.

[6] I do not want to deny that this portrayal of missionaries is support by evidence from the history of European colonialism. However, as I argued in Chapter 2, this portrayal does not accurately describe the Lakota Catholic missions.

[7] Julian Rice, *Before the Great Spirit: The Many Faces of Sioux Spirituality* (Albuquerque: University of New Mexico Press, 1998), 5, emphasis added.

it was lost or corrupted. Consequently, the anthropologist becomes an editor rather than a reporter.

In addition to the Boasian method, many modern scholars embrace the second assumption that what Westerners classify as Native American religion is foundational for Native American identity.[8] In the same work Rice writes, "Tim Giago, the Oglala Lakota editor of *Indian Country Today* (the country's largest Indian newspaper), reminds us that authentic spirituality is the one thing Euro-Americans cannot steal."[9] Such an argument believes that Lakota religion must be kept pure, as it is the most authentic aspect of Lakota culture. Pure Lakota religion guarantees Lakota identity. This assumes that cultures themselves have permanent, well-defined boundaries that can and must be maintained.

The third assumption used by many scholars is that Christianity threatens the uniqueness of Lakota tradition. Any association of Lakota tradition with Christianity is a threat to its survival:

> It may be that these "blenders" wish to avoid having to study Native American cultures in and of themselves. . . . The Sioux people that I know have little patience for such a view. They are too busy restoring a unique consciousness that Euro-Americans, using first Christianity and now syncretism, are trying to erase.[10]

Rice sees Christianity as a destructive force that acts only to erase a unique Lakota tradition. He claims that the Lakota he knows share this view of Christianity and are engaged in reconstructing a pure Lakota worldview.

Since Rice does not name these Lakota, an examination of Lakota society is necessary to determine who shares these assumptions. In the next part of this chapter, I demonstrate that the Lakota Rice refers to—those who share his assumptions about Christianity—are those Lakota who have not inherited an intact Lakota worldview. Continuing Sanneh's argument from Chapter 2—that indigenous worldviews are contained in indigenous languages—I maintain that hostility to Christianity found in both Rice and his informants at least partially stems from the fact that they do not speak Lakota. As a result, involvement in Christianity does not have the internal dynamic that Sanneh describes. Non-Lakota speakers may well feel that Christianity exists externally to Lakota tradition and demands a choice, either a Western version of Christianity or a Boasian reconstruction of a pure Lakota tradition. Native American Russell Means is a primary representative of this group.

I also maintain that Lakota raised in a traditional environment and speaking the Lakota language (like Black Elk) have a very different understanding of Christianity. Along with the Lakota language, they inherit a relatively intact

---

[8] The term *religion* is a Western concept developed during the Enlightenment; it is used to separate culture into different spheres of varying degrees of value. This division is not inherent in Lakota culture in the way that modern Western thought uses the term.

[9] Rice, *Before the Great Spirit*, 4.

[10] Ibid., 11–12.

Lakota worldview. Consequently, Christian conversion is able to inhabit this part of the Lakota world. Christianity and Lakota tradition are not inherently opposed but obtain a type of continuity described by Sanneh in the form of a "Lakota-ized" Christianity. A primary representative of this group is Lakota Frank Fools Crow, a nephew of Black Elk.

Finally, I use this discussion to contextualize the Black Elk debate, arguing that because Black Elk was raised in a traditional environment and spoke Lakota, he encountered Christianity with the same internal dynamic as Fools Crow and the other traditionals. Consequently, there is no reason to assume that Black Elk would share the assumptions of Rice and the modern Lakota who are attempting to reconstruct a pure Lakota worldview. In other words, there is no reason to assume that Black Elk's Catholicism was insincere.

## THE AMERICAN INDIAN MOVEMENT AND THE URBAN LAKOTA

The modern Western assumptions exemplified by Rice and described above are not foreign to contemporary Native American thought. They first became evident relatively recently in Lakota society through the American Indian Movement (AIM). AIM is a Pan Indian political group that advocates a rejection of American culture, native cultural revival, and an aggressive political-action platform. This platform includes political autonomy of tribal groups and the just enforcement of treaties signed with the American government. Most important, AIM takes a strong stance on many social and economic problems that plague Native Americans. A major focus of AIM's platform includes the revival of traditional religion and the rejection of Christianity.[11]

Russell Means, one of the founders of AIM, is of Lakota descent and one of AIM's most visible media figures. Means was born November 10, 1939, on Pine Ridge Reservation in South Dakota. Means grew up primarily in California, attending American public schools and socialized in the English language. He became an accountant in Cleveland before founding a chapter of AIM in 1970.[12]

Like Rice, Means is clear about his hostility to Christianity. At the funeral of Frank Fools Crow in 1989, Means was one of several people who spoke. "I reminded everyone that Fools Crow was always a beacon to his people. Never a Christian, he maintained the honorable traditions of our ancestors by living as

---

[11] I do not wish to denigrate AIM or its political activism, which seeks to address the many problems facing contemporary Native American communities. I solely wish to show that their understanding of Lakota ceremonial life and tradition is an innovation with its sources in American secular culture and that it is not native to the Lakota of Black Elk's generation.

[12] Raymond Wilson, "Russell Means: Lakota," in *The New Warriors: Native American Leaders since 1900*, ed. R. David Edmunds (Lincoln: University of Nebraska Press, 2001), 147–49.

an example of their beauty."[13] The AIM group that came from different reservations objected to the Christian elements. Means states that "to [the AIM group], burying Fools Crow with the trappings of Christianity was blasphemous."[14] Means stressed that Fools Crow "was never a Christian," and that, for AIM, any association of Christianity with Native American tradition is blasphemy.

AIM equates Christianity with colonialism. Clyde Bellecourt, a leading member of AIM, summed up AIM's position at a protest of a Catholic celebration at the Ojibway Reservation in Sault Sainte Marie, Michigan: "The missionaries came with the Bible in one hand, and the sword in another."[15] Means agrees with this view of Christianity as a form of colonization: "Christianity serves only to further colonize Indians and rob us of dignity and self-worth."[16]

As with Rice, Means views Lakota religion as foundational for native identity. In speaking about a Sun Dance at Pine Ridge in 1971, he stated that AIM leaders decided to return to the reservations in order to better understand Lakota culture. "To set an example for everyone else, we leaders would return to our reservations. We would get involved in Indian ceremonies to find out more about who we are, what we are, and where we are going."[17] For Means, Lakota identity is discovered and understood primarily through Lakota religion.

Means makes the same claims about Lakota religion as Rice. First, traditional people, such as Fools Crow, are not Christians. Second, Christianity is only a tool of colonization and serves to destroy pure Lakota culture. Third, Lakota religion is the foundation of Lakota identity.

What is important to highlight is that Means's and Rice's views are dependent on similar social locations, formation, and time periods. Both were raised in secular America, in the English language, during the mid-twentieth century. In the Lakota context, these views are new. As we will see below, they are not found in the older Lakota generations raised in the Lakota language and cultural context.

## FOOLS CROW AND OTHER TRADITIONALS

Frank Fools Crow is perhaps the best representative of the early Lakota reservation period. Born around the time of the Battle of Wounded Knee in 1890, he served as the ceremonial chief of the Lakota nation from 1960 until his death in 1989. He represented the Lakota in treaty claims with the U.S. government and was perhaps the most respected holy man of his generation. Russell Means

---

[13] Russell Means, with Marvin J. Wolf, *Where White Men Fear to Tread: The Autobiography of Russell Means* (New York: St. Martin's Press, 1995), 534.

[14] Ibid.

[15] Ibid., 160.

[16] Ibid., 78.

[17] Ibid., 182.

calls him "the most renowned Lakota holy man" and understands him to be a symbol of Lakota tradition and resistance to colonialism.[18]

However, Fools Crow describes a much different relationship to Christianity than is attributed to him by Means. Fools Crow became a Catholic in 1917, ten years after Black Elk converted. Writing in 1979 in his autobiography, Fools Crow states:

> I am still a practicing Roman Catholic. I go to Mass once or twice a month, and I receive Holy Communion whenever I can. My first wife did not attend church. My second wife, Kate, whom I married in 1958, is also a Roman Catholic, and we attend worship services together. At the same time, we live according to the traditional religious beliefs and customs of our people, and we find few problems with the differences between the two.[19]

According to Fools Crow's testimony, Means's statement that he was "never a Christian" is false. In his own words, Fools Crow states that Christianity is not antithetical to Lakota tradition, does not erase it, and that he finds little conflict between the two.

Fools Crow also expresses that traditional Lakotas were sincerely attracted to the Christian message. In explaining his daily life in the 1970s, he describes entertaining fellow Lakotas who visited his home:

> Indian friends often visit us in the early evening, ordinarily staying for only a little while. . . . Sometimes they ask me to tell them a story. The kinds of stories they prefer may surprise you, because many people ask me about this extraordinary holy man who lived way back, Jesus Christ, who did such spectacular things as walking on water and changing a few fish and loaves of bread into enough food to feed thousands. So I tell them stories from the Bible as the priests have told them to me. And these really interest my visitors. Even today, the middle-aged and older Sioux are not able to understand and deal with Bible stories until they hear them told by an Indian and in their own Lakota language. Then they are able to sense the greatness of them and to feel their impact on their personal lives.[20]

Fools Crow's story makes clear that traditional Lakota people (at least the ones he knows), speaking their own language, were interested in the stories of Jesus Christ, and preferred them to other stories. Fools Crow, as a holy man and political leader, actively passed on those stories.

Fools Crow was not alone among traditionals in his participation in Catholicism. Many other important holy men respected as leaders among the Lakota

---

[18]   Ibid., 189.

[19]   Thomas E. Mails, *Fools Crow*, with Dallas Chief Eagle (New York: Doubleday, 1979), 45.

[20]   Ibid., 174.

were Catholic, including Edgar Red Cloud, Pete Catches, and George Plenty Wolf.[21]

Other Lakota religious groups accepted Christian belief and did not see it as contradictory to Lakota identity. In a meeting of the Native American Church of Pine Ridge,[22] Rev. Emerson Spider describes an incident between himself and two boys, in which he responded to the accusation that Christianity was contrary to Native American culture:

> They pointed at me and asked: "Do you believe in Christ?" I said: "Yes, I believe in Jesus Christ." "You must be a white man," they said. "Once you believe in Jesus Christ, you are a white man." "No, you got me all wrong," I said. "I'm a hundred percent Indian. Not one drop of blood in me that is white. . . . When one receives Christ, that doesn't change a person into another one."[23]

According to Emerson Spider, belief in Jesus Christ in no way compromised Lakota identity. Acceptance of Christ did not erase one's cultural formation.

Even those Lakota who explicitly reject traditional religion do not see doing so as compromising their Lakota identity. An interesting case is the Body of Christ Independent Church, a nondenominational church founded by the Lakota in 1958.[24] Membership consists of "full-blooded Lakota who are unacculturated in all areas of their life except religious symbolism."[25] According to their church's view, all traditional Lakota religion must be rejected, but they do not see that as "un-Indian." According to a member, Garfield Good Plume, it is "Indian in membership, language and sharing food."[26]

These groups of traditional Lakota demonstrate very different understandings of Lakota tradition and Christianity than Means and Rice. Fools Crow and traditional Lakotas are Christian. Christianity does not erase their Lakota cultural formation. They do not see religion as the exclusive foundation for Lakota

---

[21] See Paul B. Steinmetz, S.J., *Pipe, Bible, and Peyote among the Oglala Lakota: A Study in Religious Identity,* rev. ed. (Knoxville: University of Tennessee Press, 1990). Edgar Red Cloud, Pete Catches, and Fools Crow are cited by Means and Matthiessen as important traditional Lakota leaders supporting AIM's demands in the occupation of Wounded Knee. "To the traditionals, the real power on Pine Ridge—the supreme spiritual leaders and therefore the moral authorities—lay with our eight traditional chiefs and holy men, all born in the last century . . . [who] were the legitimate heirs to leadership of the only nation that had ever forced the United States to beg for peace—the Lakota" (Means, *Where White Men Fear to Tread,* 252).

[22] The Native American Church is based on Christian and Lakota tradition and is centered around the sacramental use of peyote (see Steinmetz, *Pipe, Bible, and Peyote,* 87–151).

[23] Ibid., 155.

[24] Ibid.

[25] Ibid., 176.

[26] Ibid., 155.

identity. Finally, Lakota Christians, even those who reject Lakota religion, claim to be Lakota because of the entirety of their cultural formation.

## AMERICANIZATION AND THE REJECTION OF CHRISTIANITY

Along with different understandings of Christianity and Lakota tradition, Fools Crow and other traditionals tell a different story about colonialism and continuing Lakota problems. While many of these traditionals share the political demands of AIM, they do not attribute Lakota societal and cultural problems to Christianity. They attribute Lakota problems and the rejection of Christianity by young militants associated with AIM to the same source: conformity to secular America. Spider continues the earlier story:

> And [to] this boy . . . who was saying that I was a white man, I said: "Do you drink?" "Yes," he said, "I drink." "Do you smoke?" "Yes, I smoke." "You must be a white man," I said, "because you are using the white man's things . . . and then you tell me that I am a white man; I'm an Indian. If you don't like this Christ and you want me to say that I'm a white man, who would I be if I gave Christ back to the white man? Would you come and join me as a good Indian, representing the Indian, being a true Indian? In the early days this white man came and tricked the Indian through this liquor and now we are using and we talk big. If we are going to be Indian, let's do it the right way."[27]

In this story a militant Lakota accuses Spider (who rejects Lakota ceremonies as salvific) of compromising his Lakota identity by his belief in Christ. Spider responds that it is not religious symbolism that makes a Lakota white but alcohol consumption. For Spider, the opposite is true: belief in Christ helps the Lakota to be "good" and "true" to their Native American identity. Secular values and lifestyle compromise Lakota identity, not religious symbolism.

Fools Crow's interpretation of the roots of Lakota problems also matches this view of acculturation to secular American culture. In his autobiography he traces the roots and development of contemporary social problems. Fools Crow first states that the early reservation period was not the source of current reservation problems, and in fact was "in some ways better than the old buffalo-hunting days":[28]

> I recalled that, from 1895 to 1920, we Sioux had learned what unity was; what it was like for a family to work together, and what it was like to cooperate with relatives and neighbors. We had achieved in those days a

---

[27]  Ibid., 135–36.
[28]  Mails, *Fools Crow*, 68.

measure of self-respect, and were able to continue much of our traditional way of life.[29]

While the Lakota had lost their freedom and old economy, they were still free of contemporary social and economic problems.

Fools Crow ascribes the beginning of trouble to the years between the two world wars, particularly the 1930s. According to Fools Crow, "The years from 1930 to 1940 rank as the worst ten years I know of, and all the Oglala as old as I am will agree. In that one single period we lost everything we had gained."[30] Corrupt Bureau of Indian Affairs (BIA) programs and the Great Depression reversed early Lakota success. According to Fools Crow:

I wanted to know where things had begun to go wrong. *Wakan-Tanka* answered that. He told me then that it had started when the young men went off to fight in World War I. It had been their first real exposure to the outside world, and to what money could do . . . the worst damage came with worldly and selfish attitudes the survivors brought back. . . . Where money is, liquor follows. Many of our young people were getting drunk and fighting one another. Had I not noticed that now and then cattle and horses were missing from farms, stolen to be sold for whiskey? It was known that one young man had even argued and fought with his father, a thing unheard of in the earlier days.[31]

Fools Crow cites the importation of American secular values learned by Lakota soldiers in World War I as the source of Lakota social problems. The power of money and alcohol consumption were now important values, which led to untraditional behavior. It was this untraditional behavior that led to the loss of Lakota culture and identity:

These were the key: money and jealousy. If you can't control money and the desire for it you can't control the people. So if we Sioux were going to hold onto our traditional way of life, we would have to fight to protect it. We would need to fight against the idea of people becoming more concerned with spending money than they were about their religion, families, homes, and farms. If we did not do this, if happiness was to be based upon having as much money as one could get his hands on, then we Sioux were becoming far less red and far more white.[32]

Fools Crow explicitly links the loss of Lakota identity and the adoption of American values to money and jealousy. In order to retain Lakota identity, it was necessary for the Lakota to fight these values:

---

[29] Ibid., 109.
[30] Ibid., 148.
[31] Ibid., 111.
[32] Ibid.

The whites have invaded us and changed our entire culture and life-style, and it has not been for the better. . . . *It is the white man with his materialism and capitalism*, and his stress upon the total independence of individuals and families, who has made us poor.[33]

It is essential to highlight that Fools Crow is not ignorant or passive when faced by the problems of the Lakota, and that he attributes them to the invading white American culture. While he implicates missionaries for their complicity with government language policy and education, Fools Crow does not link Lakota problems with the Christian narrative.[34]

For Fools Crow, a practicing Catholic, Christianity is not a major threat to Lakota identity. Rather, Fools Crow explicitly equates the American focus on financial accumulation and alcohol consumption to the loss of Lakota identity and societal problems. Contrary to Means and Rice, American secularism is the major threat, not Christianity.

## DIFFERING INTERPRETATIONS OF THE SUN DANCE

In addition to different views on the relationship of Christianity to Lakota societal problems, Means and Fools Crow have different understandings of the relationship of Christianity to the Lakota religion. In 1971, in the middle of his AIM activism, Means participated in his first Sun Dance. Fools Crow was the intercessor, the Lakota in charge of the ritual.

In his description Means admits that he did not fully understand the ceremony. "I knew very little about what to do. . . . I was learning and experiencing being an Indian."[35] He was instructed by many people, including "an older man from California, a white who had been adopted by the Red Cloud family. He showed me how to make crown, wrist, and ankle bands from sage. . . . I didn't have a sunflower, so the old man lent me his. I was grateful to have the correct things to honor my ancestors."[36]

Means's discussion of the Sun Dance displays several contradictory assumptions. While learning about the Sun Dance, he admitted to not understanding the

---

[33] Ibid., 194, emphasis added.

[34] Fools Crow states: "Soon after that, young people were drinking freely on the reservation. What else would they do with nothing but time on their hands, and especially when so many of the Sioux had been separated by white teachers from our traditional life-way without at the same time being prepared to enter the white man's competitive world?" (Mails, *Fools Crow*, 147).

[35] Means, *Where White Men Fear to Tread*, 189.

[36] Ibid. This seems to contradict a statement made by Means in a speech given in 1980: "No European can ever teach a Lakota to be a Lakota" (Russell Means, "For the World to Live, 'Europe' Must Die," *Mother Jones* [September 1980], cited in Dean MacCannell, "Reconstructed Ethnicity: Tourism and Cultural Identity in Third World Communities," *Annals of Tourism Research* 11 [1980]: 376).

procedure of the Sun Dance and that he needed instruction. In "learning to be an Indian," Means sought the instruction of a non-Indian.

Means also makes clear his assumption that Christianity dilutes the purity of Lakota tradition.

> Before we could start, a Catholic priest, the biggest drunk on the reservation—a remarkable achievement—showed up. Without even removing his shoes, as is customary on the dance circle's hallowed ground,[37] he started to carry a sacred pipe around the perimeter so our sun dance could begin with the church's blessing. I was stunned, not quite believing what I was seeing. Ed McGaw, who had grown up in a Catholic boarding school and was decorated for heroism while flying Marine Jets in Vietnam, said "This is bullshit—our sun dance has nothing to do with Catholicism! We can't let him do this." He and I stopped the half-pickled priest's desecration of our holy rites.[38]

While he admits to not understanding the ceremony, Means immediately concludes that Catholicism has nothing to do with the Sun Dance and is in fact a "desecration."

However, the connection between Catholicism and Fools Crow's Sun Dance was not new. According to Steinmetz, Jake Herman, a Lakota tribal historian, initiated this association. Steinmetz was asked to celebrate mass on the Sun Dance grounds. This occurred from 1965 to 1969. Steinmetz estimates that about three hundred people attended mass, about equal to the number that attended the Sun Dance. Steinmetz describes the Sun Dance:

> In 1969, Edgar Red Cloud, the leader of the Sun Dance singers, sang a Sun Dance song, holding the Sacred Pipe during the distribution of Holy Communion. I prayed with the same Pipe during the prayers of petition. Red Cloud, Plenty Wolf, and Fools Crow all received Holy Communion on the Sun Dance Grounds, making a public profession of their Catholic faith. Fools Crow had just pierced a few minutes before.[39]

In 1970 Steinmetz was again invited to celebrate mass but was prevented by what he describes as a "militant." In 1971, the year that Means attended his first Sun Dance, Steinmetz was invited to participate in the same Sun Dance run by Fools Crow.[40]

---

[37] Interestingly, there is a photograph of Fools Crow wearing shoes while leading a dancer into position on the Sun Dance grounds (Steinmetz, *Pipe, Bible, and Peyote*).

[38] Means, *Where White Men Fear to Tread*, 187–88. I have not found any other evidence to support Means's accusation that this priest was the biggest drunk on the reservation or that he came to the ceremony drunk.

[39] Steinmetz, *Pipe, Bible, and Peyote*, 30–31.

[40] Mails, *Fools Crow*, 134. Fools Crow does not talk about the 1971 Sun Dance. In discussing an incident of the 1974 Sun Dance, Fools Crow states, "A Roman Catholic priest, who was one of the pledgers, was dancing right beside me."

The next year Fools Crow asked me to help him pray in the Sun Dance, since he knew I prayed with the Sacred Pipe as a priest. On Sunday morning he painted my face with red paint and put me into the Sun Dance with my Pipe along with three militants. He did this to show that a Catholic priest had a right to participate in the Sun Dance and to pray with the Pipe. He made a public manifestation of what he had repeatedly told me: that the Indian religion and the Catholic Church are one. . . . When one of the militants threatened to throw me out, Fools Crow told me to take a long rest. . . . The militant then proceeded to deliver a long and bitter attack against the Holy Rosary Mission and the Catholic Church. During the rest period I presented my credentials. . . . "Frank Fools Crow had asked me to help him pray in the Sun Dance and I did not feel I could turn down a request to pray." Afterwards, Lakota people remarked to me that the militant person knew nothing about Indian religion. Otherwise he would not have criticized anyone while the Pipe was in ceremony.[41]

According to the evidence, Means interpreted both Lakota tradition and its relationship to Christianity differently from the traditional participants. It appears that he did not understand the Sun Dance and violated the Sacred Pipe ceremony. Means also seemed unaware that the presence of Catholicism was not invasive but initiated by Fools Crow, the Sun Dance's intercessor. He was not familiar enough with traditional Lakota culture to grasp the subtleties of the events.

### SYMBOLIC ETHNICITY, LAKOTA SPEAKERS, AND THE INTERNAL DYNAMIC

Two distinct understandings of Lakota tradition and the relationship with Christianity are relevant for this study.[42] Fools Crow, a native Lakota speaker raised in a traditional environment, as well as a holy man and ceremonial chief of the entire Lakota nation, saw no conflict with maintaining active church membership and explaining the stories of Jesus. He ascribed much of the Lakota problems to adoption of secular American values. Fools Crow is representative of the early reservation period in which Black Elk lived.

---

[41]    Steinmetz, *Pipe, Bible, and Peyote*, 31.

[42]    There are also Lakota raised in a traditional environment who are not against Lakota ceremonies but do not view them as salvific. Emerson Spider Sr. writes: "It used to be that when we had the traditional way of worshipping, we believed in earthly life. Now we believe in the second coming of Christ, although we still have our traditional ways, we still believe in them. I believe in the Sun Dance and fasting and all the traditional ways. I believe that they are sacred and I believe that they are good. But they are earthly, so by them alone no man will be saved. The second coming of Christ is the only way to salvation" (Emerson Spider Sr., "The Native American Church of Jesus Christ," in *Sioux Indian Religion: Tradition and Innovation*, ed. Raymond J. DeMallie and Douglas R. Parks [Norman: University of Oklahoma Press, 1987], 208–9).

Russell Means, the former head of AIM, raised in an urban environment as an English speaker, saw Christianity as inherently antithetical to Lakota tradition and ascribed much of the Lakota's problems to Christianity. At the time he was apparently unaware of Fools Crow's many years of participation in the Catholic church. Means also misunderstood the dynamics of the 1971 Sun Dance, in which Catholicism played an intentional role.

The difference between these two positions in Lakota society can be attributed to socialization. Means and other Lakota raised in urban American environments demonstrate a symbolic understanding of Lakota identity. They follow the categories of symbolic ethnicity described by Herbert J. Gans. According to Gans, people formed in mainstream American culture "without assigned role or groups that anchor ethnicity" look for symbolic ways to express ethnic identity.[43] Rather than concerning themselves with

> arduous or time-consuming commitments . . . to a culture that must be practiced constantly . . . they are free to look for ways of expressing that identity which suits them best, thus opening up the possibility of voluntary, diverse, or individualistic ethnicity.[44]

According to Gans, those formed in secular America do not assert ethnic identity by learning complex communal systems that encompass a way of life, such as language. Rather, they learn expressive behavior, usually involving symbols. These symbols are taken from older ethnic culture that may still be practiced but in which they are not participants. These symbols, "are 'abstracted' from that culture and pulled out of its original moorings, so to speak, to become stand-ins for it."[45] The symbols are essentialized as the kernel of ethnic identity but are only added to a preexisting American cultural formation. Thus, while functioning as Americans, symbols stand for a different ethnic identity.

In this symbolic assertion of Lakota identity, religion becomes foundational because it is the cultural symbol that is most easily appropriated. Bea Medicine recognizes this cultural trend among urban Lakota:

> It seems obvious that a major symbolic act of being a "traditional" Native American is "to Sun Dance" and eventually, "to pierce." Participation in this ritual is rapidly becoming a symbol of traditionality and an ethnic marker for many native peoples of all tribes—those who are affiliated with the American Indian Movement, those who live in urban areas, and those whose quest for identity and individual or social change necessitates the search for a symbolic and ritual system. . . . Urban Indians of

---

[43] Herbert J. Gans, "Symbolic Ethnicity: The Future of Ethnic Groups and Cultures in America," in *Theories of Ethnicity: A Classical Reader,* ed. Werner Sollors (New York: New York University Press, 1996), 435.

[44] Ibid.

[45] Ibid.

Lakota heritage return to dance, to observe, and to obtain the benefits which accrue from attendance.[46]

By participating in the Sun Dance a Lakota participant socialized in American culture is transformed into a "traditional" Lakota, an identity that is held over and against secular America. Piercing gives the benefit of symbolically trumping years of cultural formation.

This understanding of symbolic ethnicity is read back into history. Ward Churchill, an AIM activist who teaches at the University of Colorado at Boulder, quotes researchers Mark Davis and Robert Zannis, who state, "If people suddenly lose their 'prime symbol,' the basis of their culture, their lives lose meaning. They become disorientated, with no hope. As social organization often follows such a loss, they are often unable to ensure their own survival."[47] According to this understanding of ethnicity, the source of Lakota problems is not primarily in the loss of family structure, Lakota language, cultural formation, or the Lakota economy; it is reduced to the loss of Lakota religion and the introduction of Christianity.

Means's return to the Pine Ridge Reservation is the process of constructing a symbolic ethnic identity.[48] Means "had long yearned to feel like [his] ancestors," and this pursuit of Lakota identity leads him to the Sun Dance. By dancing in the Sun Dance he "[learns] and [experiences] being an Indian."[49] Rather than cultural formation, the Sun Dance becomes the foundational symbol for establishing his Lakota identity.

It seems that this process may lead to insecurity and boundary maintenance by those attempting to assert symbolic ethnicity. A symbol is easily appropriated by individuals not socialized in a Lakota environment. Means himself demonstrates this phenomenon by appropriating the symbol of the piercing while never becoming a full participant in the life of the traditional community. If Means can do this, then non-Lakota can as well, as did the Anglo from California in

---

[46]  Bea Medicine, "Native American Resistance to Integration: Contemporary Confrontations and Religious Revitalization," *Plains Anthropologist* 26 (1981): 281. This trend is not limited to the Lakota. Medicine states that "Micmacs from New Brunswick, Canada, felt obligated to regain an Indian identity by making a pilgrimage to Pine Ridge—even if they didn't participate."

[47]  Kaye, "Just What Is Cultural Appropriation, Anyway?" *The Black Elk Reader,* ed. Clyde Holler (Syracuse, N.Y.: Syracuse University Press, 2000), 153–54.

[48]  Dean MacCannell calls Means's process of appropriating a symbolic Lakota ethnicity "constructed ethnicity." According to MacCannell, "Means is attempting to build a 'correct' image of Indian peoples in opposition to forces of assimilation into the Western mainstream, to gain widespread acceptance of that image as a model for actual behavior. In this paper, the term *constructed ethnicity* is used to refer to efforts such as Means', and to the various ethnic identities which emerged via opposition and assimilation during the colonial phase of Western history and in new 'internal colonies'" (MacCannell, "Reconstructed Ethnicity," 376).

[49]  Means, *Where White Men Fear to Tread*, 187, 189.

Means's autobiography. For Means, then, there must be a method of limiting uncontrolled appropriation, lest it become another consumer product in secular America. Constant boundary maintenance is necessary to guard the purity of the symbol from contamination by either non-native participants or Christian influence.

Despite this participation in Lakota religion, little of Means's formation sets him apart from the non-Lakota world. Based on his acculturation and inability to speak Lakota, he views Lakota culture through the lens of an outsider. Fools Crow comments on Lakota youth who do not speak good Lakota: "Besides [drinking], the youth are not able to speak enough Lakota. So when I talk to them they do not understand much of what I am saying. Even if they do catch the meaning they miss its impact."[50] Those who do not have the linguistic tools cannot adequately understand Lakota tradition because they do not inhabit an intact Lakota cultural world.

Because Means lacks this linguistic formation, anything that he knows to exist in American society cannot then be an authentic part of Lakota culture. Christianity cannot be Lakota, because it is part of the American cultural world. Holler points out that "for the AIM group, rejection of Christianity is considered absolutely essential for Indian identity."[51] Christianity can only be a contamination of the prime symbol upon which Lakota culture and individual Native American identity depend.

In addition to the desire for symbolic purity, Means and the urban Native American rejection of Christianity can also be attributed to American socialization. As early as 1946, MacGregor reported that "Christian Churches too appear to be losing some of their former hold as . . . many Indians are now following the trend of the local white population away from control by the Church."[52] MacGregor links Lakota separation from Christianity to association with Anglo American cultural trends. In the same way, Means's aggressive stance toward Christianity is a manifestation of the dominant secular trend in White America.

Fools Crow and his generation—those raised before the reservation time and families that retained similar patterns of cultural formation—are not dependent on a symbolic identity because they operate as Lakota in all facets of life. According to Holler, "Ethnic identity was hardly an issue in the days before the reservation system. In the old days, ethnic identity was not chosen, it was bestowed by birth in the tribe and by language."[53] Traditionals do not need to consciously filter out cultural influences that are non-Lakota, because there is no way to escape the Lakota cultural world embodied by their language and way of life. Cultural insecurity and identity assertion were not issues, for they

---

[50] Mails, *Fools Crow*, 197.

[51] Clyde Holler, *Black Elk's Religion: The Sun Dance and Lakota Catholicism* (Syracuse, N.Y.: Syracuse University Press, 1995), 193.

[52] Michael F. Steltenkamp, *Black Elk: Holy Man of the Oglala* (Norman: University of Oklahoma Press, 1993), 166.

[53] Holler, *Black Elk's Religion*, 194.

were formed in an exclusively Lakota context. Adoption of new religious thought did not threaten their Lakota identity, because there was nothing they could do to escape the fact that they were Lakota.[54]

Thus, Fools Crow and those raised in a traditional Lakota environment display the characteristics of indigenous conversion to Christianity that Sanneh described in Chapter 2. For individuals like Fools Crow, who are both linguistically capable and culturally secure, conversion assumes an internal dynamic *in continuity* with indigenous traditions and identity. The new religious thought inhabits an intact Lakota cultural world because they receive and experience it in their own language. Ben Black Bear, a Lakota Catholic raised in the Lakota language, demonstrated this internal dynamic. Black Bear explicitly claimed that the Lakota language and social practices allowed him to bring together Catholic and Lakota traditions into one view of the world in which the two were indistinguishable.[55]

As a result, Lakota formation for the traditionalists means that religious symbolism is not necessarily foundational for Lakota identity. Holler recognizes this when he comments on the modern traditionalist view of permitting white

---

[54] Eva Marie Garroutte quotes Julie M., a bilingual Cherokee raised in a traditional Cherokee community: "A lot of times, I think [ordinary Cherokee] people don't even understand the nuances of this whole . . . debate . . . [about] the degrees to which someone is Cherokee. . . . Just like the people who see when we go to the Stokes [Ceremonial Grounds]. You know, they're just too busy being Cherokee. . . . People who live in Cherokee homes, speak Cherokee, eat Cherokee dishes of food, and plant Cherokee Gardens, and look at the world in a Cherokee way. Basically, that's what it really boils down to: who walks in that way and sees the world in that way. . . . Those of us who are Cherokee, who grew up in the Cherokee way, in the Cherokee tradition, in the Cherokee language— and just *being* Cherokee—we don't really *think* about it, you know? You just *live* it. You just *are* (Eva Marie Garroutte, *Real Indians: Identity and the Survival of Native America* [Berkeley and Los Angeles: University of California Press, 2003], 73).

[55] Black Bear describes this in detail: "But you know, there is a whole group of our people who do not speak the Lakota language anymore and . . . it puts them out of touch with Lakota culture. Because the culture is contained in the language. This is a difficult area and I've thought a lot about this but haven't sort of brought it together to explain it in an understandable and sensible kind of way. Part of the problem is trying to figure out what is traditional Lakota culture and what isn't. . . . Part of the process of resolving this particular question is to look at white people and study them. . . . You could say something is very traditional and part of Lakota society . . . but you could find out that white people also may have the same thing!

"Part of the problem is identifying just what separates us and what distinguishes Lakota culture. It's not just secular white society where I have to learn about those people, but also in Catholic white society. How does secular white society differ from Catholic white society? How do white people differ from each other? Those who are Christian and those who are not? . . . I know what I know but then how much of that is what I've learned from the outside?" (Marie Therese Archambault, ed., "Ben Black Bear, Jr.: A Lakota Deacon and a 'Radical Catholic' Tells His Own Story, *U.S. Catholic Historian* 16/2: 93).

attendance at the Sun Dance, "The reservation traditionalists are fairly secure in their identity with respect to whites."[56] In a controversy over allowing white participants, Pete Catches, a Lakota holy man and former Catholic catechist, says that "friction here is strong against any form of white man coming here . . . and I am personally very hurt by this."[57] Christianity and outside participation do not pollute or compromise Lakota identity of those formed in the Lakota language and world.[58]

While AIM is one expression of twentieth-century Native American experience and has often gotten the most publicity in both scholarship and popular imagination, it is not normative in contemporary Lakota society. More significant, it is not the interpretive lens of Black Elk's generation but a product of secular twentieth-century American culture. It must be imported into the Black Elk sources if it is to be there at all. But this is exactly what has been done. William K. Powers exemplifies this in his work *Oglala Religion*. He observes that it is through Lakota ceremonies "that the Oglalas recognize themselves as distinct from the white man and other non-Oglalas. . . . Religion *has become* an institution which is synonymous with Oglala identity."[59]

The distinction between Oglala social and cultural identity and other possible identities should be regarded as a process rather than a category. The boundary which delineates Oglala society from non-Indians, or even non-Oglalas, is ideational. The Oglala is very much aware of the technological environment that surrounds his society. He participates in it. He wears a white man's clothing, lives in a white man's house, and works at a white man's job. But when he seeks to affirm his own identity as an Oglala, he moves along the continuum to the only institution available to him that is distinct from the white man. He seeks identity in a religious system whose structure has remained in many respects constant since European contact.[60]

---

[56] Holler, *Black Elk's Religion*, 193.

[57] Steinmetz, *Pipe, Bible, and Peyote*, 35.

[58] This conclusion is supported by Sanneh's research in Africa. Sanneh writes that "Africans best responded to Christianity where the indigenous religions were strongest, not weakest, suggesting a degree of indigenous compatibility with the gospel, and an implicit conflict with colonial priorities." Here Sanneh is not using a symbolic understanding of religion (Lamin Sanneh, *Whose Religion Is Christianity? The Gospel beyond the West* [Grand Rapids, Mich.: Eerdmans, 2003], 18).

[59] William K. Powers, *Oglala Religion* (Lincoln: University of Nebraska Press, 1977), 154–55, emphasis added.

[60] Ibid., 204. Compare Powers's statement to the views expressed by Fools Crow: "Of course, whenever I speak of customs that might be revived, I mean not only the dances and the ceremonies, but also the manners and morals. Most non-Indians just think in terms of the first two. We could, if we thought it best, revive most of the old dances and ceremonies. But the reasons for our doing many of them are not present anymore, and the attitude of many people about them is not right. The Sun Dance is performed, and we could do again the Ghost Dance and the Buffalo Dance. But Sioux

Powers description of religion as identity may be a contemporary sociological phenomenon. But the examples of Fools Crow, other traditional holy men, and Lakota Christians socialized in a traditional environment in the Lakota language do not demonstrate any evidence that they share this idea of religious symbolism as identity. Ironically, these traditionals with dual religious commitments are the very sources for the Boasian reconstructions exemplified by Rice and Means and are continually measured by the assumptions they themselves do not share. They do not see Christianity as threatening or erasing the Lakota worldview. Traditionals do not need to assert or create Lakota identity; it is inherent in their cultural formation. Religion is important and central to Lakota communal life, but it is not foundational for individual identity.

## OUTSIDER AND INSIDER VIEWS OF BLACK ELK'S CATHOLICISM

It goes without saying that the revitalization issues that confront Means and other Native Americans are important issues. Those Lakota who strive to inhabit an intact Lakota world face a difficult challenge that is a tragic result of colonialism.[61] It is not my role nor has it been my intention to advocate a particular position on the question of revitalization of Lakota tradition. Rather, the preceding analysis simply offers a framework by which to interpret Black Elk's Catholicism. This brief examination demonstrates that traditional Lakota society does not necessarily share the assumptions of AIM and some academics that Christianity is antithetical to Lakota culture. Thus, in examining the question of Black Elk's Catholicism we begin with the assumption, as do traditional Lakota, that sincere Christian participation can be a natural and even an expected characteristic of traditionally raised Lakota of the reservation period.

As a result, it is hard to build a case that Black Elk was not a sincere Catholic. In fact, only four statements in the primary sources question his life as a Catholic: two from Hilda, a daughter of Neihardt; one from the Laubin couple who visited him once a year from 1936 until his death in 1950; and one from Charles Hanson.

First, Hilda, a daughter of John Neihardt, states during an interview on November 3, 1997, at the University of Sioux Falls: "But let me recall a conversation that Neihardt and Black Elk had. It was during a break in the telling of the Great Vision, and the two were visiting. My father said: 'Black Elk, when you have

---

people do not request these, because they figure it is best to leave them alone. The stone and the war-paint powder we once used in the Ghost Dance were taken to the University of South Dakota at Vermillion, and they are on display there. I suppose we could get them back if we wanted them badly enough. But there is no reason to do so" (Mails, *Fools Crow*, 168–69).

    [61] I use "intact" here not as a synonym for "pure"; it is not meant to imply that there is only one essentialized Lakota world. Rather, it refers to a way of life that has a more integral connection to pre-reservation cultural patterns than mere symbolic appropriation, of which there are many possibilities.

such a very beautiful religion, why are you a member of a white church?' Black Elk thought for a moment, then replied: 'Because my children have to live in this world.'"[62]

The second also comes from Hilda Neihardt. In her book *Black Elk and Flaming Rainbow*, published in 1995, she refers to Black Elk's daughter Lucy, who was the main informant in Michael Steltenkamp's book, *Black Elk: Holy Man of the Oglala*. She asserts that Lucy became a pipe carrier, quit her membership in what Neihardt classifies as a "white church," and regrets telling Steltenkamp, her friend of five years when he lived and worked on the reservation, about Black Elk's life as a catechist. Neihardt reports that Lucy told her that Black Elk confessed shortly before his death that "the only thing I really believe is the pipe religion." In a similar manner, Black Elk's son Ben made a death-bed confession that Neihardt interprets as a denial of Christian belief.[63]

The third comes from Reginald and Gladys Laubin, who met Black Elk in 1936 at a Black Hills pageant. They continued to visit him each year until his death. In a personal communication to Raymond DeMallie in 1983, they stated that he never mentioned that aspect of his life. They wrote, "We had the feeling he was interested mainly in early days."[64]

The fourth, from February 1983, comes from Charles Hanson Jr. of the Museum of the Fur Trade, Chadron, Nebraska. Hanson visited Pine Ridge to meet Black Elk. Black Elk was sick and talked to him for a few minutes. Black Elk's son Ben apologized that the interview couldn't be longer. Ben went on to say "that many of their conversations then were about the old religion, and that Black Elk now felt he had made a mistake in rejecting it for Christianity."[65]

While these four sources are given normative status for determining the sincerity of Black Elk's Catholicism, it is clear that they are even farther removed from the worldview of the generation of Black Elk and Fools Crow than are Rice and Means. All of the informants are outsiders to the Lakota community. They are American, and they have no knowledge of Lakota culture or language. They have no long-term experience living with the Lakota and no commitment

---

[62] Hilda Neihardt and R. Todd Wise, "Black Elk and John G. Neihardt," in Holler, *The Black Elk Reader*, 95.

[63] Hilda Neihardt, *Black Elk and Flaming Rainbow: Personal Memories of the Lakota Holy Man and John Neihardt* (Lincoln: University of Nebraska Press, 1995), 118–19. This is a very doubtful claim. Hilda calls Lucy a "dear friend" but concedes that she does not remember much about Lucy from the interviews and does not seem to have talked to her. Hilda spent much of her free time horseback riding with Leo Looks Twice, Lucy's husband. Before Lucy's death in 1978 she visited Hilda one time. For a response to Neihardt's claims, see Michael F. Steltenkamp, "A Retrospective on Black Elk: Holy Man of the Oglala," in Holler, *The Black Elk Reader*, 109. For a discussion of the historical and cultural factors that led to the Neihardts' misinterpretation, see Chapter 6 herein.

[64] Raymond J. DeMallie, *The Sixth Grandfather: Black Elk's Teachings Given to John G. Neihardt* (Lincoln: University of Nebraska Press, 1984), 71.

[65] Ibid., 71–72.

to the Lakota community. They are people who did not have long-term relationships with Black Elk but met him for short periods of time. Most important, they all share the assumptions of the early anthropologists, and Rice and Means, who look exclusively for things that were authentically Lakota; they appear to be biased against any cultural change.

On the other hand, all the primary sources that accept the sincerity of Black Elk's life as a Catholic come from within the Lakota community. In a talk about Lakota tradition given by his son Ben at the Pine Ridge Boarding School, Ben stated that "my father was a Christian. He died a Catholic; he is buried in a Catholic cemetery."[66] The main Lakota witnesses are Black Elk's daughter Lucy Looks Twice and fellow catechists John Lone Goose, Ben Marrowbone, and Pat Red Elk, who was a young man when Black Elk was a catechist. There are also a number of Jesuits who lived and worked in the Lakota culture and community for decades who described Black Elk as a faithful Catholic. Fools Crow states that

> my uncle, Black Elk, became a Roman Catholic in 1904. . . . He was very interested in the teachings of the Roman Catholic Church, and spent many hours talking to the priests about it. . . . Black Elk told me that he had decided that the Sioux religious way of life was pretty much the same of that of the Christian churches."[67]

Fools Crow was surprised to hear that *Black Elk Speaks* even existed.[68] Even a negative source, John (Fire) Lame Deer, who dismissed Black Elk as a "catechism teacher" and a "cigar-store Indian," recognized his life as a Catholic.[69] There is no evidence that they saw Black Elk's Christianity as anything but a typical manifestation of Lakota culture of the early reservation period.

---

[66] Esther Black Elk Desersa and Olivia Black Elk Pourier, *Black Elk Lives: Conversations with the Black Elk Family*, ed. Hilda Neihardt and Lori Utecht (Lincoln: University of Nebraska Press, 2000), 18. Ben later says "but he still believed in Indian religion." This is in no way contradictory to Black Elk's status as a Catholic, as will be later clarified.

[67] Mails, *Fools Crow*, 45.

[68] Ibid., 5. When told by his potential biographer that Black Elk had described his vision to Neihardt, "Fools Crow was stunned. He knew little if nothing about the content of the famous book." Ian Frazier records a similar reaction from Charlotte, Black Elk's great-granddaughter: "I asked Charlotte about her great-grandfather, and about his book, *Black Elk Speaks*. 'To tell you the truth, I've never had the inclination to sit down and read it,' she said. 'Being related to someone like Black Elk brings a sense of responsibility that's not very gratifying sometimes, especially when you're a kid. I guess I never really felt I had to read it. As my Granpa Ben told me, "The book is about this much [thumb and forefinger an inch apart] and you already know this much [arms wide apart]"'" (Ian Frazier, *On the Rez* [New York: Farrar, Straus & Giroux, 2000], 119).

[69] Peter Matthiessen, *In the Spirit of Crazy Horse* (New York: Viking Press, 1983), xxxvii.

Ironically, those who most adamantly oppose the possibility of a sincere commitment to Catholicism on the part of Black Elk unwittingly interpret the sources with the thickest colonial lens. They assume that the authentic Black Elk was successfully obscured and hidden from his own community, from those who spoke his language, from his own people the Lakota, and that his true beliefs were communicated to people with whom he had short-term relationships and who existed completely outside of his language and cultural matrix. Rice comments: "The possibility that Black Elk could have distinctly remembered and perhaps wished to return to the spirituality he had exclusively lived until the age of thirty-seven is lost on these scholars."[70] Given the sources, Rice would have more accurately said that this possibility is lost on *all the Lakota testimony of the period*.

Rereading a contemporary position of Lakota society back into history is questionable scholarship. However, privileging the interpretations of cultural outsiders as more accurate and valuable than those living and creating the culture is anthropological discrimination that completely disregards Lakota communal memory, destroys their agency, and borders on racism.

In conclusion, the testimony of traditional Lakota, exemplified by Fools Crow, demonstrates that the assumptions of modern academics and secular American culture cannot be read back into Black Elk's life. Instead, it appears that Black Elk's life as a Catholic was as real as any other part of his life and cannot be separated from his Lakota world. The "gap" between Native American culture and Christianity is not a part of Black Elk's Lakota worldview but merely a reflection of modern academic bias.

---

[70] Rice, *Before the Great Spirit,* 11. Rice appears to mean any scholar who takes Black Elk's Catholicism seriously.

# 4

# Redescribing the Lakota World

*Remember the words you have said in making declarations. You speak the words but your lives are lives of the old way. Therefore my relatives unify yourselves. Perhaps you cannot live lives split in two, which does not please God. Only one church, one God, one Son, and only one Holy Spirit—that way you have only one faith, you have only one body, and you have only one life and one spirit. Thus we have three but really we have One—thus he who unifies himself will have victory. So it is; read carefully.*
—Black Elk, Letter to Lakota Catholics, November 2, 1911

As we saw in Chapter 3, there seems to be no adequate historical reason to dismiss Black Elk's Catholicism. Lakota-speaking traditionals, such as Fools Crow, did not see Christian participation as a threat to their identity. It is possible, therefore, to begin with the assumption that Black Elk's Catholic life was sincere.

However, scholars do distort and dismiss Black Elk's Catholicism using contemporary Western definitions of religion. For example, Julian Rice states:

Though he spent many years after 1904 as a Catholic missionary, [the idea that Black Elk] made a complete transition to twentieth century Catholic consciousness is improbable. Habitual ways of thought would have had to be erased, not simply dismissed as a wrongful creed. Black Elk may not have wished to adopt any aspect of the white man's culture.[1]

Rice understands religions to be unchanging systems. He would perceive both Catholicism and the Lakota tradition as static, monolithic systems of beliefs that do not change or adapt. As a result, Lakota religious belief and Christian

---

[1] Julian Rice, *Black Elk's Story: Distinguishing Its Lakota Purpose* (Albuquerque: University of New Mexico Press, 1991), 10.

belief could not exist simultaneously. For Rice, acceptance of Christian truth claims would *erase* Lakota cultural formation. Consequently, evidence of Black Elk's continuing Lakota religious expression or activity is proof that he cannot be Catholic.

Anthropologist William K. Powers also uses the definition of religion as an exclusive monolithic system:

> How do we explain the tendency of native people to participate in two discrete religious systems? Do they in fact "adore" two gods, one represented in the ritual paraphernalia of the Grandfathers, the other in the beaded chasuble, maniple, and stole of the priest? Are there in fact two separate sets of pantheons, cosmologies, and cosmogonies? Are the adepts, participants, or members living a religiously dualistic life; or do, in fact, the two religious systems represent for them two systems of quite different orders?[2]

In response to his own question Powers answers that Lakota tradition and Christianity are "best explained as a coexistence of two disparate religious systems."[3] Because they compete for truth, the native participant cannot believe in both.[4] Both systems compete for the allegiance of the Lakota but do not overlap. However, a Lakota can participate in both, and Powers attempts to resolve this dilemma by focusing on the function of these distinct systems. Powers writes:

> The native system satisfies needs we may call religious, in the sense that people require a belief in supraempirical beings and powers whom they call upon in culturally prescribed ways to address epistemological questions unanswerable by purely empirical means. . . . Christianity represents a system that . . . satisfies other kinds of exigencies, needs not normally associated with the supernatural, [and] provides an infrastructure upon which older, dysfunctional institutions may persist, clothed with the trappings of a new age.[5]

According to Powers's model, Lakota tradition and Christianity are separate systems that serve different purposes. Lakota tradition serves a religious function and therefore may be "believed."[6] Christianity serves a social or economic function, but in the realm of "belief does not affect dual participants." For Powers, Lakota tradition survives by inhabiting an external and superficial Christian framework.

---

[2] William K. Powers, "Dual Religious Participation: Stratagems of Conversion among the Lakota," in *Beyond the Vision: Essays on American Indian Culture*, ed. William K. Powers (Norman: University of Oklahoma Press, 1987), 99.

[3] Ibid., 123.

[4] Ibid., 100.

[5] Ibid., 123–24.

[6] Powers also makes the modern Western assumption that "religious needs" encompass only inquiry that cannot be answered by empirical needs.

Thus, both Rice and Powers take what I call an *external dynamic* to Lakota Christian conversion. Christianity exists separately and in competition with Lakota tradition. And because Lakota tradition must be protected, scholars view Lakota Christian participation as superficial or less sincere.

While I argue that Rice's and Powers's use of an external dynamic does not accurately describe Black Elk's Lakota Catholic life and thought, the external dynamic was, and is, a sociological phenomenon. Because of the Jesuit acceptance of the government ban of the Sun Dance and *yuwipi*, Christianity and Lakota traditions during the early reservation period and even today exist as separate organizations.

Despite external control, the Lakota did not separate themselves from Lakota traditions. Chapter 2 described how, albeit perhaps unintentionally, missionary use of the Lakota language challenged this external control. Sanneh writes that "with the shift into native languages, the logic of religious conversion assumed an internal dynamic, with a sharp turn away from external direction and control."[7] So, despite missionary attempts to control interpretation, Lakota Catholics retained the agency to judge the relationship between Lakota tradition and Catholic life. This created what scholars call dual participation: participation in both Lakota and Catholic rituals. Black Elk's son Ben described this phenomenon to Lakota high school students:

We became Christians. We wanted to keep some of our old ceremonies. When we pray, we don't read from a book. It comes from our hearts. But the government outlawed some of our worship, like the sun dance, so we had to do our ceremonies secretly—where we would not be caught. That made us feel bad. It was like the early Christians who had to worship secretly.[8]

Ben identifies government bans on certain Lakota ceremonies as the factor that prevented a true integration of Lakota tradition and Catholicism. He indicates that at least some Lakota Catholics continued to participate in the Lakota ceremonies while practicing Catholicism.[9] Fools Crow echoes the same idea:

---

[7] Lamin Sanneh, *Whose Religion Is Christianity? The Gospel beyond the West* (Grand Rapids, Mich.: Eerdmans, 2003), 24.

[8] Esther Black Elk DeSersa and Olivia Black Elk Pourier, *Black Elk Lives: Conversations with the Black Elk Family*, ed. Hilda Neihardt and Lori Utecht (Lincoln: University of Nebraska Press, 2000), 8–9.

[9] Lucy alludes to many ways in which Black Elk continued participating in Lakota ceremonial life. She remembers him praying and crying on a hill for his brother (17), doing the *inipi* (60), dancing (67), having a pipe (107), attending a Sun Dance (107), meeting the keeper of the Sacred Calf Pipe (107), and stopping a tornado (117). Her husband was one of the men responsible for finding and setting up the tree for the Sun Dance at Pine Ridge (188n.). These references are casually discussed despite her adamant insistence that Black Elk was a sincere Catholic. For Lucy, this participation is not an

Many of the things we believe about God are the same [in Lakota tradition and Catholicism]. Today, most other Sioux feel as we do, but it was not always this way. Some of the things the new faiths said were hard to take, especially their belief that we did not know the true God and that Sioux medicine and ceremonies were things of the Devil. So we rejected these views until their positions began to change.[10]

According to Fools Crow, Catholicism and Lakota tradition believe similar things about God. However, the missionary interpretation created a separate Lakota Catholicism. Ben Black Bear expands on Fools Crow's dual point:

They were willing to accept explanation of doctrine of what the Catholic Church is. They were willing to listen and accept that but when the missionaries started giving their opinion and say . . . "Now, you've got to do things this way." Then they said [quietly] "Wait a minute, let me look at it from another angle."[11]

According to Black Bear, the majority of Lakota who accepted Catholicism rejected the standard missionary interpretation of the Lakota tradition.

These three Lakota Catholics describe the sources of dual participation. First, they insist that the missionaries were too extensive in their criticism of Lakota tradition. Second, all three emphasize that, despite this, the Lakota did not find it necessary to reject Catholicism or the Lakota tradition. They remained active participants despite the missionary misinterpretation and the tension it created. Third, the Lakota Catholics were not powerless victims of religious change or missionary interpretation. Rather, they had agency to, in the words of Black Bear, "look at it from another angle." Fools Crow explained how he worked out the tension himself: "I never talked about the Pipe to a Catholic priest in the early days, but I brought the two religions together on my own."[12] The Lakota, not the missionaries, resolved the theological tensions and brought together the two traditions.

Lucy recounted a story that emphasizes the Lakota agency in resolving theological tension. After Black Elk had a stroke near the end of his life, Lucy and

---

issue, which she makes clear with her discussion of Black Elk's conversion: "After he became a convert and started working for the missionaries, he put all his medicine practice away. He never took it up again" (34). The *yuwipi*, not Lakota tradition in general, conflicts with Christianity and must be rejected (Michael F. Steltenkamp, *Black Elk: Holy Man of the Oglala* [Norman: University of Oklahoma Press, 1993]).

[10] Thomas E. Mails, *Fools Crow,* with Dallas Chief Eagle (New York: Doubleday, 1979), 45.

[11] Marie Therese Archambault, ed., "Ben Black Bear, Jr.: A Lakota Deacon and a 'Radical Catholic' Tells His Own Story," *U.S. Catholic Historian* 2/16: 92.

[12] Paul B. Steinmetz, S.J., *Pipe, Bible, and Peyote among the Oglala Lakota: A Study in Religious Identity*, rev. ed. (Syracuse, N.Y.: Syracuse University Press, 1990), 191.

Little Warrior wanted to perform a healing ceremony. However, the *yuwipi* was out of the question. As we have seen, the Jesuits condemned the *yuwipi* for the alleged duplicity of the healer and what they considered to be incantation of spirits. During the time of the official ban on Lakota religious ceremonies, the *yuwipi* became the most important ceremony on the Lakota reservations. Before becoming Catholic, Black Elk worked as a medicine man and made a substantial living from performing the *yuwipi*.

There is no evidence that Black Elk did not accept the Jesuits' critique of the *yuwipi* ceremony. The story of his conversion focuses on his rejection of the *yuwipi* in favor of Catholicism. There is no evidence that after his conversion he continued his *yuwipi* practice. While Black Elk performed many rituals while telling his vision, Neihardt's daughter Hilda "recalled that her father repeatedly asked Black Elk to perform a *yuwipi* ceremony for him, but the old man steadfastly refused."[13] More significant, Black Elk makes no mention of the *yuwipi* in *The Sacred Pipe*.

Black Elk's cousin Little Warrior, who was Catholic, offered to do the *wanagi wapiya* [Ghost ceremony of healing], perhaps as an alternative to the *yuwipi*. Lucy said Black Elk did not want to but agreed to out of respect for her and Little Warrior. Little Warrior said: "[*Yuwipi* men] tell you to take down from the wall the holy pictures [of the Sacred Heart] and rosary. I say no. Those are the ones we are going to pray to. . . . If you have a rosary, you'd better say it while I'm doctoring your father."[14] After the ceremony, Black Elk's condition improved.

This story manifests a certain amount of tension as the Lakota Catholics struggle to reinterpret their tradition in a way that both respects tradition and is faithful to their Catholic commitments. In the need to find a cure for Black Elk, the *wanagi wapiya* is proposed as an alternative to the *yuwipi*. Black Elk does not want to participate, but Little Warrior introduces and recenters the prayer on the Catholic elements. In the unresolved question of how to retain Lakota tradition without denying their Catholicism, the Lakota Catholics make a theological judgment about the consistency of the ceremony with Catholic tradition.

While this process may be a struggle at times, it is not accurate to describe this process as the combination of two external religious systems. According to Fools Crow, Black Bear, and Ben Black Elk, despite sociological divisions, the early Lakota Catholics themselves inhabited one cultural world. The one Lakota Catholic world is a result of the internal dynamic to Lakota conversion examined

---

[13]   Raymond J. DeMallie, *The Sixth Grandfather: Black Elk's Teachings Given to John G. Neihardt* (Lincoln: University of Nebraska Press, 1984), 15.

[14]   Steltenkamp, *Black Elk*, 124. Lucy said her father did not talk about his medicine practice much, but she once asked him if he believed in the *yuwipi*: "No! That's all nonsense—just like the magicians you have in the white people. It's just like that. Praying with the pipe is more of a main thing. . . . But this other one, *yuwipi*, it's just like a magician trying to fool. I know because I've done it myself." According to Lucy, Black Elk claims that the ceremony is duplicitous and claims that the pipe is the main focus of Lakota tradition (Steltenkamp, *Black Elk*, 26).

in Chapters 1 and 2. As we saw in Chapter 2, Sanneh argued that indigenous people who discover Christianity in their own language tend to see Christianity within the indigenous culture. New Christian thought comes to inhabit the indigenous cultural world. Chapter 3 described concrete examples of traditional Lakota, particularly Fools Crow, who demonstrated this internal dynamic in their conversion to Christianity. Through the Lakota language they lived in the Lakota cultural world *and* embraced the new Christian thought.

I maintain as well that Black Elk's Lakota thought is a further manifestation of the same internal dynamic. For Black Elk, Lakota tradition and Catholicism were not the two disparate systems that Rice and Powers describe. Rather, as Ben Black Bear argued, they composed one way of looking at the world.

It is helpful at this point to expand somewhat on the internal dynamic employed by Lamin Sanneh. Sanneh highlights the tendency for indigenous people to incorporate new thought into their indigenous cultural world through language. An important reason for this tendency is that the cultures described by Sanneh are oral cultures.

Walter Ong, who describes the fluid categories of conceptualization and organization of knowledge in oral cultures, can help illuminate more clearly Sanneh's dynamic. The rigid analytical and philosophical categories of Rice's and Powers's external dynamic are dependent on the permanence of writing.[15] In contrast, oral cultures must conserve and pass on all knowledge by the spoken word. Consequently, oral cultures cannot retain the necessary tools to build and maintain distinct systems of knowledge. Ong states:

> Oral cultures must conceptualize and verbalize all their knowledge with more or less close reference to the human lifeworld, assimilating the alien, objective world to the more immediate, familiar interaction of human beings.[16]

There can be little room for objective distance to allow the division of knowledge into abstract categories. Knowledge does not exist in separate systems as Powers and Rice propose, but in only one real—if changing—world.

In oral cultures knowledge that is not often repeated aloud disappears. This fosters a conservative set of mind that tends to inhibit intellectual experimentation. Originality does not come from completely new systems of knowledge but by incorporating new ideas into the established framework of knowledge. The old formulas and themes are made to interact with new and complicated situations, "but the formulas and themes are reshuffled rather than supplanted with new materials."[17] This process applies to all aspects of culture. Ong goes on to say:

---

[15] Although I focus on the fluidity of oral cultures, even literate modern Western cultures change and absorb new cultural influence over time, contrary to the impression given by Rice and Powers.

[16] Walter J. Ong, S.J., *Orality and Literacy: The Technologizing of the Word* (New York: Methuen, 1982), 42.

[17] Ibid.

Religious practices, and with them cosmologies and deep-seated beliefs, also change in oral cultures. Disappointed with the practical results of the cult at a given shrine when cures there are infrequent, vigorous leaders . . . invent new shrines and with these new conceptual universes. Yet these new universes and the other changes that show a certain originality come into being in an essentially formulaic and thematic noetic economy. They are seldom if ever explicitly touted for their novelty but are presented as fitting the traditions of the ancestors.[18]

According to Ong, oral cultures must change in order to respond to new challenges, but they must retain the traditional framework of knowledge in order to survive. Any new knowledge must be presented and understood within the traditional framework.

The characteristics of oral cultures are important for this study. Because oral cultures lack the permanence of writing, discourse closely reflects the current practices of a changing world. However, oral agents do not develop this change as an alternative system to the traditional framework. Rather, change inhabits the traditional cultural framework.

Ong's description of the fluid nature of oral cultures is nothing new, nor is it contradictory to Lakota tradition. Lakota Plains culture itself was a recent development, as the Dakota fanned out from woodlands in the 1700s and took up the horse to follow the buffalo on the western Plains. According to Steltenkamp, "Demographic convulsions of the frontier era created for Plains groups a kind of utilitarian behavioral mode whereby expedience vied equally with convention."[19] The creation of the Lakota Plains traditions is a product of innovation and reinterpretation that evolved internally in the previous Dakota framework.

Consequently, Lakota tradition was a changing, evolving body of thought and practice. It was never codified in the way that Christianity has been in the Roman Catholic tradition.[20] The Lakota modified and transformed ceremonies to deal with new problems that the Lakota people encountered. These new problems demanded new answers from holy men. O. Douglas Schwartz explains the role of the holy man in this process:

The holy man has a "vision" of the world—its nature, its history and its destiny—and a sense of humanity's place within that scheme. Through that vision, the holy man can hope to solve problems for which the tradition offers no ready-made solutions. The *wicasa wakan* is then the theoretician—the theologian—of the Plains religion.[21]

---

[18]  Ibid.

[19]  Steltenkamp, *Black Elk*, 10.

[20]  Contrary to the assumptions of Rice and Powers, the history of the comparatively codified Catholicism demonstrates incredible change over time.

[21]  Clyde Holler, *Black Elk's Religion: The Sun Dance and Lakota Catholicism* (Syracuse, N.Y.: Syracuse University Press, 1995), 181. DeMallie elaborates on the role of the holy man in Lakota religion: "In Lakota culture, the quest for knowledge of the

Such agency to enact innovation and reinterpretation in response to new problems was a central virtue embodied by the holy man.

Black Elk was explicitly aware of the historical nature of this dynamic process of Lakota change. In *The Sacred Pipe* Black Elk describes the process of Lakota religious adaptation. The ritual of *hunkapi*, or the making of relatives, originated with the Lakota, Matohoshila, who received a vision from *Wakan Tanka*.[22] Through the cooperation of the Ree tribe, a traditional enemy with an agricultural economy, a new rite using corn was established to make peace between nations.[23] New religious power was actively incorporated into Lakota tradition through the symbol of another nation.

Black Elk explicitly applies the internal dynamic of Lakota tradition to his understanding of Christian thought. After the Lakota first settled on the reservation, Black Elk decided to join Buffalo Bill's Wild West Show. He stated that he wanted to see "the ways of the white man" and "if the white man's ways were better, why I would like to see my people live that way."[24] Writing two months after returning from Europe, Black Elk articulated the results of his investigation into the white man's customs:

> So thus all along, of the white man's customs, only his faith, the white man's beliefs about God's will, and how they act according to it, I wanted to understand. I traveled to one city after another, and there were many customs around God's will. "Though I speak with the tongues of men and of angels, and have not charity, I am become as sounding brass, or a tinkling cymbal. And though I have the gift of prophecy, and understand all mysteries, and all knowledge, and though I have all faith, so that I could remove mountains, and have not charity, I am nothing. And though I bestow all my goods to feed the poor, and though I give my body to be burned, and have not charity, it profiteth me nothing" [1 Cor 13].
>
> So Lakota people, trust in God! Now all along I trust in God. I work honestly and it is good; I hope the people will do likewise. . . . Across the big ocean is where they killed Jesus; again I wished to see it but it was four days on the ocean and there was no railroad. [It would require] much money for me to be able to go over there to tell about it myself.[25]

---

*wakan* was largely a personal enterprise, and it was predominately the work of men . . . there was no standard theology, no dogmatic body of belief. Fundamental concepts were universally shared, but specific knowledge of the *wakan* beings was not shared beyond a small number of holy men. Through individual experience, every man had the opportunity to contribute to and resynthesize the general body of knowledge that constituted Lakota religion" (DeMallie, *The Sixth Grandfather,* 82).

[22] Joseph Epes Brown, *The Sacred Pipe: Black Elk's Account of the Seven Rites of the Oglala Sioux* (1953; repr., Norman: University of Oklahoma Press, 1989), 101.

[23] Ibid., 102–3.

[24] DeMallie, *The Sixth Grandfather*, 245.

[25] Black Elk, letter to *Iapi Oaye* (Santee Agency, Nebraska), 18/12 (December 1889), 37, trans. Raymond J. DeMallie in collaboration with Vine V. Deloria Sr., cited in DeMallie, *The Sixth Grandfather*, 10.

Black Elk concludes that the white man's beliefs about God's will *are the only customs worthy of understanding*. There is no wholesale adoption of an external white cultural system or separation from the Lakota framework. Rather, Black Elk makes it clear that he continues to be Lakota while incorporating new Christian thought into the Lakota world.

## THE INTERNAL DYNAMIC OF BLACK ELK'S CONVERSION

As we return to Black Elk's conversion, we need to keep this cultural context in mind. Black Elk was part of a Lakota culture that had been consciously reshaping itself in response to the colonial pressure that pushed it onto the Plains. Black Elk appropriated new Christian thought in the language of this fluid oral Lakota culture. As a result, we should not expect Black Elk's conversion to conform to the external approach suggested by Rice and Powers. Separation between Lakota tradition and Christianity is not the natural or necessary result of Lakota conversion to Christianity. Rather, it comes from an external source (government and missionaries) that does not fully understand Lakota tradition and yet controls the power of interpretation.

Instead, despite a sociological division that continued through his life, Black Elk's conversion should broadly follow the internal dynamics of oral culture present in Lakota tradition and exhibit a dual effect. First, as described above in oral cultures, cultural innovation should be manifested in the same indigenous formulaic and thematic noetic economy. Knowledge is not organized in discrete systems but reflects the one world that the people of oral cultures inhabit. Consequently, Black Elk's conversion should be understood as the introduction of new Catholic knowledge within the traditional Lakota framework. From here on, I refer to this process as the incarnation of Christ into the Lakota world.

Second, Black Elk's conversion also has implications for Lakota culture. The new knowledge introduced in the traditional framework does not consist of isolated beliefs. New beliefs by their very nature affect the whole cultural world as the agents reread the framework in light of the new knowledge. As a result, Black Elk's conversion should be understood as a recentering of the Lakota framework around the new Catholic knowledge. Nothing in Black Elk's presentation of Lakota tradition should explicitly contradict the new center. I refer to this second process as the redescription of the Lakota world based on the incarnation of Christ.

While the following chapter examines the first process, the incarnation of Christ into the Lakota world, I focus here on the second aspect of the process, the redescription of the Lakota world. In addition to the rejection of the *yuwipi*, I argue that Black Elk recentered Lakota tradition in light of Catholicism in four major ways: the rejection of violence, the reinterpretation of Lakota tradition as the Old Testament, the adoption of a universal emphasis on Lakota tradition, and the reinterpretation of *Wakan Tanka* as the Christian God. Black Elk's "Lakota" discourse in the Neihardt interviews and *The Sacred Pipe*, then, is an integral part of his Catholic conversion and a demonstration of Lakota agency.

It is his attempt to "look at it from another angle," as Black Bear said, to do theology, and to understand the Lakota world in light of the incarnation of Christ.

## VIOLENCE AND THE LAKOTA TRADITION

The first theme of the Lakota tradition that Black Elk reinterprets is violence. Historically, the Lakota engaged in violent conflicts with neighboring tribes and then the U.S. government. As a result, Lakota culture viewed proficiency and success in war as central virtues. Because of his Christian conversion, Black Elk reinterpreted Lakota tradition in two ways. First, he de-emphasized the role of violence in Lakota tradition in general, and second, he explicitly rejected the opportunity to use violence.

Black Elk's general de-emphasis on violence in the Lakota tradition is most evident in his account of the Sun Dance in *The Sacred Pipe*. Early accounts of the Sun Dance ascribe success in war as a primary motive for the Sun Dance.[26] Holler states that unlike these earlier accounts, Black Elk's Sun Dance "is generally disassociated [*sic*] from war."[27] Black Elk never explicitly links the vow or purpose of the Sun Dance to success in war. He also reinterprets the symbolism of the rabbit skin of the Sun Dance. While Lakota holy man George Sword states that it is "an emblem of fleetness and endurance," Black Elk interprets it as representing humility and meekness, which Holler states are "decidedly not the traditional virtues of the Lakota warrior."[28]

In addition, Black Elk reinterprets the symbolism of the black face paint, which traditionally represented proficiency in war.[29] Brown quotes Black Elk: "By going on the warpath, we know that we have done something bad, and we wish to hide our faces from *Wakan-Tanka*."[30] Unlike earlier Lakota tradition, success in war is now viewed as negative and contrary to the will of *Wakan Tanka*.

Black Elk embodies this general de-emphasis on violence in the Lakota tradition by his explicit rejection of its use. Black Elk's most important critique of war is found in the account of his vision. In his great vision Black Elk is given the soldier weed of destruction, a rare herb that grows only in certain parts of South Dakota, which "could be used in war and could destroy a nation."[31] Black Elk describes a battle seen in his vision, in which he hears rapid gunfire, women and children wailing, horses screaming in fear, and shouts of victory. Black Elk says:

---

[26] For a detailed history of the Sun Dance and its historical change, see Holler, *Black Elk's Religion.*

[27] Ibid., 149.

[28] Ibid.

[29] James R. Walker, *Lakota Belief and Ritual*, ed. Raymond J. DeMallie and Elaine A. Jahner (1980; repr., Lincoln: University of Nebraska Press, 1991), 273–75.

[30] Brown, *The Sacred Pipe*, 92.

[31] DeMallie, *The Sixth Grandfather*, 135.

I am glad I did not perform this killing, for I would have not only killed the enemy but I would probably have killed the women and children of the enemy, but I am satisfied that I have not been well off. Perhaps I would have been a chief if I had obeyed this, but I am satisfied that I didn't become a chief. . . . War itself is terrible.[32]

Black Elk sacrifices the opportunity to obtain great power with the soldier weed because "war itself is terrible." Shortly after, Neihardt comments in his notes, "at the age of thirty-seven, Black Elk was to use this herb. . . . At this time he gave it up for the Catholic religion."[33] Neihardt explicitly links the rejection of war and violence to Black Elk's conversion. This statement is all the more significant as it is the only reference to Black Elk's Catholic life in the transcripts.

This is reinforced in *The Sacred Pipe*, where Black Elk explicitly links Christ to peace. According to Black Elk, "God sent men His son, who would restore order and peace upon the earth; and we have been told that Jesus the Christ was [his Son]." Black Elk recenters Lakota tradition and his own life around Christ and his restoration of peace. The rejection of war, the incorporation of peace, and a modification in Lakota tradition demonstrate Sanneh's internal dynamic. The indigenous agent reformulates the indigenous cultural framework around the Christian story.

## THE CHRISTIAN CLAIM OF UNIVERSALITY

In addition to accepting the Christian critique of war and violence, Black Elk reinterprets the object of Lakota ceremonial life. Ceremonies are no longer conducted primarily for personal power for war and the survival of the tribe. Instead, they are performed for all nations and peoples.[34] This modification is demonstrated in Black Elk's interpretation of the Sun Dance. Holler develops this point by describing the Sun Dance:

Although the theme of the survival of the people is attested to in the classic period, it is never interpreted as the reason for making a pledge. In the classic period, pledges are made primarily for success in war. Black Elk does not mention this benefit, or the acquisition of shamanic power by the individual pledger, the power acquired by the dance accruing instead to the people as a whole.[35]

For Black Elk, the motivation for involvement in the Sun Dance changes from the acquisition of personal power to the survival of the people as a whole. What

---

[32]  Ibid., 136.

[33]  Ibid., 137.

[34]  For a description of the intent of classic Lakota religion, see Holler, *Black Elk's Religion*, chap. 3, "The Classic Sun Dance Remembered," 75–109.

[35]  Ibid., 150. By "classic period" Holler means the period of time between the first European contact with the Lakota and the government ban on the Sun Dance.

Holler does not make clear is that "people" for Black Elk's is not restricted to the Lakota alone. In addition to the Lakota, Black Elk states that the sacred hoop of his vision is "the continents of the world and the people shall stand as one."[36]

Black Elk's universality is emphasized in his description of *hanblecheyapi*, or what is typically called the vision quest. He describes the lamenter as seeing the light of wisdom, for "it is Your [*Wakan Tanka*'s] will that the peoples of the world do not live in the darkness of ignorance."[37] *Wakan Tanka*'s will is not for Lakota survival alone but for all peoples.

Fools Crow agrees with this universalist understanding of Black Elk. In his autobiography he says: "Like myself, Black Elk prayed constantly that all people would live as one and would co-operate with one another. We have both loved the non-Indian races, and we do not turn our back on them to please those of our own people who do not agree."[38] According to Fools Crow, Black Elk extends the boundaries of the Lakota tradition to embrace all peoples, regardless of other interpreters of Lakota traditions.

Again we see the dual dynamic described by Sanneh and Ong. Black Elk's elimination of the focus on war in Lakota tradition and the insertion of universality into the Lakota framework follow the description of orality provided by Ong. Black Elk absorbs new Christian thought within the old culture, which in turn is reinterpreted to be in continuity with the new thought.

## LAKOTA TRADITION AND THE OLD TESTAMENT

As we have seen so far, Black Elk eliminates those aspects of Lakota tradition that are not consistent with the new center of Christ. In addition, Black Elk reinterprets his understanding of Lakota tradition as a whole. Lucy Looks Twice says that her father equated the Lakota to the Israelites:

He and Father Buechel would talk. They talked about my father's visions . . . and the Sun Dance, and all the Indian ceremonies that my father said were connected to Christianity. My father said we were like the Israelites, the Jews, waiting for Christ. . . . They knew, somehow, that in the future our Lord Jesus Christ would come one day to his people. . . . And they somehow already practiced it in the Sun Dance.[39]

According to Lucy, Black Elk believes that the Lakota practiced Christianity in their ceremonies. Black Elk states in an interview recorded in 1944 that "the peace pipe was the Bible to our tribe."[40] Black Elk not only reinterpreted the present and future based on religious innovation, but also the past.

[36] DeMallie, *The Sixth Grandfather*, 139.
[37] Brown, *The Sacred Pipe*, 65.
[38] Mails, *Fools Crow* (1979), 45.
[39] Steltenkamp, *Black Elk*, 102.
[40] DeMallie, *The Sixth Grandfather*, 334.

This theme is continued by Ben Marrowbone. Marrowbone was a highly respected reservation elder and one of leaders pressing claims to the U.S. government that the Black Hills should be returned to the Lakota. He also worked as a catechist when Black Elk was still an active missionary.[41] Marrowbone claims that Black Elk equated the Lakota framework with the Old Testament.

A heavenly woman once came and gave us a pipe. Every family had to keep a pipe of its own—use it every day, at night too. That woman gave it to us and told us to talk to the Almighty—pray for whatever we need—for rain or good crops. You didn't have to see any great vision. The almighty hears. Take this pipe. Pray that he hears you. That's what the holy woman said. That kind of order was given to our grandfathers. So they followed.

Before he converted, Nick Black Elk talked to Almighty God with that pipe. He learned that same god talked to white people. That's why those catechists believed in the Catholic church. Nobody said: "Oh, you fool you!" No. That's the great Almighty you are respecting and honoring—in a new way. And just as we were brought the sacred pipe, we now had the sacred bread [the Eucharist] from heaven.

Nick Black Elk used to use that pipe in his *wapiya* [curing ceremony], and he believed in it. At that time there weren't any doctors, so different ceremonies were used for healing. So I think Black Elk worked according to the Almighty. These old people used the pipe and prayed to one Spirit. That was their foundation. That's what he said.

The catechists would get together, have meetings, encourage each other—show interest in one another. At one such gathering, Nick Black Elk stood up and said: "*Yuwipi* come from Santee [the Dakota-speaking Sioux from the Minnesota area]. We have a pipe here. We use that. God gave us that pipe from heaven through a woman. Two young men met her while out hunting. One had bad thoughts about her and was punished. But the other one was a good man. She told him, 'I want to explain to the Lakota people how to pray.' She brought that pipe and gave it to an old man—a good man with a good conscience.

"That pipe—it's a road to take—a road of honesty—a road to heaven. It teaches how to lead a good life, like the Ten Commandments. They understood what that woman was saying, and that worship was my formation—my foundation. But my foundation is deepening.

"God made me to know him, love him, serve him. To make sure I do this, God sent us his Son. The Old way is good. God prepared us before the missionary came. Our ancestors used the pipe to know God. That's a foundation! But from the old country came Christ from heaven—a wonderful thing—the Son of God. And the Indian cares about this."[42]

---

[41] Steltenkamp, *Black Elk*, 52.

[42] Ibid., 104–5.

According to Marrowbone, Black Elk understood the Lakota tradition of the Pipe to be good and foundational. Christ is for the Lakota, and to accept Christianity does not erase the foundation or mean a separate existence. Christ is incorporated into the Lakota tradition and deepens the foundation.

Black Elk illustrates these positions in *The Sacred Pipe*. Here he organizes Lakota traditions into seven rites. Holler states that "since there is no mention of a seven-rite Lakota ritual complex in the literature before *The Sacred Pipe*, Black Elk has clearly conformed traditional religion to the Catholic model for the purpose of comparing and equating the two."[43] Lakota scholar DeMallie agrees: "The teachings seem to represent the end point in Black Elk's synthesis of Lakota and Christian beliefs. . . . Perhaps this was Black Elk's final attempt to bridge the two religious traditions that his life had so intimately embodied."[44]

However, Black Elk is not primarily bridging what is essentially an artificial sociological division. Rather, Black Elk makes an explicit theological connection between Lakota and Catholic tradition. According to Black Elk, the two traditions are not similar or parallel; rather, they are internally connected in a way that *precedes* separation. This clearly follows Sanneh's internal dynamic and Ong's categories of oral cultures. Cultural innovation (Christ) is incorporated into the old noetic framework (Lakota tradition), and that framework is interpreted in light of the innovation.

## *WAKAN TANKA* AND THE CHRISTIAN GOD

The fourth aspect of Black Elk's reformulation of Lakota tradition is his understanding of *Wakan Tanka*. While it is unclear today what the exact nature of the Lakota tradition was before contact with Christianity, it is generally agreed that it was not monotheistic. Both DeMallie and Lavenda, as well as Powers, agree that *Wakan Tanka* "is a single term that refers to sixteen aspects, all of which are related to each other in a special way."[45] DeMallie and Powers agree that *Wakan Tanka* is an impersonal "animating force" as well as an impersonal creator.[46] Rice also states that Sioux narrators shared "the tolerance of diverse spiritual thought without universal reverence for any one divinity."[47] Rice refers to Good Seat, born in 1827 and one of oldest Lakota interviewed by James R. Walker, for a typical early Lakota understanding: "The white men have made [the Lakota] forget that which their fathers told them. . . . In old times the Indians did not know of a Great Spirit. . . . There is no Nagi Tanka [Great Spirit]."[48]

---

43  Holler, *Black Elk's Religion*, 141.

44  DeMallie, *The Sixth Grandfather*, 71.

45  William K. Powers, *Sacred Language: The Nature of Supernatural Discourse in Lakota* (Norman: University of Oklahoma Press, 1986), 119.

46  Rice, *Before the Great Spirit: The Many Faces of Sioux Spirituality* (Albuquerque: University of New Mexico Press, 1998), 152.

47  Ibid., 13.

48  Ibid., 20.

Because there was no central figure, Lakota tradition employed a great diversity of spirits in ritual supplication. Rice writes: "Since there was no consensus of devotion to a single *Wakan Tanka* (God), adherents of competing spirits like Wakinyan and Unktehi felt no obligation to pray to each other's several *wakan tanka* (great spirits)."[49] According to Rice, Lakota tradition did not recognize a single all-powerful god or practice a uniform worship to the same deities.

In contrast to earlier Lakota traditions, Black Elk reinterprets the Lakota pantheon and focuses it on a unified *Wakan Tanka*. In the introduction of *The Sacred Pipe* he declares: "It is my prayer . . . that through this book. . . [the white men] will realize that we Indians know the One true God, and that we pray to Him continually."[50] Black Elk directly equates *Wakan Tanka* with the Christian God, which the Lakota "know as the One true God" and then proceeds to discuss the Lakota religion.

Throughout *The Sacred Pipe*, Black Elk consistently describes *Wakan Tanka* as one united being: "Give us the knowledge to understand that they [powers of the universe] are all really one Power."[51] According to Raymond DeMallie, this association of a unified *Wakan Tanka* has "no parallel in recorded Lakota religious tradition."[52] Black Elk has actively transformed the Lakota tradition and united the Lakota pantheon.

In addition, Black Elk uses Christian language to describe *Wakan Tanka* and his action. Steinmetz lists the following examples:

Any man . . . who is attached to the senses and to the things of this world, is one who lives in ignorance and is being consumed by the snakes which represent his own passions. . . . It should also be a sacred day when a soul is released and returns to its home, *Wakan-Tanka*. . . . Further, my relatives, our Father, *Wakan-Tanka*, has made His will known to us here on earth, and we must always do that which he wishes if we should walk the sacred path . . . and as the flames of the sun come to us in the morning, so comes the grace of *Wankan-Tanka*, by which all creatures are enlightened.[53]

According to Steinmetz, "These expressions are paraphrases, and sometimes almost direct quotations from the Bible and Catholic catechism."[54] To his list Steinmetz could add the descriptions of creation: "It is You who have placed us upon this island; we are the last to be created by You who are first and who always have been . . . remembering the goodness of *Wankan Tanka*, and how it was He made all things."

Finally, Black Elk directly quotes the Baltimore Catechism to explain the purpose of *The Sacred Pipe*:

---

[49] Ibid., 33.
[50] Brown, *The Sacred Pipe*, xx.
[51] Ibid., 37.
[52] DeMallie, *The Sixth Grandfather*, 91.
[53] Steinmetz, *Pipe, Bible and Peyote,* 186.
[54] Ibid.

When we do understand all this deeply in our hearts, then we will fear, and love, and know the Great Spirit, and then we will be and act and live as He intends.[55]

Q. 126. What do we mean by the "end of man"?

A. By the "end of man" we mean the purpose for which he was created: namely, to know, love, and serve God.[56]

According to Black Elk and the Baltimore Catechism, the purpose of human life is to know and love God. As a result, *Wakan Tanka* acts within the Lakota story and history, even though the language Black Elk uses to describe *Wakan Tanka* is Christian. God creates all, enlightens humanity, is good, eternal, and worthy of our knowledge, fear, and love.

Of the Christian characteristics that Black Elk ascribes to *Wakan Tanka*, the judgment of sin is perhaps the most unlikely. Rice argues that in addition to the lack of the monotheistic *Wakan Tanka*, there was no divine judgment or eschatological harmony in the Lakota tradition.[57] Yet, as we will see in both Chapters 5 and 7, for Black Elk judgment of sin and the institution of the Promised Land is one of most important aspects of *Wakan Tanka*.

Overall, Black Elk's understanding of *Wakan Tanka* has been transformed. Not only does Black Elk unify the previously multifaceted *Wakan Tanka* to one divine being, but he explicitly equates him to the Christian God. Again we see Black Elk's innovations inserted into Lakota tradition. Black Elk does not hold the belief in one God and the Son of God over and against Lakota tradition, but, in continuity with Sanneh's internal dynamic, Black Elk makes them part of Lakota tradition.

## FOOLS CROW: THE BLACK ELK TRADITION EMBODIED

Black Elk's reformulation of Lakota tradition is demonstrated in his interviews and recollections of family and contemporaries, and it also survives in the Lakota religious tradition. Fools Crow exemplifies this influence. Black Elk, Fools Crow's uncle, served as one of Fools Crow's mentors in becoming a holy man. Holler claims that Fools Crow is the most influential interpreter of the Black Elk tradition.[58] Fools Crow describes his relationship with Black Elk:

My uncle, the renowned Black Elk, has earned a place above all of the other Teton holy men. We all hold him the highest. I have never heard a bad word about him, and he never said a bad word about anyone. All he wanted to do was love and serve his fellow man. Black Elk was my father's first cousin, and so he is my blood uncle. But in the Indian custom, he was

---

[55] Brown, *The Sacred Pipe*, xx.

[56] The Baltimore Catechism is available online.

[57] Rice, *Before the Great Spirit*, 20.

[58] Holler, *Black Elk's Religion*, 164.

also a father to me. I stayed with him quite often, and sometimes for long periods of time. We also made a few trips together, and over the years talked about many things. I learned a great deal about *Wakan-Tanka*, prophecy and medicine from him.[59]

Fools Crow identifies Black Elk as a mentor who greatly influenced his understanding of *Wakan Tanka*. Fools Crow's interpretation of the Lakota tradition embodies the Christian innovations of Black Elk.[60] Like Black Elk, he rejects violence and war. Fools Crow cites violent tactics as the reason why traditionalists withdrew their support from AIM. Fools Crow states that even the corrupt tribal president knows that "traditionalists do not resort to violence."[61] War is not emphasized in Fools Crow's Sun Dance.

Fools Crow accepts the universal focus of the Sun Dance. It is not only the pledgers who participate and benefit, but "everyone is profoundly involved, and because of this the Sioux nation and all of the peoples of the world are blessed by *Wakan Tanka*."[62] The efficacy of the Sun Dance affects the whole world.

Fools Crow also interprets *Wakan Tanka* as the Christian God. In the words of Fools Crow, "There is only one true God, and we Sioux have believed this for as far back in time as we can remember";[63] Fools Crow even compares the Lakota understanding of divinity to the Trinity.[64] Throughout his autobiography, God is used interchangeably with *Wakan Tanka*. As we will see in Chapter 7, it is *Wakan Tanka* who now judges the sins of humanity. Mails draws attention to this presence in Fools Crow's Sun Dance:

> The primary source of power called upon in the Sun Dance is the same God that Christians worship, and it is not without consequence that the men who lead and pledge in the dances often claim to be both traditionalist and Christian. Fools Crow, whose memory takes him as far back as 1897, declares that his people have always believed in a Supreme Being who is identical with the God of the Bible.[65]

---

[59] Mails, *Fools Crow* (1979), 53.

[60] The only difference between Black Elk's and Fools Crow's interpretations of Lakota tradition is the *yuwipi*. Black Elk completely rejected the *yuwipi*, while Fools Crow continued to practice it. This discrepancy may have a number of roots. The first is the difference in commitment to Catholic life. Both were sincere, but Black Elk spent over two decades as a leader of the Lakota Catholic Church. Fools Crow never occupied a leadership position. Even though Black Elk rejected the *yuwipi*, he allowed a modified healing ceremony to be conducted on him. Thus, a hard distinction between Black Elk's and Fools Crow's interpretation of the *yuwipi* should be avoided.

[61] Mails, *Fools Crow* (1979), 216. This in an innovation because military success through violence was a central virtue for traditionalists from pre-reservation times.

[62] Ibid., 44.

[63] Ibid., 119.

[64] Ibid., 120.

[65] Ibid., 193. These innovations are not unique to Fools Crow. Stephen Feraca, writing in 1963, reported that Gilbert Bad Wound considered the Sun Dance a Christian

Fools Crow worked to embody these innovations in a way that challenged the external pressure that separated Lakota Catholicism and Lakota tradition. By the mid-twentieth century the sociological separation between Catholicism and Lakota ceremonies began to dissolve. The Sun Dance was revived, and Lakota Catholics began to openly participate in it. The church also began to reassess its interpretation of the Sun Dance as some Jesuits began to engage Lakota ceremonies and use the pipe in Catholic liturgical contexts. Perhaps the best example of this was Fools Crow's Sun Dance described in Chapter 3. Mass was said at the Sun Dance grounds, and Fools Crow invited Father Steinmetz to pierce. This led Steinmetz (and some others) to embrace the Lakota tradition as a type of Old Testament.[66] While still unresolved,[67] Black Elk's son Ben said that he was happy, because Lakota and Catholic tradition were now embodied in the church:

> So I used to live two lives: one, Indian religion, and one as a Christian. To us, the Indian pipe is sacred; it has meaning for us. It used to be that when I would speak about the pipe, when I used the pipe, it seemed to me that it clashed with Christianity. But now, I know they come together in our Church. Behind the altar, we have the tipi design. In our Christian ceremonials, we use the pipe. We see that there is no clash. After these years it comes together. Now, I live only one way.[68]

## RETELLING THE STORY: BLACK ELK'S AGENCY

In light of the preceding analysis, Rice's claim that Catholicism erased Lakota tradition and Powers's description of Catholicism as a superficial framework fail to account for Black Elk's dedicated Catholic life and his continuing discourse on a Lakota tradition that has been redescribed in light of new Catholic thought. The five areas of religious change in Black Elk's thought—the *yuwipi*,

---

ceremony. Feraca states that "he is by no means alone in this belief" (Holler, *Black Elk's Religion*, 154). Eagle Feather, Thomas Mails's main informant for his book *Sundancing at Rosebud and Pine Ridge* (Sioux Falls, S.D.: Center for Western Studies, 1978), also equates *Wakan Tanka* with the Christian God. In discussing his 1975 Sun Dance, Eagle Feather states, "I sincerely believe in Almighty God in both the non-Indian and Indian ways, because we pray to one and the same God" (Mails, *Sundancing at Rosebud and Pine Ridge*, 152). Plenty Wolf states that "the piercing of the flesh in the Sun Dance is a reminder of the piercing of Jesus. When a man pierces his flesh, he is doing it in remembrance of Christ" (Steinmetz, *Pipe, Bible and Peyote*, 190).

[66] For autobiographical accounts of missionary conversion to this perspective, see Steinmetz, *Pipe, Bible, and Peyote;* William Stolzman, *The Pipe and Christ: A Christian-Sioux Dialogue* (Chamberlain, S.D.: Tipi Press, 1995).

[67] According to Black Bear, the majority of people are still waiting for "a sort of blending where you establish a basically Lakota Catholic Church" (Archambault, "Ben Black Bear, Jr.," 99).

[68] DeSersa and Pourier, *Black Elk Lives*, 8–9.

war and peace, universality, Lakota tradition as an Old Testament, and *Wakan Tanka* as the Christian God—all demonstrate the same pattern of change. First, Black Elk incorporated new religious thought into the Lakota framework. He then reinterpreted the Lakota framework in light of the new thought, so as to avoid contradiction and unify the new worldview. Finally, and most important, Black Elk retained the Lakota framework. Innovation did not erase the Lakota world it now inhabited.

So, rather than using an external dynamic that views Black Elk's conversion in opposition to Lakota tradition, Black Elk guides us to see his conversion *in continuity* with Lakota tradition. Sanneh's internal dynamic, the categories of primary orality, the Lakota tradition itself, the role of the *wicasa wakan* (holy men), and Black Elk's understanding of Lakota tradition all demonstrate that the reformulation of Lakota tradition is an expected product of economic and demographic change. It is also an expected result of his conversion to Christianity. Christian belief was not a thin illusion of insincere necessity that hid a pure Lakota tradition. Rather, Black Elk incorporated Christian thought into the Lakota cultural world. To deny this imposes foreign categories on the sources. More important, it denies the agency of the Lakota to live according to their own cultural standards and to use their creativity to confront a changing world.

# 5

# Black Elk's Vision:
# The Incarnation
# of the Lakota Christ

*And so I say to you, you are* Inyan,
*and upon this rock I will build my church.*
—MATTHEW 16:18

*James, son of Zebedee, and John the brother*
*of James, whom he named Boanerges, that is,*
*sons of* Wakinyan.[1]
—MARK 3:17

Black Elk made Catholicism an integral part of the Lakota world. Chapter 2 demonstrated how the missionary practice of using the Lakota language made this possible through what Sanneh calls the internal dynamic to indigenous conversion. Chapter 3 gave examples of Lakota-speaking traditionals such as Fools Crow, a holy man and a ceremonial chief of the Lakota nation, who embodied the internal dynamic in both sincere Christian participation and traditional Lakota

---

[1] Unless otherwise noted, all English biblical citations are taken from the New American Bible. In passages in the Riggs Dakota Bible *inyan* is rock and *wakinyan* is thunder (*Dakota Wowapi Wakan: The Holy Bible in the Language of the Dakotas*, trans. Tomas S. Williamson and Stephen R. Riggs [New York: American Bible Society, 1880]). See note 5 for an explanation of the Riggs Dakota Bible and the significance of the translation. I am indebted to Jan Ullrich, a Lakota linguist, who provided all of the biblical translations as well as invaluable insight into Lakota culture. He is currently translating Buechel's *Bible History* (Eugene Buechel, S.J., *Wowapi Wakan, Wicowoyake Yeptecelapi: Bible History in the Language of the Teton Sioux Indians*, ed. Paul Manhart [New York: Benzinger Brothers, 1924]; hereafter referred to as *Bible History*) as well as textbooks to teach the Lakota language. His work can be found online.

lifestyle. Chapter 4 showed how traditional Lakota lived in one Lakota Catholic world, despite external sociological division, and how Black Elk made this clear in his discourse; he redescribed the Lakota world in light of the incarnation of the Christian story.

But what of the incarnation of the Christian narrative in the indigenous world? Of course, communal storytelling, public ritual, and personal devotion incarnated the Christian story into the Lakota world. But did Black Elk's Lakota discourse reflect only the redescription of the Lakota world, or did it also reflect the actual incarnation of the Christian story?

Black Elk told Neihardt about the great vision he had at the age of nine. Two men descended from the clouds and brought Black Elk to the sacred tipi of the six grandfathers. They called the young Lakota boy to "create a nation" and lead his people down the red road into the sacred hoop. Black Elk would be an intercessor for his people and make the sacred tree bloom with the power given to him by the six grandfathers. This vision dominated the rest of Black Elk's life as he strove to fulfill the call of the six grandfathers.

Most academics portray Black Elk's vision as a pure, pre-contact view of the Lakota tradition. In addition, they often assume that Black Elk's conversion to Catholicism was a turning away from the six grandfathers' call. Raymond DeMallie states that "by accepting Catholicism he at last put himself beyond the onerous obligation of his vision."[2] Julian Rice claims that the "largely 'pure' Lakota content of [the Neihardt] interviews may express a desire to wholeheartedly return to traditional religion."[3] Thus, for many academics, Black Elk's vision represents the antithesis of his life as a Catholic.

Despite the position of most academics, my thesis—that Black Elk lived in one Lakota Catholic world—is not new. Black Elk's daughter Lucy indicates that Black Elk's vision is a reflection of Black Elk's Lakota Catholicism and that the central symbol of Black Elk's great vision, the sacred tree, is in fact a Christian symbol:

> The Great Spirit has promised one day that the tree of my father's vision was to root, grow, and blossom—to give out its flourishing sweet scent for everyone, and become a symbol of life. I know this. He meant it's like the Catholic faith. Our Lord told St. Peter to establish the religion just like that. The Great Spirit gave the Sioux people a knowledge of Christianity through the sacred pipe. But this tree would grow and spread out strong, flowing branches. He had that vision and learned the tree was to be the Christian life of all people.[4]

---

[2] Raymond J. DeMallie, *The Sixth Grandfather: Black Elk's Teachings Given to John G. Neihardt* (Lincoln: University of Nebraska Press, 1984), 14.

[3] Julian Rice, *Before the Great Spirit: The Many Faces of Sioux Spirituality* (Albuquerque: University of New Mexico Press, 1998), 14.

[4] Michael F. Steltenkamp, S.J., *Black Elk: Holy Man of the Oglala* (Norman: University of Oklahoma Press, 1993), 109.

This chapter will examine Lucy's claim that "the tree was to be the Christian life of all people," beginning with the strong correlation between the language and imagery of Black Elk's vision and the biblical narrative. The remainder of the Black Elk corpus—Neihardt's notes, *The Sacred Pipe*, and Black Elk's letters—provide greater depth for the symbols of Black Elk's vision, as does a comparison of Black Elk's discourse with the Riggs Dakota Bible, which, according to Lakota linguist and ethnographer Jan Ullrich, is the biblical text that Black Elk used.[5] In addition, other Lakota sources ascribe similar Christian interpretations to Black Elk or make similar Christian interpretations independently of Black Elk as evidence. In the end, I argue, we find Black Elk's vision not to be a "pure" Lakota remnant but rather a Lakota-Catholic narrative of salvation history. The vision is remarkably similar to the imagery and plot of the book of Revelation, and its central theme is christological.

Of course, Black Elk's vision is not a mere repetition of salvation history. It is another reflection of the first part of Sanneh's internal dynamic, the incarnation of Christ into the indigenous world. The vision is uniquely Lakota in that Black Elk reads salvation history internal to the Lakota cultural world of the early reservation period. Black Elk's vision appears to be an intentional historical account of the Lakota, their discovery of Christianity, and the problem of colonialism. In other words, Black Elk's vision is an imaginative exploration of the history and implications of the Lakota's conversion to Catholicism.

This chapter also illuminates the second process of the internal dynamic, the redescription of the indigenous world in light of the incarnation and how the christological nature of the vision is found in Black Elk's refashioning of the entire Lakota tradition. Black Elk redescribed the Lakota tradition to avoid contradiction with the Christian story and also to show how Christ permeated the entire Lakota tradition as its central theme.

---

[5] In response to my question, "Why you are so certain that Black Elk had access to the Riggs Bible?" Jan Ullrich replied in an informal communication: "I have NO DOUBT about it. Riggs's Bible was widely used by all Christian Dakota and Lakota, because there weren't any other biblical texts in dialects of Sioux available until Buechel's *Bible History*. And that was not published until 1924. Black Elk became Catholic in 1904, and soon after that (sometime around 1906) the missionaries appointed him to the position of catechist, because he was extremely familiar with the content of the Bible. He could not speak English, so the only source he could learn from was the Riggs Dakota Bible. The Dakota and Lakota dialects are perfectly mutually intelligible. Another piece of evidence is Black Elk's vision. . . . By 1917 Black Elk was practically blind so even if he knew how to read, he was not able to read Buechel's *Bible History* published seven years later. Although he might have had some of his children read from Buechel's *Bible History* for him, most of his biblical knowledge must have originated earlier, perhaps in the period of 1904 to 1917. And this means that his source was Riggs!" DeMallie also states that Black Elk used the Riggs Dakota Bible in a letter written about his trip to Europe in 1889 (see DeMallie, *The Sixth Grandfather*, 11n.). Also, Buechel's *Bible History* presents very brief and simplified narratives of the biblical events, while the Riggs Dakota Bible presents a complete verse-by-verse translation.

## MULTIPLE-SOURCE EVIDENCE OF BIBLICAL THEMES
## IN THE BLACK ELK SOURCES

To argue that Black Elk's vision ought to be understood as a Lakota-Catholic narrative challenges most interpretations of Black Elk's corpus. Despite the presence of biblical references at central points in Black Elk's Lakota works, many scholars quickly dismiss their relevance. For unspecified reasons, DeMallie, for example, assumes that "such expressions as phrases from the Bible . . . are readily transparent and not especially significant."[6] On the other hand, I maintain that multiple occurrences of the same biblical references are not incidental but rather demonstrate the centrality of Catholicism in Black Elk's world.

What, then, was Black Elk's relationship to the biblical text? According to the testimony of his community, Black Elk was known for his knowledge of Christian scripture. His daughter Lucy states that Black Elk "had poor eyesight, but he learned to read Scripture and prayer books written in the Indian language."[7] According to Lucy, he was quite proficient: "Everything in the Scriptures he understood."[8] John Lone Goose remembers Black Elk's dedication to study:

> Nick said he wanted to teach God's word to the people. So he kept on learning, learning, learning. Pretty soon, he learned what the Bible meant, and it was good. . . . All he talked about was the Bible and Christ.[9]

Missionaries also recorded Black Elk's knowledge and skill. His companion Father Westropp wrote before 1916 that "though half blind, [Black Elk] has by some hook or crook learned how to read, and he knows his religion thoroughly."[10]

Black Elk used this textual knowledge to relate scripture to the Lakota cultural world. Lucy remembers that

> he related Scripture passages to things around him, and he used examples from nature—making comparison of things in the Bible with flowers, animals, even trees. And when he talked to us about things in creation, he brought up stories in the Bible. That's why he was a pretty strong Catholic—by reading the Bible.[11]

According to Lucy, the Bible was not abstract or separate from Black Elk's everyday experience. Rather, he connected scripture to the world around him, especially the natural world. In addition, discussions about creation led to connections with biblical tradition.

---

[6]  DeMallie, *The Sixth Grandfather*, 89.
[7]  Steltenkamp, *Black Elk*, 56.
[8]  Ibid., 63.
[9]  Ibid., 54.
[10]  Ibid., 65.
[11]  Ibid., 47.

Black Elk was also known for his ability to remember accurately specific details from scripture. In discussing Black Elk, Pat Red Elk emphasizes the ability of the early converts to remember and quote the Bible.

> Even though they didn't have any formal education, those old converts were really trained to preach. They'd say that Saint John says this here and there, and when I'd get the Bible and read it—they were right! That's what was written. I read Scripture, but I can't remember the right words like they used to be able to do.[12]

Black Elk not only referred to general ideas or images from the Bible, but he also wove scriptural passages into his speeches and writings. Such direct biblical references are present in all the known writings attributed to Black Elk. One letter from Europe quotes a passage from 1 Corinthians. His letters printed in the Catholic newspaper *Sinasapa Wocekiye Taeyanpaha* frequently made scriptural allusions. Black Elk's interviews with Neihardt and *The Sacred Pipe* likewise contain biblical allusions. For example, relating his vision with the grandfathers and his calling to "help mankind," Black Elk states that "many are called, few are chosen," a citation of Matthew 22:14.

A biblical theme found in diverse Black Elk sources is "love your neighbor" (Lv 19:18; Dt 6:5; 10:12; Jo 22:5; Mt 19:19; 22:37–39; Lk 10:27; Rom 13:9; Gal 5:14; Jas 2:8). During the 1944 interviews Black Elk describes a talk given during the mourning period after a death. The people are reminded to "love your neighbors."[13] He also uses this language in the 1931 interviews to describe the defeat of the Lakota: "Here's where the Indians made their mistake. We should treat our fellowmen all alike—the Great Spirit made men all alike. Therefore, we made a mistake when we tried to get along with the whites. We tried to love them as we did ourselves."[14] Black Elk takes up this theme in a letter written to the Lakota Catholic community published in *Sinasapa Wocekiye Taeyanpaha*.

> In the Bible, Jesus told us that "You should love your neighbor as you love Me." So remember if you get in trouble with your neighbor, remember that God has said, "Love your neighbor." So whatever you have said or if you have done some bad thing to them, go over there and please tell them you are sorry.[15]

---

[12] Ibid., 120.

[13] DeMallie, *The Sixth Grandfather*, 382.

[14] Ibid., 290. While Black Elk's statement may seem to be a negative judgment against this Christian teaching, it must be read in context. On the preceding page Black Elk clearly states his faith in the Great Spirit and his just judgment: "Now, when I look ahead, we are nothing but prisoners of war, but the Great Spirit has protected us so far, and this Great Spirit takes care of us. . . . It is up to the Great Spirit to look upon the white man and they will be sorry and this great thing that happens might be just among themselves." See also ibid., 127.

[15] Black Elk, letter to friends and relatives and the Lakota Catholic Community, no date, published in *Sinasapa Wocekiye Taeyanpaha,* date unknown, ca. 1907–8. Translated

Black Elk preached this theme to the Lakota community and also used it to challenge American colonialism. Lucy remembers Black Elk using this theme to preach to whites about the guilt of their participation in colonialism on a trip east with some missionaries:

> At one place he said he was up there talking and saying to the audience: "You white people, you come to our country. You came to this country, which was ours in the first place. We were the only inhabitants. After we listened to you, we got settled down. But you're not doing what you're supposed to do—what our religion and our Bible tells us. I know this. *Christ himself preached that we love our neighbors as ourself. Do unto others as you would have others do unto you.*" At that early time, he said those words. He told us that when he was finished speaking, everybody clapped.[16]

In summary, the biblical theme "love your neighbor" appeared in four of the Black Elk sources, three of which scholars usually interpret as having no relation to his life as a Catholic. The diversity and number of sources, as well as their use to discuss key topics (colonialism), suggest that a reexamination of these sources will show that scriptural themes and passages permeate all aspects of Black Elk's life and discourse.

Indeed, this use of Christian scripture is neither unique nor sporadic. In *The Sacred Pipe* Black Elk describes a prayer during the *inipi* (sweat lodge), in which he supplicates, "May we be as children newly born! May we live again, O *Wakan-Tanka!*"[17] He also describes how often little children poke their heads inside the sweat lodge. Black Elk makes it clear that "we do not chase them away, for we know that little children already have pure hearts."[18] This easily overlooked passage is in fact a reference to Matthew 18:3.

Lucy states that Black Elk always taught Matthew 18:3. "When [my father] taught, he said, 'Unless we become as children, become like those little children'—he would point at some—'we cannot enter the Kingdom.' This was his main topic."[19] In Luke's version of the story, the disciples chasing away those who brought children to Jesus precede this teaching (Lk 18:15). The language of Black Elk's *inipi* prayer and the Dakota Bible both use the phrase *newborn children.*

---

from Lakota to English under Michael F. Steltenkamp, S.J., in Ivan M. Timonin, *Black Elk's Synthesis: Catholic Theology and Oglala Tradition in The Sacred Pipe*, dissertation proposal. See also Matthew 5:23–24: "Therefore, if you bring your gift to the altar, and there recall that your brother has anything against you, leave your gift there at the altar, go first and be reconciled with your brother, and then come and offer your gift."

[16] Steltenkamp, *Black Elk,* 67–68, emphasis added.

[17] Joseph Epes Brown, *The Sacred Pipe: Black Elk's Account of the Seven Rites of the Oglala Sioux* (Norman: University of Oklahoma Press, 1989), 40.

[18] Ibid., 43.

[19] Steltenkamp, *Black Elk,* 109.

Dakota text: K'a heyá; Awíčakhehaŋ hečíčiyapi; Nihdúhomnipi šni, k'á hokšíyok'opa iyéničhečapi šni kiŋháŋ, maȟpíya wókičuŋze kiŋ én yaípi kte šni.

English gloss: *and / he said as follows / really / I say that to you / you turn yourself round / not / and / babies / you are alike / not / if / sky / reign / the / in / you arrive there / will / not.*

English text: *And said, Verily I say unto you, Except ye be converted, and become as little children, ye shall not enter into the kingdom of heaven* (KJV).

In Black Elk's *inipi* prayer, he uses the same phrase, "children newly born," and assures the listener that he, unlike the disciples, does not turn away the children because, like Christ, he knows they have pure hearts. This demonstrates a three-source correlation: Lucy describes one of Black Elk's favorite teachings; it is present in a source attributed to Black Elk; and it is present in that source using the same language as the Dakota Bible.

An important example of a Christian reference that Black Elk uses intentionally in his discourse to convey meaning is found in the 1944 interviews with Neihardt. In discussing the origins of the Lakota, Black Elk states that "the Indian, if we came from Asia, we should have iron, because Christ was nailed on the cross with iron nails. I just cannot believe we came from Asia."[20] What may seem like a tangential or transparent remark emphasizes what Black Elk holds to be true. He uses the Christian story as a frame of reference by which other truth-claims are measured. Native Americans cannot come from Asia, because the truth of the Christian story cannot be contradicted. Black Elk measures the origins of the Lakota against the centrality of Christ.

Black Elk's understanding of symbols and language reinforces the significance of biblical language. In describing the details of the Sun Dance, Black Elk states: "You see, *there is a significance for everything*, and these are the things that are good for men to know, and to remember."[21] Black Elk carefully chose what to an outsider might seem trivial or insignificant details to shape his discourse. It would be inconsistent to view biblical references as accidental or foreign because, as we saw in Chapter 4, Black Elk lived in one Lakota Catholic world. His biblical allusions, especially at focal points in the text, appear to be both intentional and significant modes of meaning.

## BLACK ELK'S GREAT VISION

Black Elk's vision of the six grandfathers demonstrates a similar integration of biblical imagery. It shows a strong correlation between the vision and biblical tradition, and taken as a whole, it also forms a Lakota-Catholic narrative of salvation history.

---

[20] DeMallie, *The Sixth Grandfather*, 318.
[21] Brown, *The Sacred Pipe*, 80, emphasis added.

## BLACK ELK IS TAKEN UP INTO THE CLOUDS

When Black Elk was nine years old, he fell ill. His vision began while he was lying in his family's tipi. Two men descend from the sky and say, "Hurry up, your grandfather is calling you." Black Elk gets up to follow them:

> Just as I got out of the tipi I could see the two men going back into the clouds and there was a small cloud coming down toward me at the same time, which stood before me. I got on top of the cloud and was raised up, following the two men.[22]

The beginning of the vision is similar in structure to Acts 1:9–11.

> When [Jesus] had said this, as [the disciples] were looking on, he was lifted up, and a cloud took him from their sight. While they were looking intently at the sky as he was going, suddenly two men dressed in white garments stood beside them. They said, "Men of Galilee, why are you standing there looking at the sky? This Jesus who has been taken up from you into heaven will return in the same way as you have seen him going into heaven."

Jesus ascends to the clouds, and as the apostles watch the clouds, two men appear and address them. One could imagine a continuation of the story in which two men bring a believer to the clouds on the same cloud that "took" Jesus. Christians are urged to expect this. Paul writes: "Then we who are alive, who are left, will be caught up together with them in the clouds to meet the Lord in the air. Thus we shall always be with the Lord" (1 Thes 4:17). According to Paul, believers will be brought to the clouds where they will meet the Lord.

In addition, many biblical call stories include an ascension to the heavens or clouds. In Revelation, John is called to heaven to be shown what will happen. "After this I had a vision of an open door to heaven, and I heard the trumpetlike voice that had spoken to me before, saying, 'Come up here and I will show you what must happen afterwards'" (Rv 4:1–2).

A significant point is the translation for heaven. The Dakota word used is *maȟpíya*, which translates as sky or clouds. Black Elk hears in this passage that John is taken up to the clouds to see *Wakan Tanka*. A supporting detail is the translation for angels: *maȟpíya ohníȟde* (cloud messengers).[23]

Following this trend, the kingdom of heaven, an important theme of the gospels, was translated "kingdom of *maȟpíya*." The kingdom of the clouds was a subject in Black Elk's Catholic teaching. As we saw in the first section, Matthew 18:3 was one of Black Elk's favorite teachings; it says that unless one becomes like a newborn, one will not enter the kingdom of *maȟpíya*. In one of

---

[22] DeMallie, *The Sixth Grandfather*, 114.
[23] See Rv 8:3–4 (Jan Ullrich, personal communication).

his Catholic letters Black Elk urges Lakota Catholics to "always look towards heaven and prepare yourselves. God has promised the Kingdom of Heaven for us. When we die, if we have faith in God, the place that we go is the Kingdom of Heaven."[24]

On many levels, then, there is a correlation between Black Elk's ascension to the clouds and Christian tradition. The Dakota biblical tradition describes Jesus, John of Revelation, and Christians in general ascending to the clouds (heaven). In the Dakota Bible both concepts are unified in the one word *mahpíya*. The particulars of Black Elk's vision mirror the details of Jesus' ascension in Acts. Most important, Black Elk's Catholic teaching centers on the kingdom of heaven.

## THE HORSES AND THE FOUR DIRECTIONS

On his way to the six grandfathers, Black Elk sees four groups of twelve horses, each group positioned at one of the four directions. They are grouped according to color: black, white, buckskin, and sorrel.

> I followed those men on up into the clouds and they showed me a vision of a bay horse standing there in the middle of the clouds. One of the men said: "Behold him, the horse who has four legs, you shall see. . . . " Then these horses went into formation of twelve abreast in four lines—blacks, whites, sorrels, buckskins. . . . Then the bay horse said: "Make haste." The horse began to go beside me and the forty-eight horses followed us.[25]

In the book of Zechariah the prophet has an almost identical vision of horses:

> Again I raised my eyes and saw four chariots coming out from between two mountains; and the mountains were of bronze. The first chariot had red horses, the second chariot black horses, the third chariot white horses, and the fourth chariot spotted horses—all of them strong horses. I asked the angel of the angel who spoke with me, "What are these, my lord?" The angel said to me in reply, "These are the four winds of the heavens, which are coming forth after being reviewed by the LORD of all the earth" (Zec 6:1–5).

The horses in Black Elk's vision are structured similarly. In both visions the horses appear in groups of the same colors—black, white, sorrels/reds—with the only difference being the spotted and buckskin. For both Black Elk and Zechariah the horses represent the four winds or directions.

---

[24] Black Elk, letter to friends and relatives written at Pine Ridge Reservation, Manderson, South Dakota, April 21, 1907, published in *Sinasapa Wocekiye Taeyanpaha*, June 15, 1907. Translated from Lakota to English under Michael F. Steltenkamp, S.J., in Timonin, *Black Elk's Synthesis*.

[25] DeMallie, *The Sixth Grandfather*, 114–15.

## The Cloud Tipi of the Six Grandfathers

After seeing the horses, the bay horse leads Black Elk to the Cloud Tipi, where he meets the six grandfathers.

> One of the grandfathers said to me: "Do not fear, come right in" (through the rainbow door). So I went in and stood before them. The horses in the four quarters of the earth all neighed to cheer me as I entered the rainbow door.[26]

There the grandfathers address Black Elk and tell him that they are having a council:

> Your grandfathers all over the world and the earth are having a council and there you were called, so here you are. Behold then, those where the sun goes down; from thence they shall come, you shall see. From them you shall know the willpower of myself, for they shall take you to the center of the earth, and the nations of all kinds shall tremble.[27]

The grandfathers' declaration to Black Elk contains two biblical themes. The first is the willpower of the grandfather. While DeMallie identifies this as a Lakota concept,[28] it is also a central Christian theme that Black Elk would have used every time he prayed the Our Father (see Mt 6:10):

Dakota text: Nithókičuŋze ú kte; Nitháwačiŋ ečhéŋ ečhúŋpi nuŋwé, maȟpíya kiŋ éŋ iyéčheča, nakúŋ makhá akáŋ:

English gloss: *your order (kingdom) / come / will / your will / thus / they do / oh if / sky / the / in / as it is / also / earth / upon*:

English text: *Thy kingdom come, Thy will be done in earth, as it is in heaven*: (KJV)[29]

Black Elk, then, uses *will* in a Christian context as well. Writing about his trip to Europe two months after his return, he states:

> So thus all along, of the white man's customs, only his faith, the white man's beliefs about God's will, and how they act according to it, I wanted to understand. I traveled to one city after another, and there were many customs around God's will.[30]

---

[26]  Ibid., 116.
[27]  Ibid.
[28]  Ibid., 116n.
[29]  Jan Ullrich, personal communication.
[30]  DeMallie, *The Sixth Grandfather* 9–10.

Black Elk states that the only good thing about white culture that interested him was the whites' customs about the will of God. As a result of his search, he writes later in the letter that he embraces this custom about God's will: "So Lakota people, trust in God! Now alone I trust in God."

The grandfathers' declaration that "the nations heard and quaked" is a second biblical theme. Moses and the Israelites sing a song in the book of Exodus after the Lord frees them from the Egyptians and is leading them to the Promised Land: "The nations will hear and tremble" (Ex 15:14). This is picked up by the prophets and in the psalms: "The LORD is king, the peoples tremble" (Ps 99:1). The book of Revelation associates this theme with Christ, who comes on the clouds:

Dakota text: Waŋyáŋka po, maȟpíya šápa kiŋ akáŋ ú; uŋkháŋ wičhíšta owás'iŋ waŋyáŋkapi kta, k'a tóna hé čhaphápi k'uŋ hená nakúŋ, k'a iyé uŋ oyáte makhá ohnáka kiŋ owás'iŋ aíč'iphapi kta. Héčhetu nuŋwé. Amen.

English gloss: *Look / plural imperative / clouds / dark / the / upon / he comes / and then / human eyes / all / they see him / will / and / those / he (him) / they pierced him / the aforesaid / those / also / and / he / on account of (because of) / people / earth / on / the / all / they strike themselves / will / it be so / may / Amen.*

English text: *Behold, he cometh with clouds; and every eye shall see him, and they also which pierced him: and all kindreds of the earth shall wail because of him. Even so, Amen.* (KJV)[31]

The *oyáte* (peoples/nations) of the earth will strike themselves upon seeing Christ come upon the clouds.

The setting where Black Elk meets the grandfathers, the cloud tipi, is similar to the heavenly temple described in the book of Revelation, where the Lord calls John:

At once I was caught up in spirit. A throne was there in heaven, and on the throne sat one whose appearance sparkled like jasper and carnelian. Around the throne was a halo as brilliant as an emerald. Surrounding the throne I saw twenty-four other thrones on which twenty-four elders sat, dressed in white garments and with gold crowns on their heads. From the throne came flashes of lightning, rumblings, and peals of thunder. Seven flaming torches burned in front of the throne, which are the seven spirits of God (Rv 4:2–5).

Like Black Elk's vision, the temple in Revelation is located in the clouds, or *maȟpíya*. Throughout Revelation, temple is translated *tipi wakan* (sacred/holy

---

[31] Rv 1:7 (Jan Ullrich, personal communication).

tipi), which matches the tipi of the six grandfathers.[32] Both the *tipi wakan* of Revelation and the tipi of Black Elk's vision are associated with a rainbow.[33]

While both visions place the *tipi wakan* in the clouds, they are also located on a mountain. As Black Elk is leaving the grandfathers to return home, he looks back: "I looked back and the cloud house was gone. There was nothing there but a big mountain with a gap in it."[34] In the last part of John's vision, he is brought to the New Jerusalem, which is the new dwelling of God and God's people. "He took me in spirit to a great, high mountain and showed me the holy city Jerusalem coming down out of heaven from God" (Rv 21:10). In both visions God's dwelling is associated with a great mountain where there is always light. The cloud tipi "shall be set where the sun shines continually."[35] The New Jerusalem will need no sun or moon, "for the glory of God *(Wakan-Tanka)* gave it light" (Rv 21:23). This is brought together in *The Sacred Pipe*, where Black Elk compares *anpetu wi* (the sun) to the light of *Wakan Tanka*.[36]

Revelation 4:2–5 also demonstrates that while Christianity is monotheistic, it is metaphorically possible to describe God faithfully in other ways. In Revelation, John sees the seven spirits of God, as Black Elk sees the six grandfathers. However, both interpret divinity monotheistically. While Black Elk sees the six grandfathers throughout the vision, he states that "the fifth grandfather represented the Great Spirit."[37] This equation of the fifth grandfather with the Great Spirit is consistent with Black Elk's monotheism, as discussed in Chapter 4.

While Black Elk is in the cloud tipi, the first grandfather tells Black Elk why they called him there:

> Take courage and be not afraid, for you will know him. And furthermore, behold him, whom you shall represent. By representing him, you shall be very powerful on earth in medicines and all powers. He is your spirit and you are his body and his name is Eagle Wing Stretches.[38]

The content of the grandfathers' explanation of Black Elk's call contains six Christian biblical themes. The first is the command to "be not afraid." In the biblical tradition God repeatedly tells those he calls or appears to "be not afraid." In an example from the book of Judges, Gideon sees the Lord and is afraid he will die.

---

[32] Father Craft often said mass outdoors with the altar in a tipi (see illustration in Thomas W. Foley, *Father Francis M. Craft: Missionary to the Sioux* [Lincoln: University of Nebraska Press, 2002], 51).

[33] See also Ezekiel's call story (Ez 1:28—2:10). Here Ezekiel sees the Lord surrounded by a rainbow, filled with the spirit of the Lord, and sent to the Israelites to prophesy.

[34] DeMallie, *The Sixth Grandfather*, 141.

[35] Ibid.

[36] Brown, *The Sacred Pipe*, 71–72.

[37] DeMallie, *The Sixth Grandfather*, 119.

[38] Ibid., 116.

Gideon, now aware that it had been the angel of the LORD, said, "Alas, Lord GOD, that I have seen the angel of the LORD face to face!" The LORD answered him, "Be calm, do not fear. You shall not die" (Jgs 6:22–23).[39]

This also occurs in Revelation when Jesus appears to John:

When I caught sight of him, I fell down at his feet as though dead. He touched me with his right hand and said, "Do not be afraid. I am the first and the last, the one who lives" (Rv 1:17–18).

In the Bible and Black Elk's vision, the Divine assures those he calls and tells them not to be afraid.

Second, Black Elk is told that he will "represent" Eagle Wing Stretches. This command mirrors the sending of the prophets, who represent God by speaking and acting for him. Moses is called to represent the Lord:

"Come, now! I will send you to Pharaoh to lead my people, the Israelites, out of Egypt." . . . "Thus shall you say to the Israelites: The LORD, the God of your fathers, the God of Abraham, the Isaac, the God of Jacob, has sent me to you" (Ex 3:10, 15).

Like Black Elk, Moses is called to lead his people to the Promised Land. In addition, the calling of Isaiah mirrors that of Black Elk. Like Black Elk, Isaiah is called to the *tipi wakan* of *Wakan Tanka* and sent to the people to prophesy (Is 6).

Third, by representing Eagle Wing Stretches, Black Elk will be powerful with "medicines and all powers." This echoes Jesus giving his disciples authority over unclean spirits and the power to cure (Mt 10:1). In the Gospel of Matthew Jesus sends the disciples out, telling them to "cure the sick, raise the dead, cleanse lepers, drive out demons" (Mt 10:8). To facilitate this mission Black Elk is given healing herbs throughout his vision. While herbs are an important part of Lakota tradition, there are also important biblical correlations. Psalm 147 urges readers to "sing to the LORD with thanksgiving," for among various other blessings, he also gives "*peji* [herbs] for the service of men" (Ps 147:7, 8). The trees of Ezekiel and Revelation, important images that will be examined in greater detail below, provide leaves that will serve as "medicine for the nations" (Rv 22:2; see also Ez 47:12).

Fourth, Black Elk is told that "he is your spirit." In biblical tradition those who are chosen to go in the name of the Lord are given his Spirit. The messianic prophecy of Isaiah says that "the spirit of the LORD shall rest upon him" (Is 11:2). This is taken up in the Christian scriptures where the Holy Spirit descends upon Jesus: "On coming up out of the water he saw the heavens being torn open and the Spirit, like a dove, descending upon him" (Mk 1:10). Later, Paul tells the Galatians

---

[39] For similar stories see Gn 15:1; 21:17; Dn 10:12; Mt 1:20; 28:10; Lk 1:30.

that he has been crucified with Christ, "Yet I live, no longer I, but Christ lives in me" (Gal 2:20). In other words, Paul's spirit is now Christ's spirit.

Fifth, the grandfather tells Black Elk that "you are his body." In biblical tradition baptism incorporates Christians into the body of Christ. Paul writes in his first letter to the Corinthians, "For in one Spirit we were all baptized into one body, whether Jews or Greeks, slaves or free persons, and we were all given to drink of one Spirit" (1 Cor 12:13). Like Black Elk's description, Paul asserts that the Christian actually becomes that body: "Now you are Christ's body" (1 Cor 12:27).

These two concepts that the grandfather links together—"he is your spirit and you are his body"—are also linked together in biblical tradition:

> In a little while the world will no longer see me, but you will see me, because I live and you will live. On that day you will realize that I am in my Father and *you are in me and I in you* (Jn 14:19–20, emphasis added).

> Those who keep [Jesus'] commandments *remain in him, and he in them*, and the way we know that he remains in us is from the Spirit that he gave us (1 Jn 3:24, emphasis added).

The believer and Christ are united in that they are of the same body and spirit and remain in each other.

Sixth, the one who Black Elk represents is named Eagle Wing Stretches. As the vision progresses, Black Elk becomes identified with the name. In the biblical tradition the eagle is a symbol of God.

> He found them in a wilderness, a wasteland of howling desert. He shielded them and cared for them, guarding them as the apple of his eye. As an eagle incites its nestlings forth by hovering over its brood, So he spread his wings to receive them and bore them up on his pinions. The LORD alone was their leader, no strange god was with him (Dt 32:10–12).

In this passage the author of Deuteronomy describes God as a great eagle who has stretched out his wing over his people and led them out of slavery into the Promised Land. This theme is also taken up in the psalms.

> How precious is your love, O God!
> We take refuge in the shadow of your wings.
>                    (Ps 36:7; see also Ps 63:8)

Humanity trusts in the shadow of the great eagle, *Wakan Tanka*. Black Elk also used this metaphor: "The voice of the Spotted Eagle; our Grandfather, *Wakan-Tanka*, always hears this, for you see it is really His own voice."[40] The voice of the spotted eagle is *Wakan Tanka*, or God.

---

[40] Brown, *The Sacred Pipe*, 71.

While the eagle has always been a symbol of divinity in the Lakota tradition, there are indications that during the early reservation period it gained a specifically Christian connotation. The Lakota gave many of the Jesuits eagle names: Eugene Buechel became *Wanbli Sapa* (Black Eagle); Otto Moorman, *Wanbli Ska* (White Eagle); Joseph Zimmerman, *Wambli Wankatuya* (High Eagle); Leo Cunningham, *Wambli Makeskan Un* (Eagle of the Lonely Country); and William Ketcham, *Wambli Wakita* (Watching Eagle).[41] The Lakota named the diocesan priest of Mohawk descent, Francis Craft, *Wabli chica aglahpaya* (The Eagle Covers Its Young, or Hovering Eagle).[42]

The three-source connection—biblical tradition, Black Elk's description of the eagle, and the frequent association of the name Eagle with the Catholic missionaries—indicates a strong correlation between Black Elk's use of the eagle symbol and Christian meaning.

Viewed as a whole, then, the concentration of Black Elk's description of his call by the grandfathers demonstrates a very strong correlation with biblical imagery.

## THE SACRED ROAD

The main action of the vision is the walking of the sacred red road. The fourth grandfather tells Black Elk that "he shall make a nation."[43] Black Elk leads the nation down the road "so that they will all be prosperous. As I walk I am going to pray to the Great Spirit."[44] He guides them through the difficult ascents.

In *Black Elk: Holy Man of the Oglala*, Michael Steltenkamp claims that the road imagery in Black Elk's vision is in fact borrowed or influenced by a catechetical teaching aid known as the Two Roads Map that depicts the Catholic story of salvation history.[45] According to Steltenkamp:

---

[41]  Ross Alexander Enochs, *The Jesuit Mission to the Lakota Sioux: Pastoral Theology and Ministry 1886–1945* (Kansas City, Mo.: Sheed & Ward, 1996), 141.

[42]  Foley, *Father Francis M. Craft*, 17.

[43]  DeMallie, *The Sixth Grandfather*, 118.

[44]  Ibid., 125.

[45]  Steltenkamp describes the Two Roads Map: "In an attempt to communicate Catholic theology nonabstractly, early missionaries made use of a picture catechism. On a strip of paper about one foot wide and several feet long were contained illustrations depicting what Christians have traditionally called salvation history. Goll described this mandalalike device as follows: 'Beginning with the Blessed Trinity and Creation at the bottom of the strip, the student follows the connected pictures of God in heaven at the top. The Apostles Creed, the life and death of Christ, the Church, the sacraments, the theological virtues, the capital sins—all are there between two roads, a golden road leading to heaven and a black one ending in hell.' Native catechists were instructed as to the chart's meaning by means of individual and group lessons conducted by priests, and by written explanations in both English and Lakota. . . . The Two Roads Map (as it was popularly called) in use among the Lakota was a colorful, engaging depiction of human beings and preternatural creatures. The pantheon of Judeo-Christian figures is arresting,

Black Elk used the Two Roads Map during his life as a catechist, and
many references within his vision correspond directly to the old picture
catechism. Some of the surprising parallels include thunder beings, a day-
break star, flying men, tree imagery, circled villages, a black road, a red
road, friendly wings, an evil blue man living in flames, a place where
people moaned and mourned, emphasis on people's history, and gaudily
portrayed, self-indulgent individuals. Other, more detailed segments of
Black Elk's vision are either explicitly or implicitly present on the Two
Roads Map.[46]

According to Steltenkamp, Black Elk's road imagery connected with the concrete practices of his life as a catechist. No substantial critique of Steltenkamp's
assertion has yet been offered, and the following linguistic evidence reinforces
his theory.

The first example comes from Steltenkamp's interviews with Black Elk's
daughter Lucy Looks Twice. Lucy remembers the first Catholic hymn that her
father taught her, one that alludes to the gathering of the Lakota nation:

> O God *(Wakan Tanka)* most good, Who wants to make
>     himself known,
> All rejoice rightly, He asks of you your hearts.
> You Lakota are a nation, Quickly may they come
>     together;
> Jesus would have it so, Because he has called you all.[47]

In the hymn Jesus calls the Lakota to come together as a nation, and as a catechist, Black Elk worked to gather the Lakota nation together and to help make
the Lakota sacred.

The second example comes from a prayer that Lucy says her father said at
Thanksgiving; it uses the image of the road in Christian eschatological terms:

> One day, we shall go and arrive at the end of the road.
> In that future, we shall be without any sin at all.
> And so it will be in the same manner for my
>     grandchildren and relatives
> who will follow as well.[48]

---

as winged angels and bat like demons are pictured fluttering about the course of world
history. Crowds of people are variously portrayed—at the mercy of natural disaster, in
the clutches of a leviathan monster, under the embrace of a grandfather-creator, and all
in seeming constant motion. In short, the Two Roads Map imaginatively captured in
picture form the basic worldview of traditional Christian theology" (Steltenkamp, *Black
Elk*, 94–95).

[46]  Ibid., 95.
[47]  Ibid., 56–57.
[48]  Ibid., 118–19.

In Black Elk's prayer the road is a journey through time that the Lakota and their descendants should travel to the destination where they will be without sin. Black Elk's description of the road in his vision carries this Christian understanding of a durational quest for holiness: the red road is "a good road for good spirits."[49]

Black Elk uses the same metaphor of road as an eschatological journey in a letter written in the summer of 1909 to the *Catholic Herald*: "We are here on this earth temporarily and for he who walks the straight path and dies, there is rest waiting for him."[50] For Black Elk, the Christian life is the walking of the straight path.

The Dakota Bible strengthens this concrete image of road as journey. The translation for *saint* in Revelation is "those straight" (Rv 8:3). Buechel's Lakota dictionary translates this word concretely first as "straight, not crooked."[51] This concept is also used to translate righteousness in 1 Corinthians 1:30. Jan Ullrich writes: "'Righteousness' is translated as 'wóowothaŋna' which is a noun formed from the verb owóthaŋna ('straight, frank, honest') used for translating the concept of Saint."[52] This translation occurs numerous times throughout both testaments of the Dakota Bible.

Road imagery is also central in the call of John the Baptist. In the Gospel of John, John the Baptist tells the priests and Levites: "I am 'the voice crying out in the desert, "Make straight the way of the Lord."'" (Jn 1:23). The Dakota Bible translates "straight" as wóowothaŋna and "way" as Čhaŋkú. The Gospel of John later associates Jesus with the road, Čhaŋkú.

Thomas said to him, "Master, we do not know where you are going; how can we know the way?" Jesus said to him, "I am the *way* and the truth and the life. No one comes to the Father except through me" (Jn 14:5–6).

The Dakota Bible translates *way* with Čhaŋkú, which means "road."[53] When Thomas says they do not know on what road Jesus will go, Jesus replies by saying that he himself is the Čhaŋkú. He is the road that must be followed to come to the Father, *Wakan Tanka.*

Black Elk's description of the nation walking down the red road reinforces the connection with Jesus, the Messiah. Four spirit horsemen, who correlate with the four horsemen of Zechariah, lead the people. The only people from the nation that Black Elk describes are old men with canes and old women with canes. Zechariah, when describing the days of the Messiah and the New Jerusalem, says, "Thus says the LORD of hosts: Old men and old women, each with staff in hand because of old age, shall again sit in the streets of Jerusalem" (Zec 8:4).

---

[49] DeMallie, *The Sixth Grandfather*, 118.
[50] Ibid., 21.
[51] Eugene Buechel, S.J., *A Dictionary of the Teton Sioux Language*, ed. Paul Manhart (Pine Ridge, S.D.: Red Cloud Indian School, 1970), 416.
[52] Jan Ullrich, personal communication.
[53] Jan Ullrich, personal communication.

Black Elk's description of the road demonstrates a strong correlation with Christian imagery. Steltenkamp's argument for the catechetical map, Black Elk's prayer given by Lucy, one of Black Elk's Catholic letters, the translation of *saint,* and the words of Jesus all connect Christian ideas to the concrete image of road. The goal of Christianity, holiness, is expressed in terms of the road. To become holy is to follow the road to the end. Black Elk expresses this Christian concept when he attributes the second grandfather with saying, "Hundreds shall be sacred, hundreds shall be flames."[54] The journey down the red road ends in sanctification or, alternately, retribution.

Before Black Elk starts on his journey down the road, he is given "sacred relics" by the grandfathers while he is in the cloud tipi. These relics—a cup of water, a bow and arrow, some soldier weed, the pipe, a flowering stick—have power and serve particular purposes. In addition, other symbols—the morning star, the wind, a man painted red, the sacred hoop—appear during the course of the journey. Both the relics and symbols correlate with the biblical narrative.

## CUP OF WATER

The first grandfather gives Black Elk a cup of water. He is told, "Behold, take [the cup of water], and with this you shall be great." Throughout the vision the purpose of the cup is developed and clarified. Black Elk comments that "with the wooden cup of water I was to save mankind."[55] Black Elk later states that "this cup will be used for me and my nation—that they will all be relatives to each other, and the water is the power to give them strength and purify them. This water will make them happy."[56]

The Christian concept of salvation of all humanity is linked to the cup, which we will return to later. One of the aspects of the cup, purification, is directly linked to the Christian concept of sanctification in the Dakota Bible. In 1 Corinthians 1:30 the Dakota word for purification is used to translate sanctification. Jan Ullrich writes:

> The Dakota word used in the [Dakota Bible] for sanctification— "wóyučedaŋ" is new for me, I have never encountered it before; Riggs does not give this word in his dictionary, he only gives "yučedaŋ" which he says means "to purify." The prefix wo- forms nouns of verbs, thus "wóyučedaŋ" should mean "purification" or more freely perhaps "purity."[57]

For Black Elk, to purify the people with the cup can mean to sanctify the people, using Christian terminology.

---

[54]  DeMallie, *The Sixth Grandfather,* 139.
[55]  Ibid., 119.
[56]  Ibid., 138.
[57]  Jan Ullrich, personal communication.

Catholic liturgical language also makes a connection with Black Elk's description of the cup. While the Dakota Bible uses a "Dakotacized" version of the Greek, the Catholic context used a word describing the concrete physical action of baptism. Buechal translates "to baptize" or "one who baptizes" in his *Bible History* as mniákaštaŋ. According to Ullrich this translates literally as: *mní*—water; akáštaŋ—to pour upon.[58] In Lakota, to baptize is to pour water on.

Lucy alludes to the use of a cup of water in a Christian context. She recalls a story in which she imitates baptism as practiced among the Lakota.

> Another time Father Lindebner came over to baptize my grandma and her cousins. . . . They were going so slow that I took my fancy little cup. I had it ever since I was a small girl. I took my cup, filled it with water, and went around baptizing my three grandmas. That Father Lindebner—I really liked him. He just stood there looking at me pouring water on each one and said, "Hurry up with the prayers, Lucy has already baptized all the old ladies!"[59]

Lucy's story indicates that the use of a cup in baptism was an accepted, if not standard, practice among the Lakota. This concrete link between the imagery of the cup and baptism would be reinforced every time Black Elk performed or attended a baptism.[60]

The link is further strengthened by the cup's absence from sources that record Lakota ceremonial tradition. Black Elk makes no mention of a cup in *The Sacred Pipe*, where he is ostensibly describing Lakota religious traditions. Because it is not present in discussions of "pure" Lakota tradition, the cup appears to be a Christian innovation.

Black Elk's description of water deserves further attention. After the interviews Black Elk and Neihardt went to Harney Peak. There Black Elk prays, "You presented to me from where the sun goes down a cup of water—the living water that makes the two-leggeds live. And thus you have said that my people will be saved."[61] According to Black Elk, the cup contains living water that will save his people. The concept of living water is a major theme of Christian tradition and is described in the two following passages from the Gospel of John:

> Whoever drinks the water I shall give will never thirst; the water I shall give will become in him a spring of water welling up to eternal life (Jn 4:14).

---

[58]   Text taken from Buechel, *Bible History.* Translation provided by Jan Ullrich (personal communication).

[59]   Steltenkamp, *Black Elk*, 74.

[60]   One of the catechists' responsibilities was to administer the sacrament of baptism when there was no priest available. Lucy remembers this in Steltenkamp, *Black Elk*, 50. See also Mary Claudia Duratschek, O.S.B., *Crusading along Sioux Trails* (St. Meinrad, Ind.: The Grail Press, 1947), 206–7.

[61]   DeMallie, *The Sixth Grandfather*, 295.

On the last and greatest day of the feast, Jesus stood up and exclaimed, "Let anyone who thirsts come to me and drink. Whoever believes in me, as scripture says: 'Rivers of living water will flow from within him'" (Jn 7:37–38).

According to these two passages, Jesus gives the living water of everlasting life. The water of life is more concretely described in Revelation as a river in the New Jerusalem:

Then the angel showed me the river of life-giving water, sparkling like crystal, flowing from the throne of God and of the Lamb (Rv 22:1).

The most explicit indication of the correlation with water as a Christian symbol is found in Black Elk's vision. Shortly after the establishment of the flowering stick, a cloud rains on the nation, which Black Elk describes as a "christening."[62] Christening, of course, is a popular way of referring to baptism.

Again we see a strong correlation between Black Elk's vision and Christian tradition. Black Elk's description of the cup of "living water" that "will save mankind" matches Christian descriptions in the Dakota Bible. Black Elk's description of the cup is concretely embodied in the translation of baptism used by Catholics and in the description of baptism by Lucy.

### BOW AND ARROW AND THE SOLDIER WEED OF DESTRUCTION

The six grandfathers also give Black Elk two instruments of war: the bow and arrow and the soldier weed of destruction. During the vision Black Elk uses the bow and arrow to kill various evil spirits. He interprets this as meaning, "if I had gone to war much, I would have been able to do much damage to the enemy, but the enemy couldn't fight back."[63] Black Elk describes being sent to battle:

I was on the bay horse now that had talked to me at first. . . . Then [the riders on the horses] all hollered: "He is coming!" and ran. They said: "Eagle Wing Stretches, make haste, for your nation all over the universe is in fear, make haste." I could hear, at this time everything in the universe cheering for me. At this time my bow and arrow turned into a big spear.[64]

In his vision he is victorious over all his enemies. This imagery is similar to a description of a rider found in Revelation.

I heard one of the four living creatures cry out in a voice like thunder, "Come forward." I looked, and there was a white horse, and its rider had a bow. He was given a crown, and he rode forth victorious to further his victories (Rv 6:1–2).

---

[62]   Ibid., 130.
[63]   Ibid., 132.
[64]   Ibid., 119, 121.

Both Black Elk and the rider are called, sent to battle, and are victorious.

Black Elk also states that "the bow and arrow represent lightning."[65] While DeMallie claims that this represents the destructive power of the thunder beings, this is also a biblical reference. Zechariah writes, "The LORD shall appear over them, and his arrow shall shoot forth as lightning" (Zec 9:14; see also 2 Sm 22:15; Ps 18:14; 144:6). Habakkuk also compares lightning to arrows and a spear, which Black Elk's bow and arrow turn into in his vision (Hb 3:11).

Toward the end of his vision he receives the soldier weed of destruction which is so powerful it kills with only a touch. Black Elk says that "this medicine belongs only to me."[66] He explains:

> I am glad I did not perform this killing, for I would have not only killed the enemy but I would probably have killed the women and children of the enemy, but I am satisfied that I have not been well off. Perhaps I would have been a chief if I had obeyed this, but I am satisfied that I didn't become a chief.[67]

Neihardt connects this decision not to kill to Black Elk's conversion to Christianity: "At the age of thirty-seven, Black Elk was to use this herb. . . . At this time he gave it up for the Catholic religion."[68] Neihardt's only explicit reference to Christianity in this case correctly explains how Black Elk interprets the violent aspects of his vision. Consequently, not only is Black Elk's imagery similar to the apocalyptic battles of Revelation and the prophets, but Black Elk decides to reject the embodiment of violence on earth—and its potential for power and material reward—because of his Christian faith.

## MORNING STAR

Another important symbol is the morning star, to which the third grandfather first alludes.[69] In the biblical tradition the morning star is a symbol of Christ. Balaam's prophecy in Numbers, "a star shall advance from Jacob," is interpreted as a messianic prophecy (Nm 24:17). In the Gospel of Matthew a star guides the magi to Christ (Mt 2:2). The book of Revelation associates the morning star with Christ in two different ways. First, Christ gives the morning star to the victor, who holds fast to Christ's ways (Rv 2:28). In the last chapter of the Bible, at the end of the apocalyptic battle of Revelation and the establishment of the New Jerusalem, Jesus explicitly calls himself the morning star: "I am the root and offspring of David, the bright morning star" (Rv 22:16).

---

[65] Ibid., 131.
[66] Ibid., 132.
[67] Ibid.
[68] Ibid., 137.
[69] Ibid., 117.

The southern spirit tells Black Elk that from the morning star his nation will have knowledge[70] and wisdom.[71] Paul associates wisdom and knowledge with Jesus in the Letter to the Ephesians:

Dakota text: Jesus Messiya Itháŋčhaŋ uŋkíyapi Wakháŋthaŋka tháwa, k'a wówitaŋ Atéyapi kiŋ hé é wóksape wówiyukčaŋ khó oníya kiŋ nič'úpi kta, hé iyé sdonyáyapi kta é heúŋ:

Dakota gloss: *Jesus / Messiya / chief / we have him for (a chief) / God / his / and / glory (pride) / their father / the / that / it is him / wisdom / also / breathing / the / the give you / will / that / he / you (plural) know him / will / that is it / on account of that:*

English text: *That the God of our Lord Jesus Christ, the Father of glory, may give unto you the spirit of wisdom and revelation in the knowledge of him:* (KJV)[72]

The morning star, like Jesus, imparts wisdom and knowledge.

The morning star is explicitly equated with Christ in one strand of Lakota tradition. Bernard Ice, a member of The Native American Church of Pine Ridge, states, "In the Cross Fire they use the star. Jesus Christ, the offspring of David, is the morning star."[73] It is likely that this association with Christ is implicit in Black Elk's vision as he personifies the Morning Star: "Behold him who shall appear, from him you shall have power."[74]

## PIPE

A very important Lakota symbol, the pipe, also plays a central role in Black Elk's vision. The third grandfather gives Black Elk a peace pipe.

[The southern?] spirit speaks again: "Behold him they have sent forth to the center of the nation's hoop." Then I saw the pipe with the spotted eagle flying to the center of the nation's hoop. The morning star went along with the pipe. They flew from the east to the center. "With this your nation's offering as they walk. They will be like unto him. With the pipe they shall have peace in everything. Behold your eagle, for your nation like relatives they shall be. Behold the morning star, relative-like they shall be, from whence [*sic*] they shall have wisdom." Just then the morning star appeared and all the people looked up to it and the horses neighed and the dogs barked.[75]

---

[70]  Ibid., 124.
[71]  Ibid., 129.
[72]  Eph 1:17 (Jan Ullrich, personal communication).
[73]  Steinmetz, *Pipe, Bible, and Peyote among the Oglala Lakota*, 103.
[74]  DeMallie, *The Sixth Grandfather*, 120.
[75]  Ibid., 129.

While there is no parallel to the pipe in Christian tradition, Black Elk connects it to the biblical tradition as a whole in other sources. Looks Twice's and Black Elk's contemporaries assert that he considered the pipe to be an "old testament" and foreshadowing of Christ.[76] Black Elk states in interviews recorded in 1944 that "the peace pipe was the Bible to our tribe."[77] Black Elk strengthens the correlation of the pipe with Christian tradition by the positioning of the pipe with the eagle, a Christian symbol for God, and the morning star, a Christian symbol for Christ.

The use of the pipe as a representative of Lakota tradition and Black Elk's equation of the pipe with the Old Testament is a significant theme for this study. Black Elk is explicitly claiming that he has connected the entirety of Lakota tradition with the Christian story. Thus, Black Elk indicates that individual biblical allusions, such as those identified above, should not be viewed as scattered fragments but as parts of a whole unified Lakota Catholic world.

## WIND

As Black Elk is walking the sacred red road from south to north, a wind starts to blow from the south. He is told by the northern grandfather, "Give [your nation] your sacred wind so they shall face the wind with courage. Also they shall walk as a relative of your wind."[78] Black Elk uses three images to describe the wind in his description of his vision: life, breath, and strength.

The northern grandfather later refers to the wind as "the wind of life."[79] Black Elk describes the action of the wind:

Then a little breeze came from the north and I could see that the wind was in the form of a spirit and as it went over the people all the dead things came to life.[80]

This event mirrors the description of valley of the dry bones given in Ezekiel:

From the four winds come, O spirit, and breathe into these slain that they may come to life. I prophesied as he told me, and the spirit came into them; they came alive and stood upright (Ez 37:9–10).

In both stories, the wind, described as spirit, blows over the dead and brings them back to life. Acts 2 explicitly connects the Holy Spirit to wind:

When the time for Pentecost was fulfilled, they were all in one place together. And suddenly there came from the sky a noise like a strong driving wind, and it filled and the entire house in which they were. Then there

---

[76] For a more detailed discussion, see Chapter 4 herein.
[77] DeMallie, *The Sixth Grandfather*, 334.
[78] Ibid., 122.
[79] Ibid., 139. DeMallie later states that the wind symbolizes life, 286n.
[80] Ibid., 129.

appeared to them tongues as of fire, which parted and came to rest on each one of them. And they were all filled with the holy Spirit and began to speak in different tongues, as the Spirit enabled them to proclaim (Acts 2:1–4).

Black Elk's correlation of the wind of his vision and the Holy Spirit is strengthened by his description of the wind as breath and strength. During his first cure Black Elk states: "Through this wind I shall draw power. The sacred wind, as he passes, the weak shall have strength. Through this wind I will breathe the power on the weak that they may see a happy day."[81] Black Elk uses this wind to "breathe the power on the weak." The Gospel of John also uses the image of the Holy Spirit as breath: "And when he had said this, [Jesus] breathed on them and said to them, 'Receive the holy Spirit'" (Jn 20:22). Black Elk associates the sacred wind with strength; Acts associates strength with the Holy Spirit. Jesus tells his disciples before he ascends: "You will receive power when the holy Spirit comes upon you" (Acts 1:8). The wind as Holy Spirit gives strength.

Black Elk's descriptions of wind correspond to biblical descriptions of the Holy Spirit. In addition, these three concepts—spirit, breath, and strength—are unified in the definition of Holy Spirit *(Woniya Wakan)* given by Buechel. The noun *woniya* translates as "spirit, life and breath."[82] The verb *woniya* translates "to resuscitate by blowing." This is comes from the verb *niya* "to breathe."[83] To breathe is to live, as the verb *niya(y)* expresses: "to cause to live, make life, revive."[84] *Wakan* translates as "sacred," which Ben used to translate his father's description of wind: "You have given me a sacred wind."[85] Consequently, when Black Elk spoke or heard the term *Woniya Wakan*, its connotations would correspond to the images of wind in his vision. As a whole, there is an integral relationship between Black Elk's sacred wind and the Holy Spirit.

## The Man Painted Red

Just before the establishment of the sacred stick at the center of the sacred hoop, a man painted in red appears:

As I looked upon the people, there stood on the north side a man painted red all over his body and he had with him a lance (Indian spear) and he walked into the center of the sacred nation's hoop and lay down and rolled himself on the ground and when he got up he was a buffalo standing there in the center of the nation's hoop.[86]

---

[81] Ibid., 238.

[82] Buechel, *A Dictionary of the Teton Sioux Language*, 605.

[83] Ibid., 364.

[84] Ibid.

[85] DeMallie, *The Sixth Grandfather*, 238.

[86] Ibid., 128.

The man painted red later turns into an herb and then wind "in the form of a spirit."[87] The transformation of the red man into a buffalo links him to White Buffalo Woman, the one who brought the Lakota the pipe. Black Elk describes White Buffalo Woman in *The Sacred Pipe* undergoing a similar transformation into a buffalo:

> The mysterious woman left, but after walking a short distance she looked back towards the people and sat down. When she rose the people were amazed to see that she had become a young red and brown buffalo calf. Then this calf walked farther, lay down, and rolled, looking back at the people, and when she got up she was a white buffalo. Again the white buffalo walked farther and rolled on the ground, becoming now a black buffalo. This buffalo then walked farther away from the people, stopped, and after bowing to each of the four quarters of the universe, disappeared over the hill.[88]

Catholic Lakota equated White Buffalo Woman with the Virgin Mary. Lucy remembers that "Father Buechel accepted the Blessed Virgin as the same one who brought the pipe, and that was what we always believed."[89] Similarly, Black Elk's description associates the red man with Christ.

Black Elk depicts the red man in his later Ghost Dance vision with explicitly Christian language and imagery:

> I saw twelve men coming toward me and they stood before me and said: "Our Father, the two legged chief, you shall see." Then I went to the center of the circle with these men and there again I saw the tree in full bloom. Against the tree I saw a man standing with outstretched arms. As we stood close to him these twelve men said: "Behold him!" The man with outstretched arms looked at me and I didn't know whether he was a white or an Indian. He did not resemble Christ. He looked like an Indian, but I was not sure of it. He had long hair which was hanging down loose. On the left side of his head was an eagle feather. His body was painted red. (At that time I had never had anything to do with the white man's religion and I had never seen any picture of Christ.)
>
> This man said to me: "My life is such that all earthly beings that grow belong to me. My father has said this. You must say this." I stood there gazing at him and tried to recognize him. I could not make him out. He was a nice-looking man. As I looked at him, his body began to transform. His body changed into all colors and it was very beautiful. All around him

---

[87]  Ibid., 129.
[88]  Brown, *The Sacred Pipe*, 9.
[89]  Steltenkamp, *Black Elk*, 107.

there was light. Then he disappeared all at once. It seemed as though there were wounds in the palms of his hands.[90]

In this vision, there are twelve men, like the apostles. Like Christ, the red man has wounds on the palms of his hand. DeMallie compares his transformation to the transfiguration.[91] Like the crucifix, the red man stands with outstretched arms against the blooming tree in the center of the circle. Later in the interview Black Elk tells Neihardt, "It seems to me on thinking it over that I have seen the son of the Great Spirit himself."[92] The red man of his great vision is also described with christological language:

Behold you have seen the powers of the north in the forms of man, buffalo, herb and wind. The people shall follow the man's steps; like him they shall walk and like the buffalo they shall live and with the herb they shall have knowledge. They shall be like relatives to the wind.[93]

If this red man is interpreted as the red man of the Ghost Dance vision, then Black Elk clearly understands him as the Son of God. The language reinforces this theory. The people are to follow the steps of the Son of the Great Spirit and be like relatives to "the wind." We have already seen the equation of the wind with *Woniya Wakan* (Holy Spirit). To follow the red man's steps reinforces the earlier equation of Jesus and the red road. This is strengthened by Jesus' often repeated call for people to follow him. First, there is the call of the disciples (Mt 4:19; Mk 1:17; Lk 5:27; Jn 1:43). Second, Jesus calls Christians to pick up the cross (equated to the flowering stick) and follow him (Mt 16:24; Mk 8:34; Lk 9:23). In his vision Black Elk picks up the flowering stick and follows the road.

Black Elk's use of biblical language, the depiction of the red man in his Ghost Dance vision, and his declaration that he saw the Son of the Great Spirit strongly indicate that the red man of his vision is a Christ figure. Based on the evidence, it seems likely that, just as the Lakota equated White Buffalo Woman with the Virgin Mary, Black Elk interpreted the red man as Christ.

## FLOWERING STICK

The most important symbol in Black Elk's vision is the flowering stick, also called the sacred tree. The fourth grandfather gives it to Black Elk and says,

---

[90] DeMallie, *The Sixth Grandfather*, 263. Little Wound states in his description of the *hunka* ceremony that "red is the most beautiful color. The spirits are pleased with red. *Inyan* is the Spirit of the Earth that dwells in the stone. It pleases *Inyan* to have red placed on a stone. When you would please the spirits put red paint on a stone" (James R. Walker, *Lakota Belief and Ritual*, ed. Raymond J. DeMallie and Elaine A. Jahner [1980; repr., Lincoln: University of Nebraska Press, 1991], 197).

[91] DeMallie, *The Sixth Grandfather*, 263n.

[92] Ibid., 266.

[93] Ibid., 129.

"Behold this, with this to the nation's center of the earth, many shall you save."[94] The action of the journey down the sacred road culminates in the establishment of the sacred stick at the center of the sacred hoop.

> They put the sacred stick into the center of the hoop and you could hear birds singing all kinds of songs by this flowering stick and the people and animals all rejoiced and hollered. The women were sending up their tremolos. The men said: "Behold it; for it is the greatest of the greatest sticks." This stick will take care of the people at the same time it will multiply. We live under it like chickens under the wing. We live under the flowering stick like under the wing of a hen. Depending on the sacred stick we shall walk and it will be with us always.[95]

As the centerpiece of the Sun Dance, the tree has been an important symbol in Lakota tradition. Lucy claims that this tree is also a Christian symbol. Evidence of this was noted above: the red man, whom Black Elk interprets as the Son of God, is portrayed with an outstretched hand in front of a blooming tree. Indeed, Black Elk's description of the sacred stick directly supports Lucy's claim, when he uses two biblical references where Jesus is the subject.

> Jerusalem, Jerusalem, you who kill the prophets and stone those sent to you, how many times I yearned to gather your children together, as a hen gathers her young under her wings, but you were unwilling! (Mt 23:37; cf. Lk 13:34).

In this passage Jesus is the one who gathers his children under his wing like a mother hen. In Matthew 28 Jesus, also the subject, assures his disciples that "I am with you always, until the end of the age" (Mt 28:20). Like the flowering stick of Black Elk's vision, Jesus will always be with his disciples. Both references explicitly connect the flowering stick with Christ.

Black Elk continues, stating that this sacred stick is the cottonwood tree. *The Sacred Pipe* and a prayer given during the 1931 Neihardt interviews give a more detailed description of the cottonwood tree used in the Sun Dance. They both contain many biblical allusions connecting the tree to Jesus:

> The weak will lean upon you, and for all the people you will be a support.[96]

> Oh Great Spirit, Great Spirit, my Grandfather, may my people be likened unto the flowering stick. Your stick of sticks, tree of trees, forest of forests, tree of trees of the earth, trees of all kinds of the earth. Oh, flowering tree, here on earth trees are like unto you; your trees of all kinds are likened unto

---

[94] Ibid., 118.
[95] Ibid., 129–30.
[96] Brown, *The Sacred Pipe*, 74.

you, but yet they have chosen you. Oh tree, you are mild, you are likened
to the one above. My nation shall depend on you. My nation on you shall
bloom.[97]

These two passages taken together describe the tree as mild, likened to the one
above, and a support for all peoples, especially the weak. The same concepts are
found in a passage from Matthew:

Come to me, all you who labor and are burdened, and I will give you rest.
Take my yoke upon you and learn from me, for I am meek and humble of
heart; and you will find rest for yourselves. For my yoke is easy, and my
burden light (Matthew 11:28–30).

Like Black Elk's description of the cottonwood, Jesus is meek and supports
those who are burdened or weak.

Black Elk calls the flowering stick "tree of trees and forest of forests." Black
Elk used this construction in the first passage of this section, in which he referred to the flowering stick as "the greatest of the greatest sticks."[98] This construct strongly echoes a christological refrain used in the New Testament. In the
book of Revelation, Christ is depicted riding a white horse and is called "King
of kings and Lord of lords" (Rv 19:16; see also Rv 17:14 and 1 Tm 6:15).

Black Elk's description of the cottonwood highlights the shelter it provides
for birds:

You are a kind and a good-looking tree; upon you the winged peoples
have raised their families; from the tip of your lofty branches down to
your roots, the winged and four-legged peoples have made their homes.[99]

This description echoes Ezekiel's passage on the messianic king, a tree that God
will plant:

On the mountain heights of Israel I will plant it. It shall put forth branches
and bear fruit, and become a majestic cedar. Birds of every kind shall
dwell beneath it, every winged thing in the shade of its boughs (Ez 17:23).

In both Black Elk's description and the passage from Ezekiel, the tree is described as good or kind, sheltering the creatures of the earth. According to Black
Elk, the cottonwood will stand at the center of all peoples.

May we two-leggeds always follow your sacred example, for we see that
you are always looking upwards into the heavens.

---

[97] DeMallie, *The Sixth Grandfather*, 287.
[98] Ibid., 129–30.
[99] Brown, *The Sacred Pipe*, 74.

Of all the many standing peoples, you O rustling cottonwood have been chosen in a sacred manner; you are about to go to the center of the people's sacred hoop, and there you will represent the people and will help us fulfill the will of *Wakan-Tanka*. . . . Soon, and with all the peoples of the world, you will stand at the center; for all beings and all things you will bring that which is good.[100]

This description evokes the tree of life that God establishes in the New Jerusalem, found in Revelation. "On either side of the river grew the tree of life that produces fruit twelve times a year, once each month; the leaves of the trees serve as medicine for the nations" (Rv 22:2). In both Black Elk's vision and the book of Revelation, the tree is a symbol of unity. Established in the center, it brings goodness to all peoples.

The cottonwood tree and the Sun Dance are linked to the cross in the Black Elk tradition. Fools Crow compares the tree to Jesus on the cross: "So the tree . . . becomes a living thing for us. It becomes human, and it dies for us like Jesus on the cross for everyone."[101] He also compares the Sun Dance sacrifice to Jesus' sacrifice:

The Sioux received the Sun Dance from *Wakan-Tanka*, and we honor him by doing it as he told us to. Since the white man has come to us and explained how God sent his own son to be sacrificed, we realize that our sacrifice is similar to Jesus' own. As to how the white man feels about what we do, there was a far more terrible thing done by Jesus Christ. He endured more suffering and more pain. He was even stabbed on his side, and he died.

The Indian tribes must speak for themselves, but the Sioux feel a special closeness to God in the dance and in the piercing and flesh offerings. We even duplicate Christ's crown of thorns in the sage head wreath the pledgers wear.[102]

According to Fools Crows, the Sun Dance brings a special closeness to God and bears a similarity to the passion of Christ, even to the point that the dancers replicate Christ's crown of thorns. Other Lakota agree with Fools Crow. Stephen Feraca, writing in 1963, reports that one of his informants, Gilbert Bad Wound, considers the Sun Dance a Christian ceremony. Feraca states that "he is by no means alone in this belief."[103]

Lucy remembers Black Elk viewing the Sun Dance in the same way, ascribing the same Christian interpretation to it:

---

[100] Ibid., 74. This passage also develops Black Elk's understanding of will and connects it to the sacrifice of Jesus. For a discussion of will as a Christian theme, see pages 100–101 above.

[101] Thomas E. Mails, *Fools Crow*, with Dallas Chief Eagle (Garden City, N.Y.: Doubleday, 1979), 133.

[102] Ibid., 136.

[103] Holler, *Black Elk's Religion*, 154.

They pray and say to the Great Spirit, "Without any sinful thoughts or actions, we're going to do this for you." That's the way they feel when they do these Sun Dance ceremonies. They purify themselves—that's why they wear the sage crown, which resembles the crown our Lord wore— and they start dancing. So the Indian, early before sunrise, had to stand there and had to go with the sun—watching it until it went down. That's the suffering, you see. And some of them even shed their blood. Christ did that too, before he died on the cross. That was the way he suffered.[104]

In *The Sacred Pipe* Black Elk uses the language of the passion to describe the Sun Dance. In preparing for the dance, the dancer echoes Jesus' agony in the Garden of Gethsemane. "All this may be difficult to do, yet for the good of the people it must be done. Help me, O Grandfather, and give to me the courage and strength to stand the sufferings which I am about to undergo!"[105] Later, the dancer says, "I shall offer up my body and soul that my people may live."[106] This resembles the message of Jesus in John: "I am the living bread that came down from heaven; whoever eats this bread will live forever; and the bread that I will give is my flesh for the life of the world" (Jn 6:51). Both Black Elk's sun dancer and Jesus offer their bodies for the life of the world.

The culmination of the passion is Jesus' death on the cross: "When Jesus had taken the wine, he said, 'It is finished.' And bowing his head, he handed over his spirit" (Jn 19:30).

This is a major theme in Black Elk's vision and Sun Dance. When Black Elk completes his vision, the western grandfather, Kablaya, tells him, "All over the universe you have finished."[107] At the end of the Sun Dance, Kablaya says: "O *Wakan Tanka*, this sacred place [the Sun Dance grounds] is Yours. Upon it all has been finished. We rejoice."[108] Holler agrees with this reading, noting that Kablaya's words echo Jesus' words on the cross in the Gospel of John.[109]

The connection between the Sun Dance sacrifice and the passion of Christ was concretely embodied by communal practice. During the summer Catholic conferences a Sun Dance pole was erected. An altar was constructed underneath it, and mass was said.[110] Like the summer conferences, Black Elk's account of the Sun Dance has an altar next to the Sun Dance pole.

---

[104] Steltenkamp, *Black Elk*, 103.

[105] Brown, *The Sacred Pipe*, 79.

[106] Black Elk uses "my people" in a universal sense.

[107] DeMallie, *The Sixth Grandfather*, 132.

[108] Brown, *The Sacred Pipe*, 100.

[109] Holler, *Black Elk's Religion*, 148.

[110] Ross Alexander Enochs, "Black Elk and the Jesuits," in *The Black Elk Reader*, ed. Clyde Holler (Syracuse, N.Y.: Syracuse University Press, 2000), 296. For a detailed history of the Lakota Catholic summer conferences, see Mark G. Thiel, "Catholic Sodalities among the Sioux, 1882-1910," *U.S. Catholic Historian* 16/2 (Spring 1998): 56-77.

In addition, missionaries explicitly compared the Sun Dance to the sacrifice of Christ. Ross Enochs cites Florentine Dingman, S.J., who wrote in 1907,

> The late Bishop Martin Marty, O.S.B., then Abbot of St. Meinrad's was one of the first who preached to the Sioux, taking occasion, from the cruelties they practiced at the Sun Dance to appease the Great Spirit, to point out to them our divine Savior hanging from the tree to atone for our sins.[111]

Marty demonstrates that, from the beginning, Lakota Catholicism cultivated the association between the Sun Dance and the crucifixion.

Black Elk also uses the image of root to describe the sacred tree. In Black Elk's final prayer, he refers to the sacred tree as a root. "There may be a root that is still alive, and give this root strength and moisture of your good things. . . . I prayed that you may set the tree to bloom again."[112] Lucy also remembers her father saying, "The Great Spirit has promised one day that the tree of my father's vision was to root."[113] The symbol of root is another biblical symbol. Jesse's stump, or the root of Jesse, was a messianic prophecy that foretold the lineage of the messiah.

> But a shoot shall sprout from the stump of Jesse,
>     and from his roots a bud shall blossom. . . .
>   On that day,
> The root of Jesse,
>     set up as a signal for the nations,
> The Gentiles shall seek out,
>     for his dwelling shall be glorious (Is 11:1, 11).

According to Isaiah, a branch will grow from the root of Jesse and will stand as a sign for what the Dakota Bible translates *Ikcewicasta*, meaning ordinary people, or Indians.[114] Christians interpret this passage as a prophecy for Jesus; in Revelation, for example, Jesus is called the "the root and offspring of David, the bright morning star" (Rv 22:16).

The most important biblical passages for this comparison are those that refer to the cross as a tree. In Acts, Peter tells Cornelius that Jesus was put "to death by hanging him on a tree" (Acts 10:39; see also Dt 21:23; Acts 5:30; 13:29; Gal 3:13). The First Letter of Peter depicts Jesus as a sun dancer: "He himself bore our sins in his body upon the cross [in the Dakota Bible *can*—tree], so that, free from sin, we might live for righteousness [wóowothaŋna]. By his wounds you have been healed" (1 Pt 2:24). This important passage unites all the previous themes of the flowering stick, the red man in front of the tree, and Black Elk's

---

[111] Enochs, *The Jesuit Mission to the Lakota Sioux*, 60.
[112] DeMallie, *The Sixth Grandfather*, 295–96.
[113] Steltenkamp, *Black Elk*, 109.
[114] Jan Ullrich, personal communication.

portrayal of the Sun Dance in *The Sacred Pipe*. Jesus is pierced and hung from the tree; his wounds are for the healing and life of all the world.

In summary, the evidence supports the hypothesis that Black Elk's sacred tree is a Christian symbol. Black Elk's description mirrors biblical imagery on many levels: the tree of life, the messianic root, the Sun Dance and the passion, the use of christological language, the description of Jesus dying on the tree in the Dakota Bible, and the vision of the Son of God in front of the blooming tree. Missionaries preached this, communal practice embodied it, and Fools Crow and others attested to its persistence in Lakota tradition. Lucy Looks Twice's claim must be taken seriously.

## THE SACRED HOOP/THE GREAT MULTITUDE

The destination of the journey down the sacred road is the sacred hoop. This is a symbol for what Black Elk also refers to as the Promised Land. Black Elk uses three prominent themes to describe the sacred hoop: the universality of the hoop, the end of suffering, and finishing and re-creating all things to make them live.

The first major theme, the universality of the hoop, was previously discussed in Chapter 4. For Black Elk, the hoop includes all peoples:

Behold the circle of the sacred hoop, for the people shall be like unto it; and if they are like unto this, they shall have power, because there is no end to this hoop and in the center of the hoop these raise their children. (The sacred hoop means the continents of the world and people shall stand as one.)[115]

I could see nothing but millions of faces behind the grandfathers. The west spirit said (pointing to all the people trying to see me): "Behold your nation!"[116]

Black Elk's description is similar to a vision of John recorded in Revelation:

After this I had a vision of a great multitude, which no one could count, from every nation, race, people, and tongue. They stood before the throne and before the Lamb, wearing white robes and holding palm branches in their hands. They cried out in a loud voice: "Salvation comes from our God [*Wakan Tanka*], who is seated at the throne, and from the Lamb" (Rv 7:9–10).

In both Black Elk's and John's vision, an uncountable number of people from all nations stand before divinity in a new creation. Black Elk in his Catholic teaching stressed this concept of unity:

---

[115] DeMallie, *The Sixth Grandfather*, 129.
[116] Ibid., 138.

So my friends and relatives, we should stand together and do what is right
and be patient. That way God has something good for us all the time.[117]

Those of us here on earth who are suffering should help one another and
have pity. We belong to one family and we have only one faith. Therefore,
those who are suffering, my relatives, we should look toward them and pray
for them, because our Savior came on this earth and helped all poor people.[118]

According to Black Elk, the Savior came for all suffering peoples. All belong to
one family and, like his vision, all should stand together. This reinforces the
reading of the red man as a Christ figure who tells Black Elk the same thing:
"My life is such that all earthly beings that grow belong to me."[119] All belong to
Christ, who came to help all.

A second theme is the cessation of suffering that all will experience in the
Promised Land. "One of the old men said (showing me the sacred hoop): 'Behold a good nation, a sacred nation, again they will walk toward good land, the
land of plenty, and no suffering shall there be. A nation you shall create and it
shall be a sacred nation.'"[120] Revelation discusses the new creation where God
will eliminate all suffering:

Behold, God's dwelling is with the human race. He will dwell with them
and they will be his people and God himself will always be with them (as
their God). He will wipe away every tear from their eyes, and there shall
be no more death or mourning, wailing or pain, (for) the old order has
passed away (Rv 21:3–4).

Once again, this theme of Black Elk's vision is a theme of Black Elk's Catholic
teaching:

Therefore, those who are suffering, my relatives, we should look toward
them and pray for them, because our Savior came on this earth and helped
all poor people.[121]

A third theme is the renewal of creation, where all is made alive:

[The western grandfather] says "all over the universe you have finished."
After singing, the black stallion spoke saying: "All over the universe

---

[117] Black Elk, letter to friends and relatives written at Pine Ridge Reservation,
Manderson, South Dakota, November 12, 1906, published in *Sinasapa Wocekiye
Taeyanpaha,* March 15, 1907, translated from Lakota to English under Michael F.
Steltenkamp, S.J., in Timonin, *Black Elk's Synthesis.*

[118] DeMallie, *The Sixth Grandfather,* 19.

[119] Ibid., 263.

[120] Ibid., 125–26.

[121] Ibid., 19.

everything is finished and your nation of nations is rejoicing." (Meaning that everything is living—trees, flowers, grass, and every animal is living now.) In the vision I was representing the earth and everything was giving me power. I was given power so that all creatures on earth would be happy.[122]

A similar description is found in Revelation:

> Then I heard every creature in heaven and on earth and under the earth and in the sea, everything in the universe, cry out: "To the one who sits on the throne and to the Lamb be blessing and honor, glory and might, forever and ever" (Rv 5:13).

Both Black Elk and Revelation describe the setting of divine renewal as the totality of creation.

The previous passage from Black Elk describes the totality of creation being made alive, giving him power, so that all creation will be happy. Earlier in his vision Black Elk tells of a song that the people sing on their journey down the red road: "May you behold this I have asked to be made over. A good nation I have asked to be made over." In a footnote DeMallie says, "'To make over' implies a spiritual strengthening, the making of new life for the people."[123] This newness of life is a major biblical theme. Isaiah describes the action of God in finishing creation:

> Lo, I am about to create new heavens
>     and a new earth;
> The things of the past shall not be remembered
>     or come to mind.
> Instead, there shall be rejoicing and happiness
>     in what I create. . . .
> No longer shall the sound of weeping be heard there,
>     or the sound of crying (Is 65:17–19).

The renewal of all creation is not limited to man alone but includes animals:

> Your justice is like the mountains of God;
>     your judgments, like the mighty deep;
>     man and beast you save, O Lord (Ps 36:7).

Hosea emphasizes this in describing the messianic covenant that *Wakan Tanka* will make with his people:

---

[122]   Ibid., 132–33.
[123]   Ibid., 126.

I will make a covenant for them on that day,
  with the beasts of the field,
With the birds of the air,
  and with the things that crawl on the ground. . . .
I will espouse you to me forever . . .
  and you shall know the LORD (Hos 2:20–22).

In Revelation, Jesus says he is the fulfillment of this process: "The one who sat on the throne said, 'Behold, I make all things new'" (Rv 21:5). Through *Wakan Tanka* in Christ all of creation is renewed and made to live.

In conclusion, it is clear that Black Elk's eschatological vision parallels the biblical account of God's action in the redemption of all peoples with the elimination of suffering and the creation of new life.

## THE PRAYER AT HARNEY PEAK

After relating his story, Black Elk, Neihardt, and their children ascended Harney Peak, which was the setting of Black Elk's vision. There Black Elk prayed to *Wakan Tanka* in what represents a summation of his vision. In the prayer the Christian language is even more explicit. First, Black Elk makes no mention of the aspects of his vision and Lakota tradition that do not correspond to Christian tradition, including the soldier weed and the bow and arrow. Second, he emphasizes those aspects of his vision that have the most clear Christian meanings: the sacred wind, the cup of water, and the tree. Black Elk prays for the tree that has not bloomed.

But I have fallen away thus causing the tree never to bloom again; but there may be a root that is still alive, and give this root strength and moisture of your good things that you have given to us people and through all the powers of the four quarters.[124]

Black Elk's description is almost identical to a description of a tree in Job:

For a tree there is hope,
  if it be cut down, that it will sprout again
  and that its tender shoots will not cease.
Even though its roots grow old in the earth,
  and its stump die in the dust,
Yet at the first whiff of water it may flourish again
  and put forth branches like a young plant.
                    (Jb 14:7–9)

---

[124] Ibid., 295–96.

Both descriptions are of trees, though cut and old, that live in hope that with water and strength from the Lord, they will bloom again.

During the prayer Black Elk says, "Help us and have mercy on us . . . that my people may live."[125] This is a constant theme in Black Elk's interpretation of Lakota tradition. During the *Hanblecheyapi* (crying for a vision), the lamenter continually cries: "*Wakan-Tanka onshimala ye oyate wani wachin cha!*' (O Great Spirit, be merciful to me that my people may live!)"[126] During the Sun Dance this is repeated in song: "*Wakan-Tanka*, have mercy on us, that our people may live!"[127] Black Elk's son Ben, in a talk given in 1969 to the students of the Pine Ridge Boarding School, states that "there is only one prayer the Indian uses: 'Oh, Great Spirit, be merciful to me, that my people may live.'"[128]

However, as was noted in Chapter 4, this was not the only prayer the Lakota used. In the early Lakota tradition prayers for personal power and success in war were primary themes. This exclusive emphasis on the life of the people was an innovation by Black Elk.[129] What is striking is the Christian correlation. First, *onshimala*, the word that Black Elk uses for mercy in *The Sacred Pipe*, is the same stem that is used to translate both grace and mercy in the Lakota Christian tradition.[130]

Second, salvation, the Christian understanding of the primary action of God, is translated "to make live." According to Ullrich, savior is translated as *waníkhiye* (one who brings back to life). The roots of the word make the connection more explicit:

| | |
|---|---|
| *wa* | someone (detranzitivizer, forms occupational and other types of nouns) |
| *ní* | to live |
| *-khiya* | to cause to[131] |

Consequently, Jesus Christ, the Savior of the world, is he who "causes to live." This same translation is used for salvation. An example from the Dakota Bible is Revelation 7:10:

Dakota text: K'a hotháŋkakiya hóthaŋiŋpi k'a heyápi, Wakháŋthaŋka uŋkíthawapi oíyotaŋke kiŋ akáŋ khíyotaŋke čiŋ hé é, Amnos kiŋ kičhí, niwíčhaye yuhá nuŋwé.

---

125   Ibid., 296.

126   Brown, *The Sacred Pipe*, 57.

127   Ibid., 70.

128   Esther Black Elk DeSersa and Olivia Black Elk Pourier, *Black Elk Lives: Conversations with the Black Elk Family*, ed. Hilda Neihardt and Lori Utecht (Lincoln: University of Nebraska Press, 2000), 16.

129   For example, Holler argues that "no Sun Dance in the literature resembles Black Elk's dance in its emphasis on the theme that 'the people shall live'" (Clyde Holler, *Black Elk's Religion: The Sun Dance and Lakota Catholicism* [Syracuse, N.Y.: Syracuse University Press, 1995], 141).

130   Jan Ullrich, personal communication.

131   Ibid.

English gloss: *and / with a loud voice / they proclaimed / and / they said as follows / God / our / seat / the / upon / he sits down / the / that / it is him / Amnos / the / with / making people alive / he has / may it be.*

English text: *And cried with a loud voice, saying, Salvation to our God which sitteth upon the throne, and unto the Lamb.* (KJV)[132]

According to Ullrich, the salvation that comes from God and Jesus Christ is expressed in the Dakota language as "to make people alive." The action of Jesus, the reason for Jesus' death and resurrection, the reason for the church, the reason to evangelize, is because Jesus makes the people live.

Consequently, Catholicism in its Lakota embodiment, a religion that promises mercy, grace, and salvation, is centered on the very things on which Black Elk centers Lakota tradition. When Black Elk said the words, "'*Wakan-Tanka unshimala ye oyate wani wachin cha!*' (O Great Spirit, be merciful to me that my people may live!), he was saying the same Lakota words used for the central gospel message: 'Lord, have mercy, give grace, and give us salvation.'"[133] For Black Elk, there is no separation between the central prayer of the Lakota tradition and Catholicism because the priest and the sun dancer say the same words.

## INTERPRETATIONS: BLACK ELK'S LAKOTA CATHOLIC SALVATION HISTORY

A number of conclusions can be drawn from the evidence presented here. The first is the extraordinary degree to which Black Elk refashioned Lakota tradition. The skeptic could argue that by itself Black Elk's redescription of Lakota tradition presented in Chapter 4 demonstrates at most only a negative correlation with Catholicism. That is to say, Lakota tradition is not necessarily connected to Catholicism, it simply does not contradict Catholic truth claims.

But if Black Elk's emphasis and Ben Black Elk's claim are true—that the center of Lakota tradition is "O Great Spirit, be merciful to me, that my people may live"—then at the center of Black Elk's interpretation of Lakota tradition are the two most important teachings of Catholicism: "Christ, Lord have mercy, give us salvation, that we may live." But this is more than just a random parallel. Black Elk's emphasis is clearly an intentional modification with its source in Christian thought. What has been standardized as the essence of Lakota tradition and spirituality is, in reality, the result of Black Elk's sincere faith in the Lakota Christ. Following Sanneh and Ong, Black Elk redescribed the Lakota tradition in light of the incarnation of the Christian story to the degree that Christ dwells at the very heart of Lakota rituals and permeates the Lakota world.

---

[132] "The Dakota translation of 'salvation' does not seem to relate closely to the English version. While the English seems to mean something like 'Let our God be saved,' the Dakota text says, if I understand it correctly, 'Let it be that he possess something to save the people'" (Jan Ullrich, personal communication).

[133] Brown, *The Sacred Pipe*, 57.

Returning to Black Elk's vision, there is certainly enough biblical evidence to demonstrate that at no point can Black Elk's vision be separated from Catholicism. Every aspect of Black Elk's vision has a clear correlation with biblical tradition. Even the claim that Black Elk's vision is from the thunder beings *(Wakinyan)* has a strong Christian correlation. James R. Walker's Lakota mythology describes the origin of *Wakinyan*:

> He [*Inyan*, the Rock] made a shapeless creature and named him *Wakinyan* (Winged One or Thunderstorm). *Wakinyan* is as shapeless as a cloud and terrifying to behold. He has two wings of many joints, which he can spread afar or make very small; he has neither legs nor feet, but has huge talons that can pierce the hardest of things; he has no mouth, but has a huge beak armed with sharp teeth that can rend and tear the toughest of things; he has no throat, but has one voice that is the thunder; and he has no head, but has one eye, and the glance of that eye is the lightning.[134]

In the Riggs Dakota Bible both the terms *Inyan* and *Wakinyan* are given significant Christian meaning. Jesus says that Peter is *Inyan*, the foundation of his church. Jesus calls the brothers James and John the sons of *Wakinyan*. Consequently, Black Elk would hear that Jesus' three most important disciples are equated to two of the most powerful Lakota mythical beings. He would hear that Jesus is the source of the power of *Inyan* and *Wakinyan*. The church is built on *Inyan,* and to follow Christ is to be a son of *Wakinyan*. As a result, DeMallie's claim that Black Elk's life as a Catholic was contrary to or separate from his vision is not only untenable, it is impossible. The question now becomes to what degree is Black Elk's interpretation an explicit manifestation *of* Christian thought.

Of course, a skeptic could argue that the evidence presented in this chapter is nothing more than random, unintentional allusions. In other words, the allusions consist of isolated fragments that compose a pure Lakota core. From this perspective, although Black Elk could see parallels between Catholicism and Lakota tradition, Catholicism was not necessarily the source of Black Elk's vision, which remained solely Lakota in origin.

However, we have every reason to look for a unified whole. Black Elk lived in a Lakota Catholic world to which both his community and writings attest. The number and depth of connections to Catholic tradition permeate every facet of his vision. In light of the claims of the Lakota community discussed at the beginning of this chapter—that Black Elk knew Christian biblical texts very well; that he connected the biblical texts to the world he experienced, especially the natural world; and that he had the ability to quote specific passages accurately—the connections between his vision and the biblical tradition must be intentional. Black Elk *intended* to talk about the Lakota Catholic tradition. In

---

[134] James R. Walker, *Lakota Myth*, ed. Elaine A. Jahner (1983; repr., Lincoln: University of Nebraska Press, 1989), 213.

other words, Black Elk was not presenting fragments of Catholic allusions to describe a pure Lakota whole. Rather, he intentionally shaped the whole story of the real Lakota Catholic world in which he lived.

Now we turn to the whole. The overall structure of the biblical imagery in Black Elk's vision reveals three themes. The first is the striking parallel to the book of Revelation. Black Elk's vision follows the basic plot of Revelation. Both include a call, an ascent to the heavenly temple, great battles and beasts, multiple divine beings that work for or represent *Wakan Tanka*, the victory of *Wakan Tanka* over suffering and destruction, and the establishment of universal peace and harmony. Revelation is also complemented by similar apocalyptic imagery from the prophets. The references for both Revelation and the prophets use similar language and imagery.

The second theme is the christological focus of Black Elk's vision. Black Elk places the establishment of the sacred tree at the center of the broader plot of Revelation. This is consistent with the position of the christological symbol of the lamb at the center of Revelation. As we have seen above, many symbols of Black Elk's vision carry other significant christological meanings.

A third theme is the historical nature of the vision. Black Elk organizes the vision in four historical periods, which he calls ascents. The nation walks down the red road, and each ascent represents a different generation with different characteristics. In the first ascent, the people are happy and well. In the second, conditions begin to deteriorate. In the third, the people follow their own rules and need to be brought back into the sacred hoop. The flowering stick appears at the end of the third ascent. The fourth ascent, which is in the future, will be filled with war and suffering before *Wakan Tanka* renews creation and ends all suffering.

Taken as a whole, Black Elk's vision is clearly a Lakota version of what Catholics call salvation history. Table 5–1 on page 130 demonstrates the narrative structure of Black Elk's vision for the preceding biblical references. The first ascent is the call of the Lakota, like the children of Israel, to an Exodus journey. The second ascent is the failure of the Lakota to keep the covenant with *Wakan Tanka*. The third ascent is the total failure of the people, which necessitates *Wakan Tanka*'s intervention. To emphasize this Black Elk echoes Isaiah 53:6 during the third ascent:

| *Black Elk's vision* | *Isaiah 53:6* |
|---|---|
| The third ascent represented all kinds of animals and fowls, and from there on every man has his own vision and his own rules.[135] | We had all gone astray like sheep [in the Dakota Bible *tahinca*—the common deer], each following his own way. . . . |

In this section of Isaiah, the Hymn to the Suffering Servant (52:13—53:12), *Wakan Tanka* sends the messiah to bear the guilt of Israel and redeem the people

---

[135] DeMallie, *The Sixth Grandfather*, 127.

**Table 5–1. Black Elk's Vision: Lakota Catholic Salvation History**

### Black Elk Called to Heaven

Like John of Revelation, Black Elk is called to heaven (Rv 4:1). The two men seen by the apostles after Jesus ascended to the clouds (Acts) return for Black Elk. On the way he sees the horses of the four directions (Zec 6:1–5).

### Theophany in the Throne Room

The two men take Black Elk to God's throne room, the *tipi wakan* of Revelation (Rv 4:2–6). There Black Elk sees God in the form of six grandfathers, like the seven spirits of God from Revelation (Rv 4:5). The six grandfathers tell Black Elk not to fear (Rv 1:17–18), for he will know their will (Mt 6:10). Black Elk will represent them on earth (Ex 3:10, 15) and create a new nation. They give Black Elk sacred relics, including the morning star (Rv 2:28; 22:16) and wind (Acts 2). God will be his spirit (Gal 2:20), and Black Elk will be his body (1 Cor 12:13; 12:27; 1 Jn 3:24). In this way God calls Black Elk into the Christian story and sends him to guide the Lakota as they walk through salvation history.

### Salvation History

God sends Black Elk into salvation history. The first stage is the primordial battle of the fallen angels. In Black Elk's version he vanquishes the man standing amid flames.

### Journey of the New Nation: Four Ascents

*First Ascent*: After the battle of the fallen angels, Black Elk is sent to the Lakota. The people will multiply, increase, and prosper (Gn 1—3). As in the Exodus, the Lakota start the journey down the good red road and will walk to the promised land where there is no suffering (Rv 7:15–17; 21:3–4).

*Second Ascent*: The Lakota continue the journey.

*Third Ascent*: The Lakota begin to walk in difficulty. They become like animals, all with their own visions and rules (Is 53:6). In addition, white people arrive and colonize the Lakota, putting them in reservations. The Lakota are very poor, and many people are dying.

Before the Lakota enter the fourth ascent, Christ appears in the form of the red man and the sacred tree. In addition, the wind revives the dead (Ez 37:9–10). The Lakota are christened, or baptized, and they say, "Thanks be to Eagle Wing Stretches," a reference to God (Dt 32:10–12; Ps 36:7).

*Fourth Ascent*: This is the time yet to come. While the Lakota remain in the third ascent, Black Elk journeys ahead and sees the apocalypse (Rv 6–19).

### Returns to Throne Room, Vision of Promised Land

After seeing the salvation history of the Lakota, Black Elk returns to God's throne room. Eagle Wing Stretches, the sixth grandfather and spirit of humankind, or Jesus, has triumphed (Rv 5:5). Black Elk sees the final judgment, where hundreds will be sacred and hundreds will be flames (Rv 20:11–15), the renewal of all creation (Rv 5:11–13; 21:5; 21:24–27), and the heavenly worship in the throne room (Rv 4:6—5:10) where the sun shines always (Rv 21:23).

### Returns to Earth

Black Elk is brought back to earth to the Lakota, who are between the third ascent (death and resurrection of Christ) and the fourth ascent (the apocalypse and second coming of Christ). As the spotted eagle guides Black Elk home (Rv 8:13), he looks back to see the mountain of the *tipi wakan* (Rv 21:10). Later, Black Elk tells his vision so that, like John, it may be written down (Rv 1:19; 21:5).

because they are totally lost. In Black Elk's vision all of the christological refer- ences now occur and the flowering stick is established. According to Black Elk, rain from a cloud "christens"—or baptizes—the nation with water. The nation responds, "Thanks to Eagle Wing Stretches," which means "Thanks be to God."

Black Elk sees ahead to the fourth ascent. This is what has not yet come to pass in salvation history: the final apocalyptic battles of Revelation, the last judgment, *Wakan Tanka's* establishment of peace and the renewal of all creation in Christ. In his preface to *The Sacred Pipe*, Black Elk asserted that this would happen in the last cycle:

> We have been told by the white men, or at least by those who are Chris- tians, that God sent to men His son, who would restore order and peace upon the earth; and we have been told that Jesus the Christ was crucified, but that he shall come again at the Last Judgment, the end of this world or cycle. This I understand and know that it is true.[136]

This reading directly coincides with Lakota history. Black Elk laments dur- ing the interview about the duplicitous actions of the whites and the suffering they brought to the Lakota. There are only two places where whites appear in Black Elk's vision. The first is in the third ascent, when the nation has lost its way and the whites have fenced in the Indians and the animals.

> The white people came on this continent and put us Indians in a fence and they put another fence somewhere else and put our game into it. When the buffalo and elk are all gone, the Great Spirit will look upon the whites for this and perhaps something will happen.[137]

Black Elk addresses the same thing in one of his Catholic letters:

> So I will tell you that all of you (and myself, that it or we) are like sheep among wolves ready to be eaten up. And you know when one sheep is surrounded by wolves, it has no place to go. That's how we are. We are ready to be eaten up.
>
> So my friends and relatives, we should stand together and do what is right and be patient. That way God has something good for us all the time.[138]

Black Elk then states that this will not be forgotten and that the Great Spirit will judge the whites. After the whites arrive, the flowering stick is established and the Catholic church comes to the Lakota.

---

[136] Brown, *The Sacred Pipe*, xix.

[137] Ibid.

[138] Black Elk, letter to friends and relatives written at Pine Ridge Reservation, Manderson, South Dakota, November 12, 1906.

The second place whites appear in the vision is at the end after the last judgment. Among the millions of faces of the renewed creation in the New Jerusalem an uncertain Black Elk also sees whites.

This description of Lakota salvation history is placed within the framework of Revelation. Like John, Black Elk is brought to the heavenly tipi and shown what will come to pass and what role he will play in the great drama. And like John, he returns to tell his people and spread his vision.[139]

As a result, Black Elk's Lakota discourse manifests a fundamentally Catholic orientation. The previous chapter demonstrated how Black Elk redescribed the Lakota world in light of Christ's incarnation. This chapter has shown that Black Elk incarnated Christ into the center of his own life, his manner of discourse, and the Lakota world. But the most significant feature of Black Elk's vision is its rereading of the entire history of the Lakota—including the arrival of Western colonialism—according to the incarnation of Christ. In Black Elk's vision, Christ becomes the Lord of history. I argue in Chapter 7 that this radical feature of the vision is the key to Black Elk's conversion and also his challenge to Western colonialism.

In the end, then, Lucy's claim of Black Elk's Lakota Catholic identity stands against the readings of most academics. The words of Black Elk, long interpreted as a rejection or an antithesis of Christianity, themselves carry the gospel message. Black Elk's vision is the best evidence that Catholicism was a central theme in all of Black Elk's life and the thought that shaped both his world and the one language he spoke.

---

[139] Black Elk's Lakota version of salvation history, or incarnation of Christ into the Lakota world, was at least partially influenced by the retreats that he attended with the Jesuits. Starting in 1922 the Jesuits gave three-day retreats from the Ignatian Spiritual Exercises. They called the retreats *hamble iciyope*—"crying for a vision"—which was the Lakota name for the vision quest. The Spiritual Exercises train participants to imagine themselves in biblical scenes. Black Elk attended eight retreats. As a result, it should not be surprising for Black Elk to imagine or have a vision of Christ in the Lakota world. For a history of the retreats, see Enochs, "Black Elk and the Jesuits," 292.

# 6

# Misinterpreting the Vision

*The years from 1930 to 1940 rank as the worst ten years I know of, and all the Oglala as old as I am will agree. In that one single period we lost everything we had gained.*

—Fools Crow

The primary question pursued in this study is the question of the historical Black Elk. On the one hand, there is Neihardt's essentialist Black Elk: a proud, defiant, yet vanquished warrior protecting a pure Lakota tradition. On the other hand, there is the Black Elk described by the Lakota community and the historical record: a Catholic agent actively and successfully participating in the new reservation economy.

Up to this point little evidence has pointed to the essentialist Black Elk. Chapter 2 noted how missionaries initiated "dissident" practices that allowed Catholicism to develop internally within the Lakota world. Chapter 3 then provided specific examples of traditional Lakota who, because of the Lakota language, lived comfortably as Christians while inhabiting a thoroughly Lakota world. The next two chapters demonstrated how Black Elk's Lakota discourse manifested an internal dynamic to his Catholic life. Chapter 4 told how Black Elk refashioned Lakota tradition in light of the Christian story, and Chapter 5 argued that Black Elk's great vision was the incarnation of the Christian story in the Lakota world. Taken as a whole, these chapters portray not a defender of a pure Lakota tradition but an active agent living in a unified Lakota Catholic world.

Yet, the defender of Neihardt's Black Elk could still have doubts. Maybe Neihardt found something not described in the other sources. Or perhaps Black Elk chose to reveal his "true" self to Neihardt. Thus, in order to conclude definitively in favor of the Lakota Catholic Black Elk, we need to address these nagging doubts and explain how Neihardt described a Black Elk so different from the historical record.

One possible answer might be insincerity. Perhaps Black Elk just told Neihardt what he thought he wanted to hear. Or perhaps Black Elk revealed his true self to Neihardt, having playing a duplicitous Catholic role for decades. Or perhaps Neihardt intentionally misrepresented Black Elk. While this would be an easy solution, there is no evidence that either Black Elk or Neihardt was insincere. Neihardt believed his representation reflected what he saw and heard from Black Elk. According to Neihardt, *Black Elk Speaks* was "the first absolutely Indian book thus far written. It is all out of the Indian consciousness."[1] To accuse Black Elk of duplicity—in either his Catholic life or the Neihardt interviews—would destroy his credibility as both a holy man and an ethnographic informant.

I maintain that the answer is actually quite simple and does not rely on insincerity on the part of any of the actors. Rather, the reservation context of the 1930s provides the answer. A story from Fools Crow's autobiography illustrates the same dynamics that allowed Neihardt to create the essentialist Black Elk:

> Black Elk gave me my first eagle feather headdress. It was a beautiful head bonnet, and it had thirty or more tail feathers in it. . . . During the depression, and sometime after 1930, I sold it for one hundred and fifty dollars, which was a lot of money in those days. I have many times regretted its sale.[2]

For some reason, Fools Crow decided to sell his first eagle feather headdress given to him by Black Elk. What was happening in the 1930s that caused an important holy man who would later become the ceremonial chief of the Lakota nation to go against tradition and sell an important Lakota cultural artifact, a decision he often regretted?

It is not surprising to learn that the Great Depression was the source of Fools Crow's decision. Because of the Lakota's incredible poverty, Fools Crow sold the headdress to an outsider with greater financial resources. Fools Crow does not identify the motivation of the buyer, but it was most likely a collector of symbols of Lakota culture. Apparently, economic disparity and the "commodification" of culture lay behind a decision that Fools Crow regretted.

The collaboration between Neihardt and Black Elk also took place in the 1930s, during the beginning of the Great Depression. I maintain that the cultural and economic factors that made it expedient for Fools Crow to sell his headdress also provided the setting for the Black Elk–Neihardt collaboration and enabled Neihardt to create the essentialist Black Elk.

Neihardt was an outsider to the Lakota Catholic community; he did not speak the language or know the traditional patterns of communication. He was also ignorant of the current cultural practices of the reservation. These

---

[1]  Letter to Julius T. House, June 3, 1931, in Raymond J. DeMallie, *The Sixth Grandfather: Black Elk's Teachings Given to John G. Neihardt* (Lincoln: University of Nebraska Press, 1984), 49.

[2]  Thomas E. Mails, *Fools Crow*, with Dallas Chief Eagle (Garden City, N.Y.: Doubleday, 1979), 88–89.

cultural differences were certainly compounded by his preconceived agenda. Neihardt did not visit the Lakota to observe the early reservation culture; instead, he was looking for a remnant figure from the past who would finish a work he had already begun. In the context of extreme Lakota poverty, he provided great resources for Black Elk and his family and promised much more. This unequal context prevented free discourse and contributed to Neihardt's control of the project.

As a result of these factors, the Neihardt interviews were not a spiritual meeting of two minds but an embodied communal interaction between two different and unequal cultures. This level of interaction bears a strong resemblance to the interactions between different cultures found in today's third-world tourist industry. Factors that reify culture in order to meet the expectations of economically advantaged tourists today appear also to have contributed to Neihardt's creation of the essentialist Black Elk.

These cultural and economic factors should not be minimized, as they created a context that allowed Neihardt to misinterpret Black Elk.[3] This claim is substantiated by Black Elk's reaction to *Black Elk Speaks;* he claims that Neihardt left out his Catholic life and did not pay him. Black Elk then expresses regret for the outcome of the Neihardt interview. While most commentators downplay or dismiss Black Elk's claim, I argue that his reaction is another indication of Black Elk's unified Lakota Catholic life.

## NEIHARDT'S CULTURAL LIMITATIONS

As noted above, profound cultural differences limited Neihardt's ability to accurately understand Black Elk's discourse. First, Neihardt employed what

---

[3] Ignoring these two factors has dangerous colonial implications. If one ignores Neihardt's cultural limitations and literary agenda, then there is no inherent significance in the Lakota language or substance to Lakota culture that cannot be grasped by an outsider with a preconceived agenda in a three-week visit. Neihardt apparently bypassed much of what makes the Lakota who they are—their essence. Ignoring the economic context has similar disembodying tendencies. O. Starn issued a warning to ethnographers whose romantic renderings of Andean culture missed the Peruvian revolution: "Ethnographers usually did little more than mention the terrible infant mortality, minuscule incomes, low life expectancy, inadequate diets, and abysmal health care that remained so routine. . . . They gave us detailed pictures of ceremonial exchanges, Saint's Day rituals, weddings, baptisms, and work parties. Another kind of scene, just as common in the Andes, almost never appeared: a girl with an abscess and no doctor, the woman bleeding to death in childbirth, a couple in their dark adobe house crying over an infant's sudden death." According to Starn, the Andean poverty was not just a contextual footnote to their exotic traditions, it permeated and structured Andean life (O. Starn, "Missing the Revolution: Anthropologists and the War in Peru," in *Rereading Cultural Anthropology*, ed. G. E. Marcus, 152–80 [Durham, N.C.: Duke University Press, 1992], 168).

resembled a Boasian method, arriving not to observe contemporary Lakota Reservation practices but to find remnants of the past. As a result, he did not so much observe the Lakota Reservation world as mentally reconstruct a preconceived understanding of what Lakota culture was like during the pre-reservation era. He did not see or understand the adaptations the Lakota had made to their way of life in order to survive American colonialism.

Second, Neihardt was not only looking for remnants of pre-reservation Lakota culture but for the dramatic end for his narrative of the American West: the "pure" pre-contact Lakota world and its inevitable defeat in the Ghost Dance and Wounded Knee. DeMallie argues:

> Neihardt perceived Black Elk through the lens of his own lifework, *A Cycle of the West*. The purpose of this epic poem, Neihardt had written, was "to preserve the great race-mood of courage that was developed west of the Missouri River in the 19th century." The corollary to the triumph of the "westering white men" was the inevitable defeat of the Plains Indians. It is not that Neihardt misunderstood Black Elk, but that he perceived his life as embodying the whole tragic history of defeat whose emotional tone he was trying to convey in verse in *A Cycle*.[4]

DeMallie emphasizes that Neihardt *interpreted* Black Elk as the essentialized "other," important only in his juxtaposition to westward American expansion.

Neihardt's third limitation was his unfamiliarity with the Lakota Reservation culture of the 1930s and his lack of proficiency in the dominant idioms. Neihardt never learned the Lakota language and was dependent on Black Elk's son, Ben, as an interpreter. Neihardt was also a stranger to the community and did not know Black Elk or any of the informants. This meant that not only was Neihardt not a participant in any of the actual day-to-day communal Lakota reservation practices, but neither was he familiar with what they were. As a result, he did not operate in or understand the cultural movement of the Lakota world at that time.

One of the movements Neihardt did not understand and in which he did not participate was Lakota Catholicism. Lakota Catholicism was embodied in narratives, rituals, and communal practices. Masses, retreats, sodalities, conferences, mission trips, biblical reading, and personal devotions permeated all aspects of Lakota Catholic life with particular meaning. Participants viewed activities and relationships through the interpretive lens formed by these Catholic practices. This was undoubtedly particularly true of Black Elk, who spent decades as a leader of the Lakota Catholic community, fostering the creation of its culture and its interpretive lens. Consequently, Neihardt could not have been a participant in either thread of Black Elk's integrated Lakota Catholic world.

---

[4] DeMallie, *The Sixth Grandfather*, 56. The Neihardt quotation is from John G. Neihardt, *The Song of the Indian Wars* (New York: Macmillan, 1925), 7.

And Neihardt had a fourth cultural limitation. Not only was he not familiar with Lakota Catholicism, but he was explicitly anti-Christian.[5] Like the Boasians, Neihardt viewed Catholicism as routine and sterile compared to the Lakota tradition. According to DeMallie, "For Neihardt, the beauty of Black Elk's vision made the formalism of Christian religion seem all the more stultifying."[6] Not only did Neihardt not understand Catholic culture, but he also saw the motivation behind Black Elk's conversion as an illogical mystery.

Hilda Neihardt recalls the interviews in her book *Black Elk and Flaming Rainbow*. When the whole Black Elk family—other than Black Elk and Ben—left for the annual Catholic conference, "their attendance at the council seemed almost disloyal" to the interview.[7] She proceeds to discuss Black Elk's membership in what she calls a "white church," a subject she considered "sensitive" and "vaguely unpleasant":[8]

> Black Elk told my father that later he did join the white church, and we knew he catechized young children. What he did not find it necessary to say left us with a strong sense of where his true beliefs remained. Understanding all too well, Neihardt said no more.[9]

This interaction shows evidence of Neihardt's bias. Hilda makes it clear that Neihardt did not feel a need to ask any questions or gather any information about Black Elk's conversion. Rather, he seems to have imposed the modern Western assumption examined in Chapter 4 that Lakota and Catholic tradition must exist in two exclusive systems of belief. Without specific evidence, Neihardt dismisses Black Elk's Catholic life, turning it into an "unpleasant subject." In essence, Hilda Neihardt makes the claim that it is possible to draw clear, definitive, and absolute conclusions about topics in ethnographic proceedings without actually gathering information. The difficulties of cross-cultural and linguistic communication were not addressed by more thorough investigation but instead avoided by complete silence.

Finally, because Neihardt was not a participant in the Lakota Reservation culture, he was unable to understand the nature of Lakota rhetorical style. Unlike

---

[5] I have not found a source that identifies Neihardt with any official religious affiliation. According to Lucy F. Aly, Neihardt disliked organized religion. She writes that he "shared his mother's distaste for 'church' religion but found the Hindu theories of an integrated universe and a Cosmic Will amenable to his own mysticism" (Lucy F. Aly, *John G. Neihardt* [Caldwell, Idaho: Caxton Printers, 1976], 6).

[6] Ibid., 47.

[7] Hilda Neihardt, *Black Elk and Flaming Rainbow: Personal Memories of the Lakota Holy Man and John Neihardt* (Lincoln: University of Nebraska Press, 1995), 88. Black Elk and Ben were the only members of the family being paid a salary by Neihardt (see the section below on financial concerns).

[8] Ibid., 89. There is no source that directly quotes Black Elk as referring to the Catholic church (or any church) as a "white church."

[9] Ibid.

American whites, Lakota tend not to be direct and succinct but descriptive, especially in sacred matters. William Stolzman describes a particularly relevant event. In an effort to promote greater understanding between the Christian and Lakota traditions, he gathered an ecumenical group of religious leaders. During the meetings, cultural differences displayed themselves in very different oratorical styles:

> The older Lakota waited to be officially recognized by name, stood to address everyone, and spoke formally in the traditional Lakota oratorical style. Their speeches lasted from fifteen to forty-five minutes. . . . The Lakota would respectfully go around the subject and only occasionally touch the specific matter at hand. Bringing in many personal experiences, they presented many illustrations rather than direct arguments. Each person in turn put himself on the table. One man's experiences triggered another series of reminiscences in the next speaker. Through all of these speeches, an attentive listener could perceive a fabric of a particular texture and consistency being woven. Often I found that at the end of a discussion I did not have any quick, crisp, formula-like answers, but I did find myself with a profound holistic understanding of the situation.[10]

This example presents a number of key themes of traditional Lakota discourse. In describing religious matters, Lakota discourse is indirect and personal. After a long period of description, the listener is responsible for understanding of the story that has been woven. Outsiders are left to interpret Lakota discourse.

The oral style characterized Black Elk's discourse. According to DeMallie, "Black Elk never stated succinctly what he considered the meaning of the vision to be; he left this for Neihardt to interpret."[11] Consequently, if Neihardt was not looking for—even screening out—Catholicism, Black Elk did not give him explicit directions to discover it.

As a result, a number of cultural factors combined to undermine the potential accuracy of Neihardt's essentialist interpretation of Black Elk. Like the Boasians, he went to the reservation to find and reconstruct the pre-reservation Lakota culture. Neihardt interpreted this reconstruction in light of the Manifest Destiny lens of his ongoing work of fiction on the expansion of the West. He did not observe the contemporary Lakota Reservation culture to learn the current cultural practices or idioms. In addition, he actively filtered out cultural change, particularly Catholicism. Most important, in the fashion of Lakota oral discourse, Black Elk was not explicit in explaining the context or meaning of his vision. Consequently, for Neihardt, Black Elk's vision existed without a context, in a cultural vacuum, which Neihardt could engulf with his own Manifest Destiny narrative. These factors gave Neihardt the freedom to find a home for Black Elk's vision and create the essentialist Black Elk.

---

[10]   William Stolzman, *The Pipe and Christ: A Christian-Sioux Dialogue* (Chamberlain, S.D.: Tipi Press, 1995), 16–17.

[11]   DeMallie, *The Sixth Grandfather*, 52–53.

## THE HISTORICAL CONTEXT: THE GREAT DEPRESSION

In addition to the cultural limitations that compromised Neihardt's ability to describe Black Elk's world accurately, its economic context further enabled Neihardt's creation of the essentialist Black Elk. Since their confinement to reservations, the Lakota had struggled to participate in the American economic system. After some initial success integrating into the dominant American economy, as we saw in Chapters 2 and 3, a number of factors converged to impoverish the Lakota. Continuing appropriation of reservation land, corrupt Bureau of Indian Affairs programs, and various social problems destroyed Lakota self-sufficiency and transferred economic control to outsiders.

Global economic depression further complicated the Lakota struggle. Neihardt arrived at Black Elk's home in the summer of 1931, almost two years into the Great Depression. Confined by their already marginalized reservation economies, Native Americans suffered disproportionately to the rest of America. DeMallie describes the desperate conditions on Pine Ridge caused by the Depression:

> With the financial crash of 1929, the short-lived prosperity of the entire region was ruined. The white grain farmers were entirely wiped out, and most of them moved away. The drought, with its hordes of grasshoppers and severe dust storms, ruined the Indian gardens and farms and killed the livestock. . . . Mekeel found that the average income per family (5.4 persons) in White Clay district in 1930 was $152.80. This income—supplemented with small government rations, chokecherries and other wild foods, and horsemeat—kept starvation just around the corner. There was no food surplus at all; traditional patterns of sharing leveled everyone to the same state of poverty.[12]

According to DeMallie, the Great Depression completely destroyed subsistence patterns on Pine Ridge and any hope of entering the modern economy. Social status offered no protection because the sharing patterns of Lakota tradition demanded that surplus goods be distributed to those with greater need. The danger of starvation was real.

Fools Crow's autobiography gives a firsthand account of the Great Depression and conditions during the drought:

> There was no rain at all, and nothing grew—not in the gardens, not the wild fruits, not the crops in the fields. Every year it got worse. The grasshoppers came in swarms, the grass didn't grow, and tumbleweeds were everywhere. Always the wind blew, and the air was thick with dust. It got

---

[12] Raymond J. DeMallie, "Pine Ridge Economy: Cultural and Historical Perspectives," in *American Indian Economic Development*, ed. Sam Stanley (Paris: Mouton Publishers, 1978), 259.

through everything, sifting into our homes and even our clothing. Most of the horses and cattle starved to death, and the poultry and the pigs shriveled up and died too.[13]

As we saw in Chapters 2 and 3, many social problems, such as alcohol use, merged during the 1930s. The economy was so bad that the Lakota were forced to sell their possessions, even ones necessary for daily survival. According to DeMallie "The Indians sold everything they could, even the dishes in their houses."[14]

Consequently, the economies of the Lakota reservations lay in ruin during the 1930s. After decades of struggle to survive their forced conversion to a new economy, the Great Depression destroyed any and all nascent economic structures. Regardless of previous personal success, the entire Lakota community now lived on the edge of starvation. In this context of extreme poverty, Neihardt arrived with comparatively large financial resources and promises of even greater compensation. This economic disparity would play a large role in shaping the interviews and compromising Neihardt's ability to interpret Black Elk.

## FINANCIAL CONCERNS

In the introduction to *The Sixth Grandfather*, DeMallie gives an extensive account of the financial details of the Neihardt–Black Elk collaboration. In a letter Neihardt wrote to Black Elk on November 6, 1930, to arrange the interviews, Neihardt assures Black Elk of compensation, "I would, of course, expect to pay you well for all the time that you would give me."[15] Hilda remembers that Black Elk, Ben, and the other storytellers received an unspecified daily wage.[16]

During the three weeks that Neihardt and his daughters stayed with Black Elk, Neihardt covered all of the expenses, particularly food, with his $1,000 advance from the publisher.[17] On May 15, before much work was done, Neihardt purchased a young Holstein bull from Black Elk's daughter, Lucy. It was butchered, and along with other traditional foods, fed over two hundred people from the area.[18] The continuing economic support covered more than the immediate family:

---

[13]  Mails, *Fools Crow* (1979), 145.
[14]  DeMallie, "Pine Ridge Economy," 259.
[15]  Ibid., 29. He also sent Black Elk a seven-dollar advance for materials to make the paintings of the Messiah and Wounded Knee. See the full transcript of the letter in Brian Holloway, *Interpreting the Legacy: John Neihardt and Black Elk Speaks* (Boulder: University of Colorado Press, 2003), 54. It is important to note that economic concerns are not a priority for any of my sources. Since such concerns are only tangential, any economic evidence they yield is even more significant. It is likely that additional research on the financial aspects of the Neihardt interviews, the Brown interview, and the Duhamel pageant would yield more information.
[16]  Hilda Neihardt, *Black Elk and Flaming Rainbow*, 19.
[17]  Ibid., 18.
[18]  Ibid., 33.

Hilda remembers that many others came uninvited and that each one sat on the ground a respectful distance from the house with his back to the proceedings. Then Ellen, Black Elk's wife, would ask Neihardt if the new-comer could be fed. After this invitation had been extended, the man would join the group. The women of Black Elk's family prepared three meals that day, feeding all who came.[19]

According to DeMallie, Lakota tradition called for Neihardt's resources to be distributed to the whole community. The number of Lakota was so great that Hilda remembers the advance "melting like ice in summertime."[20] According to Enid Neihardt's diary, written during the interview, "Daddy has to feed the whole Sioux Nation!"[21] This became such a burden that the project was moved ten days later to a more remote location.[22]

Black Elk prays for the success of the book, perhaps because of the arrival of this wealth. Enid wrote in her diary on the day they all visited the Badlands that Black Elk prayed "to the six grandfathers of his vision, wishing that they should help Daddy to make a success of this book."[23] Shortly after finishing the inter-views, Black Elk received a letter that must have seemed an answer to his prayer. Neihardt wrote to Black Elk on June 27, 1931, assuring him that the book would be a success:

> We are going to do something real with this book about "The Tree That Never Bloomed"; and I am sure that you are going to be a good deal happier because of this book. Keep a good heart and be patient until next spring when the book appears. I have to work hard on the book and be patient too, and I can do both with a strong heart because I know that the book is wise and good and that thousands of people will find good in it.[24]

One would expect that "thousands of people" finding good in the book would imply or be taken by Black Elk also to mean a good financial return.

During the course of the interview, after Black Elk told Neihardt about his Horse Dance, Neihardt said that he thought it would be a good subject for a movie. DeMallie records that "Black Elk offered to provide an entire village as a background and to stage the dance if Neihardt could get the backing."[25] DeMallie argues that even Neihardt recognized that a movie could provide much needed investment in the depressed Lakota economy.[26]

In the same letter of June 27, 1931, Neihardt wrote:

---

[19]   DeMallie, *The Sixth Grandfather*, 32.
[20]   Hilda Neihardt, *Black Elk and Flaming Rainbow*, 56.
[21]   Ibid.
[22]   DeMallie, *The Sixth Grandfather*, 39.
[23]   Ibid., 44.
[24]   Ibid., 54.
[25]   Ibid., 40.
[26]   Ibid.

You will see that my publisher thinks the best chance is to try to make a picture of the whole book rather than of the Horse Dance alone. I think perhaps this will be the best way, because there will be a story to tell and people like stories. Anyway, you may know that my publisher means business and knows how to do business. If anything comes of this, you can depend upon me to see that you get what is just as your portion.[27]

The picture that emerges is one of extensive financial involvement. Neihardt's advance provided him with financial resources equal to the yearly income of between six and seven Lakota families combined. From this resource, which melted "like ice in the summertime," Neihardt compensated Black Elk and the other participants in the form of wages and food. The compensation extended to the local Lakota community.

In addition to this immediate investment, Neihardt promised even greater financial reward. After the publication of *Black Elk Speaks*, Black Elk claimed that Neihardt promised him half the profit of the book. They discussed a possible movie deal with potentially even greater investment in the Lakota community. Neihardt later responded positively about the likelihood of success with both the book and the movie.

## THE THIRD-WORLD TOURIST INDUSTRY—
## A MODEL OF NEIHARDT'S PROJECT

Viewed as a whole, the context of the Neihardt interview has two important aspects. First, there were significant cultural differences between Neihardt and Black Elk. These differences were exacerbated by the fact that Neihardt did not arrive in Pine Ridge to observe reservation life but rather to fill in holes to his nearly completed Manifest Destiny narrative. Second, an extreme economic disparity existed between the colonized Lakota and Neihardt's well-funded project. The Great Depression increased this disparity, reducing the Lakota to desperate poverty.

These problems make it unlikely that Neihardt was able to interpret Black Elk's discourse accurately. An accurate interpretation would need to account for the cultural differences and the economic disparity that were the context of the Neihardt interviews. A contemporary parallel illustrates the dynamics operating in the Black Elk–Neihardt collaboration: the third-world tourist industry.

In the tourist industry, economically powerful foreigners go to what they see as an exotic place in search of a different world, an alternative to their world. They bring comparatively great financial resources to the local economies. Often, the local communities are dependent on tourism as the main or exclusive source of capital and the best source of employment for their people.

Both the economic power of the tourists and their desire to experience an exotic culture leads to what Dean MacCannel calls "reconstructed ethnicity."

---

[27] Ibid., 50.

According to MacCannell, "When an ethnic group begins to sell itself, or is forced to sell itself, as an ethnic attraction, it ceases to evolve naturally. . . . The group is frozen in an image of itself or *'museumized.'*"[28] In other words, the local community is forced in varying degrees to meet the tourists' expectations of what qualifies as exotic. The resulting ethnic product is usually based on romanticized symbols. These symbols often have little present value in the everyday life of the local culture or no longer function at all. In some cases they may directly contradict local culture. The resulting reconstructed ethnicity is not a reflection of contemporary indigenous practices, but rather what tourists expect to find in indigenous communities.

While reconstructed ethnicity is primarily composed of seemingly insignificant symbols, reconstruction affects the community's entire way of life. MacCannell articulates the totality of reconstructed ethnicity:

> Conforming to the requirements of being a living tourist attraction becomes a total problem affecting every detail of life. Your status as an attraction affects the job you have, the way you are supposed to behave off the job, the kind of authentic clothes you wear, the way you wear your hair, etc. Everything becomes a serious matter for discussion, authentification, clearance. Any deviation can be read as a political gesture that produces conflict not between groups but within the group.[29]

According to MacCannell, the economic survival of indigenous communities turned into tourist attractions now depends on meeting the tourists' standard for authentic culture. The qualifications necessary for economic participation even include such things as clothing and hair styles.

The industry reconstructs ethnicity in resorts, which are isolated from the realities of the Third World and have better living conditions and amenities than the surrounding community. Most important, tourists have much better access to nutrition than the local population. Workers may benefit from these improved conditions, since resorts often feed their workers and offer other benefits. Also, resorts must be able to conduct business in the languages of their clients. In sum, the tourist industry constructs "a bubble" for the tourist that reproduces

---

[28] Dean MacCannell, "Reconstructed Ethnicity: Tourism and Cultural Identity in Third World Communities," in *Annals of Tourism Research* 11 (1980): 388.

[29] Ibid. MacCannell goes on to emphasize that this is a continuation of colonial violence: "It appears that tourism has helped in getting beyond the phase of ethnic relations where minorities are kept in place with light salaries, heavy prison terms, and redneck cruelty. But one may have come full circle. Insofar as the larger society extends its acceptance conditional upon the minority restricting itself to an 'authentic' image of itself, one is only doing with admiration what he earlier did with dogs and guns. As the rhetoric of hostility toward minorities is replaced with a rhetoric of appreciation, the circle of their potential exploiters is dramatically expanded. Now blacks can exploit blacks, Indians can exploit Indians, etc. All with a clear conscience under the rubric of development and preservation of culture."

the economic and cultural world of the tourist and creates a venue in which the commodity of reconstructed ethnicity can be sold.

An example from the Dominican Republic demonstrates how reconstructed ethnicity functions.[30] Eric, a Dominican male in his early twenties, recently lost his job at a tourist resort and was looking for a new one. His first choice would be to emigrate to the United States, but he did not have the resources, connections, or status to obtain the necessary documentation. Luckily, he spoke English and understood some other languages, which made him a good applicant for jobs in the tourist industry. But two characteristics of the reconstructed ethnicity of the Dominican tourist industry posed a problem for Eric.

The first was the type of "authentic" entertainment offered at resorts: folkloric dance, which is no longer a functioning part of everyday Dominican society. Virtually the only place that it is practiced is at tourist resorts. In an effort to appear more exotic and "other," the tourist industry re-creates a virtually extinct cultural practice, folkloric dance, to improve its business.

A second characteristic was the tourist industry's desire for "blackness." This emphasis is in fact counter-cultural to a large degree in the Dominican Republic. Due to the Spanish colonial legacy, a history of racist dictatorships, and its juxtaposition to Haiti (its much poorer neighbor whose population is generally darker), there is a strain of Dominican culture that seeks to divorce itself from its African heritage. To be "negro" or to have tightly curled hair in the Dominican Republic is usually considered undesirable. Terms referring to such traits are often used as insults. In this context the tourist industry reverses Dominican cultural categories and makes blackness a marketable commodity because of the importance that blackness has in the tourists' imagined Caribbean.[31] In order to compete with the tourist industries of other Caribbean nations, where blackness is a positive cultural value, the tourist industry reifies Dominican culture and adopts blackness as a normative cultural value.

Both of these characteristics of the reconstructed Dominican ethnicity made it difficult for Eric to find employment in the tourist industry. First, he was not proficient in folkloric dance, second, he was not "black" enough, and his hair was not curled tightly enough.

Eric was anxious to overcome these impediments because he needed the employment for communal survival. With his salary Eric would support his mother and siblings. He would also enjoy better living conditions because employees of the resort were housed nearby and had access to much better nutrition and some health care.

Consequently, Eric attempted to transform himself. He looked for a school of folkloric dance that would teach him despite his limited resources. He grew his hair into braids, a "blacker" hairstyle associated with Haitians and African American rappers in the Dominican Republic. Despite Eric's transformation,

---

[30] This is from the author's work in the Dominican Republic.

[31] Many other examples exist, such as the extensive market for Haitian paintings and the common use of Jamaican reggae music.

the tourist industry is at liberty to find other "more qualified" candidates who meet the current demands of reconstructed authenticity.

This discussion highlights a number of cultural and economic themes. First, the unequal economic system developed and maintained by colonialism serves as the background for the creation of the tourist industry. Second, this industry must create an island of comfort within a sea of poverty where a better lifestyle is maintained, primarily for the tourists but also to a lesser extent for the workers. Despite its exotic image, this island operates using the cultural categories and language of the tourists. Third, culture becomes a commodity in places with few other resources. Fourth, the culture that is marketed is not the lived culture of the local communities; rather, it is shaped and even created by the imagination of the outsiders, taking the form of reconstructed ethnicity. Fifth, to participate in the tourist industry, local communities are forced to compromise if they wish to compete. Dissatisfied tourists will go somewhere else to find a product that better suits their demands. Consequently, a sixth theme is that tourists need to feel that they have had an authentic experience of the imagined world of the native—and one that is quite different from their own—so they will continue spending their money.

It is interesting to note that these themes are also present in the Neihardt–Black Elk collaboration. The connection becomes even more interesting when we turn to two examples in which the third world tourist industry affected Black Elk's life.

## THE WILD WEST SHOW
## AND THE DUHAMEL PAGEANT AS TOURISM

The third-world tourist industry was not a new phenomenon to Black Elk or the Lakota. A number of Wild West shows recruited Native Americans to travel the United States and Europe during the end of the nineteenth century. Black Elk spent more than two years in Wild West shows, which had all the characteristics of the third-world tourist industry.

Economically advantaged Westerners paid to see what for them were exotic cultural practices. Instead of resorts, the shows brought exotic culture to the communities of the consumers. These Native American cultural practices were not strictly speaking "reconstructed," since the participants come from communities where the practices were viable parts of the culture. As they were performed for white audiences, however, the practices were largely symbolic.

Native American participants received financial compensation for performing. All participants received $25 a month including travel, food, clothing, medical attention, and incidentals.[32] The travel also provided an escape from many of the more violent aspects of colonialism. Participants did not have to run from the army or deal with the poverty and social upheaval of the new reservation system.

---

[32] DeMallie, *The Sixth Grandfather*, 8.

In the more than two years that Black Elk spent as a traveling tourist attraction, he learned well what white people were looking for when they (often sympathetically) interacted with Native Americans. Even the queen of the largest colonial empire the world had ever known recognized the dynamics of the industry at work in the Wild West show. Black Elk described a speech Queen Victoria gave to the Native Americans of the Wild West show:

> America is a good country and I have seen all kinds of people, but today I have seen the best looking people—the Indians. . . . If I owned you Indians, you good-looking people, I would never take you around in a show like this. You have a Grandfather over there who takes care of you over there, but he shouldn't allow this, for he owns you, for the white people to take you around as beasts to show to the people.[33]

According to Black Elk, the queen declared that she would not permit the conditions that forced Native Americans to participate in the third–world tourist industry. Black Elk and the other participants all "hollered and gave cheers" to the queen's speech.[34]

A second example of "cultural commodification" in Lakota history is the Duhamel pageant. The Duhamel pageant ran during the Depression years of the mid-1930s. The pageant was a tourist attraction at Sitting Bull's Crystal Caverns, nine miles south of Rapid City, on the road to Mount Rushmore. During the pageant Black Elk and twenty to fifty other Lakota demonstrated pre-reservation Lakota life and ceremonies.[35]

Black Elk's granddaughter Olivia emphasizes the symbolic nature of the ceremonies that the Lakota performed in the pageant: "It was a pageant for tourists. We performed, and we did the acting." When the interviewer asked if they were actual sacred ceremonies, Olivia responded, "No, [Black Elk and other performers] would never do that."[36] Like the Wild West shows, the pageant sold a symbolic ethnicity to tourists looking for exotic culture.

Financial compensation was an important aspect of the pageant. According to David O. Born, the pageant originated with Black Elk with the purpose of

---

[33] Ibid., 249–50.

[34] Ibid., 250.

[35] For a description, see DeMallie, *The Sixth Grandfather*, 63–66, or David O. Born, "Black Elk and the Duhamel Sioux Indian Pageant," *North Dakota History* 61 (1994): 22–29.

[36] Esther Black Elk DeSersa and Olivia Black Elk Pourier, *Black Elk Lives: Conversations with the Black Elk Family*, ed. Hilda Neihardt and Lori Utecht (Lincoln: University of Nebraska Press, 2000), 135. These interviews are an important source because the interviewers were not looking for evidence of tourism or Catholicism but trying to separate Black Elk from those aspects of reservation culture. Fools Crow agrees with Olivia's view of the performing ceremonies for white tourists: "In our Wild West shows we Indians rode, sang, and danced. The dances were social performances, though, and never sacred ones" (Mails, *Fools Crow* [1979], 115).

employing Indians.[37] Native American participants received food, water, wood, and 25 percent of the daily gate.[38] There was additional income from the sale of arts and crafts to tourist who visited the Lakota camps.[39] Black Elk's daughter, Lucy Looks Twice, reports that "the women got a dollar and a quarter, and the men got a dollar and a half."[40] In addition, Black Elk was able to earn additional money from photographs that the tourists took of him.[41]

In the context of the Great Depression, the potential income was substantial. Lucy remembers that "it was during the depression, but they made quite a bit of money on his performance."[42] According to DeMallie, the average family on Pine Ridge earned $12.74 a month during the worst of the Depression. Even if we allow Black Elk double what the average family earned since he was considered economically successful, he would still earn almost twice by working for the pageant.[43] Other family members who participated would earn additional money.[44]

Black Elk's family identifies this work in the Black Hills as tourism. Olivia describes Ben's work at Mount Rushmore:

> At Mount Rushmore, the tourists started taking pictures of him. They asked him if he could stand there with his regalia. And he said he would, and so they said they'd pay him. Well, he came back all excited so we moved to Keystone and they started taking pictures. He was up there twenty-seven years.[45]

According to Olivia, Ben discovered the economic benefits of performing for tourists. Ben's authentic clothing was a commodity for consumers. Ben's grandson Aaron remembers working with Ben at Mount Rushmore:

> He was the one that taught us, him and Uncle Henry, how to dance, up at Mount Rushmore. . . . We used to go to Keystone all the time, every summer, and dance with them. . . . We were making money to survive; we were being taught our traditions. . . . Grandpa would go to Mount Rushmore, and then he'd come back. He used to carry his pouch with a

---

[37] Born, "Black Elk and the Duhamel Sioux Indian Pageant," 24.

[38] Ibid., 26.

[39] Ibid., 27.

[40] Michael F. Steltenkamp, S.J., *Black Elk: Holy Man of the Oglala* (Norman: University of Oklahoma Press, 1993), 114.

[41] Ibid., 113.

[42] Ibid., 114.

[43] Black Elk was probably not earning any income on Pine Ridge as he was not physically able to do any type of manual labor at this point in his life.

[44] Olivia remembers staying at the pageant with Lucy, Leo Looks Twice, George Looks Twice, Ben, one of her brothers, and her sisters Grace, Esther, and Kate with about five other families (DeSersa and Pourier, *Black Elk Lives*, 133–34).

[45] DeSersa and Pourier, *Black Elk Lives*, 41.

whole bunch of change; all of us used to sit there and count it all the
time.[46]

While Ben used the work at Mount Rushmore to teach the children about Lakota
tradition, Aaron highlights the fact that the work for tourists was an opportunity
to make money to survive. Aaron's brother, Clifton, remembers working in tourism:

> All summer long he and my Uncle Hank used to sing for us while we
> danced and performed. It was a way of showing the tourists the different
> styles of dances that we dance, and it was just another way of making
> money. We just passed the hat, and they'd give us money—donations and
> stuff for our performing.[47]

In conclusion, the third-world tourist industry was a means of survival during the early reservation period and the Great Depression. The Lakota learned
that tourists were willing to pay for exotic culture. Black Elk's family clearly
identified this work as tourism. It seems safe to conclude that Black Elk oper-
ated in and was consciously aware of the dynamics of the tourist industry. It
goes without saying that these dynamics underlay the Neihardt–Black Elk collaboration.

## BLACK ELK: THE FOCUS OF CULTURAL TOURISM

Black Elk and other Lakota participated in the Wild West shows and the
Duhamel pageant, which involved the reconstruction and marketing of ethnicity,
for financial gain due to economic conditions similar to those in many parts of
the Third World today. This is reflected in Black Elk's interviews with Neihardt.

Pine Ridge Reservation itself had the same economic conditions. It had no
resources, and in the 1930s its economy had been destroyed by the Great Depression. Cultural and economic factors prevented most residents from relocating in search of economic opportunity elsewhere. Black Elk called the Lakota
"prisoners of war."[48]

Second, the pageant also created a resort-like compound:

> Then they drove north, toward Manderson, where they met two of Black
> Elk's sons, who were borrowing beds for their visitor's use. As the Neihardts
> followed the boys to Black Elk's house in the hills beyond the town, Hilda

---

[46] Ibid., 25–26.

[47] Ibid., 63.

[48] DeMallie, *The Sixth Grandfather*, 289. In *Black Elk Lives* (DeSersa and Pourier),
Black Elk's granddaughters make numerous allusions to their family's poverty: not getting enough food (30), the family was too poor to get them from school during Christmas (37–38) and too poor to buy presents for Christmas (24–25).

noticed men busily hauling barrels of water from the creek. On a knoll in front of the house a large new tipi [for the Neihardts to stay in] of white duck had been erected, with the flaming rainbow of Black Elk's vision painted above the doorway and the vision power symbols painted on the sides. . . . Nearby, the Neihardts noticed a startlingly new privy, obviously constructed for their convenience. Around the house and the tipi a circle of freshly cut pine trees, uniformly small, had been thrust into the ground. Partway down the slope in front of the tipi was a small circular dance bower, also constructed of fresh pine boughs.[49]

DeMallie's description emphasizes the cultural novelty of the setting that Black Elk's family created for the Neihardt family. However, Black Elk worked to ensure that the Neihardt's lifestyle was accommodated, with plenty of water, beds, and a new privy.[50] Significantly, the Neihardts stayed in a new tipi, a dwelling no longer used for housing in Pine Ridge in the 1930s. Black Elk and the other Lakota lived in wood houses.

Although Neihardt went to investigate a different culture, the investigation was conducted in his own cultural medium, the English language. The lifestyle enjoyed by the Neihardts and Black Elk's family was certainly much better than average on the Depression-ravaged reservation, most significantly in nutrition. Neihardt's activities had a significant economic impact on Black Elk's extended family and friends.

Third, Neihardt was actively looking for and "buying" the commodity of culture. However, the culture he sought was not the contemporary reservation culture but a reconstructed Plains culture of a previous time. Like Eric in the Dominican Republic, in the Wild West shows and the Duhamel pageant Black Elk dressed in authentic clothes and demonstrated exotic cultural practices.

---

[49] DeMallie, *The Sixth Grandfather*, 30–31. Holloway provides an interesting, spiritual, "white focused" interpretation: "First, note the way in which Black Elk and his family and friends established a communal context, a teaching arena, for the 1931 narrative work with Neihardt that produced *Black Elk Speaks*. . . . Black Elk organized dances and feasts, decorated his home with pines, and supervised the creation of a special tipi with visionary symbols, including a flaming rainbow. He provided John, Enid, and Hilda Neihardt with a total cultural and communal immersion in which the visitors were active, physical participants. Informal interaction and traditional ceremony taught the visitors both intellectually and spiritually. The learning did not take place in the sterile classroom of the dominant culture's academe but was an experience activating senses and intuitions so the visitors would learn about culture, tradition, and the 'outer world.'" This description would not be out of place in an article describing the authentic experience that a particular third-world resort provides tourists in a contemporary travel magazine marketed to upper-class Americans. Notice that the focus of this description is what Black Elk *provided* for Neihardt and how he was affected by the experience (Holloway, *Interpreting the Legacy*, 66).

[50] This discussion should not be understood as a dismissal of Lakota hospitality, which was and is an important virtue. However, the sincere hospitality of Black Elk's family would still function to create the same conditions as in the tourist industry.

Fourth, the culture that Black Elk and the other Lakota demonstrated did not reflect the totality or authenticity of cultural practices of current reservation life. Rather, they reconstructed their ethnicity according to Neihardt's preconceived agenda, which emphasized only what was totally different from white America. There was no discussion of the current state of the Bureau of Indian Affairs and its allotments, the cattle industry, agriculture, the needs of educational systems, or current religious practices. The interview focused solely on the cultural practices of the pre-reservation era and their demise.

Fifth, Neihardt was at liberty to conclude that Black Elk did not provide the commodity he was looking for and find someone else. Consequently, Black Elk was at least implicitly under pressure to supply Neihardt's demand.

Sixth, Neihardt very quickly "bought" into all the cultural trappings, although he did not participate in any of the day-to-day activities current in the 1930s. Neihardt was certain that his search for the authentic Native American was over. He wanted to continue working with Black Elk, which meant potential future investment in the community. Practices such as adopting him into the tribe and calling him "son" would serve to heighten Neihardt's emotional commitment to Black Elk and his community.

It is not surprising that the Neihardt interviews reflect the dynamics of the third-world tourist industry. The impoverished Lakota appear to have "sold" their reconstructed ethnicity for significant financial compensation to accommodate Neihardt's desire for exotic culture. This context gave Black Elk less freedom to shape his discourse and Neihardt more freedom to create the essentialist Black Elk.

## BLACK ELK RESPONDS TO *BLACK ELK SPEAKS*

Black Elk's reaction to the completed book *Black Elk Speaks* supports the argument that the cultural and economic context of the interviews prevented Neihardt from accurately perceiving and understanding Black Elk. In two letters written in 1934 Black Elk claims that Neihardt ignored his Catholicism and did not follow through with his financial obligations. Black Elk uses language in the letters that is consistent with the language of his great vision.

Before Neihardt returned to Pine Ridge after the first interview in 1931, Black Elk dictated his first response to the book on January 26, 1934.[51] DeMallie writes

---

[51] Vecsey's interpretation of this letter deserves attention: "It would appear that when Black Elk was faced with possible death in the wagon accident, he promised to recant the book if the priest would give him last rites: 'I called my priest to pray for me and so he gave me Extreme Unction and Holy Eucharist. Therefore I will tell you the truth.' Just how much pressure was applied, we shall never know; however, it is clear that a quid pro quo took place. The recantation was apparently payment for Extreme Unction." While there may be evidence for this claim, Vecsey offers none. In order to make this claim he must have assumed two things. First, Black Elk had no problem with the manner in which Neihardt portrayed him in *Black Elk Speaks*. Both letters make it clear that

that "whether this was his own idea or that of the priests is not entirely certain, but the resulting document has all the indications of sincerity."[52]

Without denying the validity of his vision and biography up until the time of Wounded Knee, Black Elk faults Neihardt for ignoring the "current ways."[53] He proceeds to describe the particularities of his Catholic life and asserts that before his conversion he considered himself to be a proud, brave, and good Indian, "but now think I am better."[54] He states that he knows more about Catholicism "than many white men."[55]

Black Elk highlights the communal significance of his faith: reception of six of the seven sacraments, eight years in retreats, missionary work, and twenty years as a catechist in several communities. Because of this, "very many of the Indians know me."[56]

This letter contains the same use of the Lakota language and images to describe Catholicism as in Black Elk's vision. He repeatedly uses the metaphor of a road to describe Christianity. He wishes to be "straight in the righteous way" so that he will reach "the clouds." He states that "all my children and grandchildren belong to the Catholic Church and I am glad of that and wish very much they will always follow the holy road."[57] Later he writes, "I send my people on the straight road that Christ's church taught us about. While I live I will never fall from faith in Christ."[58] Black Elk directly equates the sacred road with Christ and the church, and he directs his people to always follow it.

Black Elk also quotes 2 Peter 2:20–22, which describes those who have known Christ and then returned to former ways as worse than those who have never known "the way of justice," or *Wóowothaŋna Čhaŋkú*. He says that they are like a dog returned to his vomit, or the washed sow again wallowing in the mire. This is again consistent with Black Elk's use of biblical passages; it links the road image with concrete examples, the dog and sow, that are directly related to the Lakota world.

This document is important for two reasons. First, it is consistent with the Black Elk who is remembered by the Lakota. Second, its language and imagery

---

he did have a problem with Neihardt. Second, the missionaries were manipulative and considered Black Elk's interview with Neihardt to be contrary to Catholic faith. What Vecsey and other scholars ignore is that even if the first two points could be demonstrated with evidence, it would only support the fact that Black Elk valued the Catholic sacraments more than his work with Neihardt. See Christopher Vecsey, "A Century of Lakota Sioux Catholicism at Pine Ridge," in *Religious Diversity and American Religious History: Studies in Traditions and Cultures*, ed. Walter H. Conser Jr. and Sumner B. Twiss (Athens: University of Georgia Press, 1997), 277-79.

[52] DeMallie, *The Sixth Grandfather*, 59.
[53] Ibid.
[54] Ibid., 60.
[55] Ibid.
[56] Ibid., 59.
[57] Ibid., 60.
[58] Ibid.

match the interpretation of Black Elk's vision, forming a Lakota version of Catholic salvation history, as was noted in Chapter 5.

The tension exhibited in this letter carried over to Black Elk and Neihardt's relationship.[59] Hilda, Neihardt's daughter, who was present at the interview, admitted in an interview with R. Todd Wise that "for a while [Black Elk] denied Neihardt."[60] Ben wrote to Neihardt in June 1934 that "Emil A. [Afraid of] Hawk [Catholic catechist and present at first interview] has been loading the old man about lots of things. The old man felt uneasy for a while. But he is perfectly satisfied, very glad to hear you are coming again."[61] Despite this assurance, when Neihardt returned to Pine Ridge in 1934 for part of the summer, he stayed on Ben's land on Wounded Knee Creek. There were no interviews; Neihardt worked on writing *Song of the Messiah*. According to Hilda, Black Elk did not visit the Neihardts.[62]

On September 20, 1934, after Neihardt's visit, Black Elk wrote a second, more animated letter. This time, in addition to citing cultural issues, Black Elk highlighted the economic aspects of the collaboration.

Dear Friends:

Three years ago in 1932 a white man named John G. Neihardt came up to my place whom I have never met before and asked me to make a story book with him. I don't know whether he took out a permit from the agent

---

[59] The nature of their relationship after this point is not clear. Although they seem to have reconciled their differences, they did not seem to be close. After Neihardt's visit in 1934, he was away from Pine Ridge for the next decade. Black Elk wrote him a letter in 1940 that said "for 5 yrs successive I've been to the Bl[ack] Hills for the summer & putting up a show for Duhamels so I really forget to write to my friends" (DeMallie, *The Sixth Grandfather*, 68). This suggests that they had not communicated since Neihardt left Pine Ridge in 1934. Neihardt returned in 1944 for another interview with Black Elk and other Oglala, which lasted seven days (ibid., 69). In 1945 Neihardt went to Pine Ridge for a day and spoke for the Bureau of Indian Affairs at the great Sioux victory celebration for World War II. Neihardt's last visit was September 19 to October 11 to work for the BIA. Although DeMallie says he "undoubtedly" visited Black Elk, there is no record of it (ibid., 70). Neihardt did not play a major role in Black Elk's family life or communal memory. When Black Elk's granddaughter Esther was asked if she remembers hearing Black Elk or Ben talking much about Neihardt or *Black Elk Speaks,* she responded, "Well, every now and then, but not often" (DeSersa and Pourier, *Black Elk Lives*, 133).

[60] Hilda Neihardt and R. Todd Wise, "Black Elk and John G. Neihardt," in *The Black Elk Reader*, ed. Clyde Holler (Syracuse, N.Y.: Syracuse University Press, 2000), 97.

[61] DeMallie, *The Sixth Grandfather*, 62.

[62] Hilda Neihardt, *Black Elk and Flaming Rainbow*, 106. Hilda claims that Black Elk was working in Colorado for the summer. This seems highly unlikely, as Black Elk was still recovering from being run over by a wagon in the winter. He received extreme unction and recovered, but Ben wrote to Neihardt on June 4, 1934, "Father got well but he aint the old man he used to be." DeMallie suggests that it is possible that Black Elk had already started working for the pageant by then. In any event, he did not return to see the Neihardts, nor did they visit him. (See DeMallie, *The Sixth Grandfather*, 59, 63n.)

or not. He promised me that if he completed and publish [*sic*] this book he was to pay half of the price of each book. I trusted him and finished the story of my life for him. After he published the book I wrote to him and ask [*sic*] him about the price which he promised me on the books he sold. He answered my letter and told me that there was another white man who has asked him to make this book so he himself hasn't seen a cent from the book which we made. By this I know he was deceiving me about the whole business. I also asked to put at the end of this story that I was not a pagan but have been converted into the Catholic Church in which I work [*sic*] as a catechist for more than 25 years. I've quit all these pagan works. But he didn't mention this. Cash talks. So if they can't put this religion life in the last part of that book, also if he can't pay what he promised, I ask you my dear friends that this book of my life will be null and void because I value my soul more than my body. I'm awful sorry for the mistake I made. I also have this witnesses [*sic*] to stand by me.
I'm yours truly
Nick Black Elk
My name is not Amerdian [but] he is lying about my name[63]

The second letter is also consistent with the interpretation of Black Elk offered above. Black Elk highlights certain aspects of his encounter with Neihardt. Black Elk emphasizes first that Neihardt did not listen to his initial desire to deal with his whole life, which, according to Neihardt, is exactly what Black Elk envisioned from the beginning. After the book was published, Black Elk asked him to make an addition that would describe his Catholic life, but Neihardt rejected the request.

Black Elk also distances himself from his "pagan" life, which both the missionaries and Black Elk equated primarily with the *yuwipi* practice. *Black Elk Speaks* focuses much of its material on his *yuwipi* practice, so it is not surprising that Black Elk is upset that the reader is left with the impression that he is still a *yuwipi* man.

In the first letter Black Elk discusses giving medicine at great length. He states that "medicine men sought only glory and presents from their curing," which is consistent with Lucy's memory of Black Elk. Lucy said her father did not talk about his medicine practice much. When she once asked him if he believed in the *yuwipi*, he said, "Praying with the pipe is more of a main thing. . . .

---

[63] Steltenkamp, *Black Elk*, 85, brackets in Steltenkamp. DeMallie dismisses the letter, stating: "This is a difficult document to assess; it is not signed by Black Elk, and the motive for writing it is not clear." He speculates that Lucy was the actual author. However, many factors point to its authenticity, including the reference to the soul being more important than the body. In addition, Black Elk's desire to be portrayed beyond the *yuwipi* is consistent with his continuing rejection of it. Third, Black Elk accurately reports the book's failure, even if he does not understand the publishing business (DeMallie, *The Sixth Grandfather*, 62).

But this other one, *yuwipi*, it's just like a magician trying to fool."[64] This is reinforced by the fact that Black Elk refused to demonstrate the *yuwipi* for Neihardt and had no qualms about recording Lakota tradition, minus the *yuwipi*, in *The Sacred Pipe*.

Most significant, Black Elk highlights the inequality of his relationship with Neihardt and the financial arrangements of the project. Black Elk "trusted" Neihardt to pay him half of the profits from the book and to include his Catholicism. However, when Neihardt did not come through on either of his promises, Black Elk feels that Neihardt has deceived him.[65] The fact that there may have been legitimate reasons for the book's financial failure would have had little meaning for Black Elk, who knew nothing of publishing. According to DeMallie, "As Neihardt later wrote, Black Elk 'was utterly unaware of the existence of literature'—nor did he understand it."[66] Neihardt's repeated promises would have meant more to Black Elk than any explanation Neihardt might have given.

This evidence, particularly the contents of Black Elk's two letters, makes it likely that Black Elk, like Fools Crow, made a "Great Depression compromise."[67] At a time when the Oglala were selling their dishes for food, Neihardt promised a financial return potentially much greater than Black Elk's pageant income.

---

[64] Steltenkamp, *Black Elk,* 26.

[65] The idea that Black Elk could be upset for having trusted Neihardt and receiving no financial return for his work and for having shared his vision with an outsider has been lost in many spiritual interpretations of Black Elk. Holloway writes: "Like Black Elk, Neihardt worked to disperse his message in fulfillment of a spiritual, not monetary, motivation" (Holloway, *Interpreting the Vision,* 64). When Neihardt was fighting with publishers, Holloway makes the totally unsupported claim that "soon Black Elk will direct events and open Neihardt's eyes to his view of the higher perceptions" (ibid., 56). In other words, Black Elk teaches Neihardt to move beyond concerns for the problems of physical reality. But it is the actions of the whites in the *physical* world that make Black Elk so mad about colonialism. In his book on the collaboration between Black Elk and Neihardt, Holloway never once raises the question of Black Elk's economic situation, nor does he wonder if Black Elk ever received any compensation. For that matter, I have found nothing in the extensive literature about Black Elk dealing with this question. Did Black Elk ever receive any financial compensation?

[66] DeMallie, *The Sixth Grandfather*, 37.

[67] In addition to Fools Crow's decision to sell his headdress, Fools Crow recounts another cultural compromise he made. In 1927, the agency officials approached Fools Crow about reviving the Sun Dance (minus the piercing) for white tourists. Fools Crow remembers: "I could hardly believe it! The whites, who had years ago forbidden the Sun Dance, wanted now to show us off to people who would purchase tickets to see us sing and dance! We were to become a Buffalo Bill kind of sideshow, performing so strangers could stand in a circle around us and view us as they did rodeo and wild animals, while we performed with sincerity what supposedly was the most important dance of our traditional and sacred way of life!" Fools Crow rejected the idea at first, but in 1928 he decided to participate for the sake of the Lakota community. Nonetheless, Fools Crow did not like what had happened to the Sun Dance: "I still did not like to do the dance without piercing, or for a crowd of white spectators, so all the while we danced I prayed from the bottom of my heart for more understanding and a change of attitude on the part of the agency officials" (Mails, *Fools Crow* [1979], 112, 118).

Given Black Elk's age and disabilities, which prevented him from pursuing most types of employment, Black Elk's decision to work with Neihardt had to be motivated at least partially by economic factors.[68] He later regretted his decision to adapt former cultural practices to the current need and to tell his vision to an outsider, especially when Neihardt did not keep his promises.

## THE GREAT DEPRESSION COMPROMISE

Throughout this chapter I have argued that cultural and economic factors allowed Neihardt to use the Lakota Catholic Black Elk described in the previous chapters and create the "essentialist" Black Elk. With cultural and economic factors at the center of the interpretation, a more accurate understanding of the collaboration comes to light. Neihardt arrived in Pine Ridge without the ability to speak Lakota or a cultural framework that would help him understand Black Elk and the other Lakota. He had a specific agenda that categorically excluded more than half of Black Elk's life as well as the cultural practices in which he lived at the time. Neihardt stayed a short time and left, convinced that he had captured the authentic native experience.

In his first interviews with Neihardt, Black Elk's discourse was general in nature. Like the traditional Lakota holy men described by Stolzman in *The Pipe and Christ: A Christian-Sioux Dialogue*, Black Elk respectfully went around the subject, only occasionally touching on the specific matter at hand. Black Elk presented many illustrations rather than a direct argument. Black Elk's finished narrative was a rich tapestry of the Lakota Catholic world that would have gone beyond Neihardt's ability to interpret it properly.

In addition, the economic context further compromised Black Elk's freedom to describe explicitly his Lakota Catholic vision. Black Elk appears to have smoothed the Catholic edges of his vision in order to meet Neihardt's expectations; directness could have been economically dangerous. Black Elk had lines that he could not cross because there was always the potential that Neihardt would find someone else more appropriate to his narrative. Undoubtedly Black Elk shaped his story for his audience, not deceiving or being dishonest, but sincerely telling about those aspects of his life in which Neihardt was interested.[69] Louis Owens describes this phenomenon as a "mask":

---

[68] Curiously, despite the fact that DeMallie wrote the article (cited by me) describing conditions on Pine Ridge during the Great Depression, he makes no mention of their effect on Black Elk; instead he refers to their effect on Neihardt. In discussing why Neihardt was unable to buy land on the reservation as a vacation home, DeMallie writes "the Depression and the war years were to be hard ones for the Neihardts" (DeMallie, *The Sixth Grandfather*, 51).

[69] Black Elk's response is in continuity with the nature of a dynamic storytelling event. In this event, a skilled storyteller tells his or her story to an eager audience, sees the reactions of the audience, and shapes the narrative for the audience. Thus, the storytelling event is a dialectic in which the reaction of the audience influences how the story is told, what is emphasized, and what is left out.

The mask is one realized over centuries through Euro-America's construction of the "Indian" Other. In order to be recognized, and to thus have a voice that is heard by those in control of power, the Native must step into the mask and *be* the Indian constructed by white America. Paradoxically, of course, like the mirror, the mask merely shows the Euro-American to himself, since the masked Indian arises out of the European consciousness, leaving the Native behind the mask unseen, unrecognized for himself or herself. In short, to be seen and heard at all by the center—to not share the fate of Ralph Ellison's Invisible Man—the Native must pose as the absolute fake, the fabricated "Indian," like the dancing puppets in Ellison's novel.[70]

According to the phenomenon that Owens describes, it is easy to understand why Neihardt would have misunderstood Black Elk. For Neihardt to listen to Black Elk, Black Elk had to don the "mask" of the imagined Indian. Powers agrees with this reading: "Did Black Elk enjoy dictating his teachings to men who mysteriously had been 'sent' to him? Or were his teachings carefully edited to conform to the white man's expectations of his life? In believing that Black Elk was indeed an honorable man, one possessing the charisma that attracted these authors, I opt for the latter."[71]

After giving the interview, Black Elk no longer had control over the direction of the project. Neihardt wrote from his transcripts, shaping the story as he wished without further consultation with Black Elk. Black Elk did not see the final draft and certainly was unable to read *Black Elk Speaks* for himself. It must be remembered that the differences between the transcripts and Neihardt's *Black Elk Speaks* were so great that DeMallie decided to publish the original transcripts.

Consequently, a mutually reinforcing dialectic worked to ensure that Neihardt failed to understand Black Elk's message. Neihardt arrived with preconceived notions of what Indians were all about and without the cultural tools to interpret Black Elk's discourse; at the same time, Black Elk's dependency on Neihardt for the realization of the project made him acutely aware of the boundaries that should not be crossed. The imagined Indian of Neihardt thus revealed only what he expected. Given this context, the question is not "how could Neihardt misinterpret Black Elk's vision?" but rather "how could Neihardt correctly understand Black Elk's vision?" Neihardt's misinterpretation of Black Elk was the expected result of a cultural outsider with *a priori* assumptions that categorically denied the validity of the informant's concrete way of life.

Nonetheless, Neihardt did gather some ethnographic data. He was fairly accurate in recording what his categorically limited field work allowed him to see.

---

[70] Louis Owens, "As If an Indian Were Really an Indian: Native American Voices and Postcolonial Theory," in *Native American Representations: First Encounters, Distorted Images, and Literary Appropriations*, ed. Gretchen M. Bataille, 11–24 (Lincoln: University of Nebraska Press, 2001), 17.

[71] William K. Powers, "When Black Elk Speaks, Everybody Listens," in *Religion and American Culture*, ed. David G. Hackett, 425–32 (New York: Routledge, 1995), 432.

The vision, read as a Lakota Catholic narrative, is consistent with the Black Elk of Lakota tradition, a devout Catholic, even when derided as a "catechism teacher" and "cigar store Indian." The inaccuracies appear to have been introduced when Neihardt removed the narrative from its Lakota Catholic context and inserted it into his own Manifest Destiny narrative. Thus Neihardt's mistake lay not in gathering information but in reading and interpreting it.

Both Neihardt and Black Elk were sincere in their endeavors. The evidence does not suggest that Neihardt intentionally deceived or manipulated Black Elk or the Lakota. For his part, Black Elk used the situation sincerely and creatively for the survival of his family and people. While the historical and cultural dynamics limited an accurate sharing and later telling of Black Elk's sacred vision, Neihardt enabled Black Elk's vision to survive.

# 7

# Colonialism and the Lakota Catholic Black Elk

*At one time, the ceremonies as they had been performed were enough for the way the world was then. But after the white people came, elements in this world began to shift; and it became necessary to create new ceremonies. I have made changes in the rituals. The people mistrust greatly, but only this growth keeps the ceremonies strong.*

*She taught me this above all else: things which don't shift and grow are dead things. They are things the witchery people want. Witchery works to scare people, to make them fear growth. But it has always been necessary, and more than ever now, it is. Otherwise we won't make it. We won't survive. That's what the witchery is counting on: that we will cling to the ceremonies the way they were, and then their power will triumph, and the people will be no more.*

—Old Betonie, speaking to Tayo, in Leslie Silko's *Ceremony*

The previous chapter described how Neihardt's cultural limitations and the economic context of Pine Ridge during the Great Depression allowed Neihardt to create the essentialist Black Elk, a person quite different from the Lakota Catholic Black Elk identified by the Lakota community and historical documents. Having established the historical accuracy of the Lakota Catholic Black Elk, one question remains: Why would Black Elk find Catholicism compelling enough to join the church, to seek to evangelize its message, and to make major modifications to the central themes of the Lakota tradition? Indeed, this question was asked by Neihardt during his interviews: "Black Elk, when you have such a very beautiful religion, why are you a member of a white church?"[1] Why did Black Elk convert?

---

[1] Hilda Neihardt and R. Todd Wise, "Black Elk and John G. Neihardt," in *The Black Elk* Reader, ed. Clyde Holler, 87–103 (Syracuse, N.Y.: Syracuse University Press, 2000), 95.

The first possible reason, government repression of Lakota ceremonial life, probably played a role, but it does not seem to have been foundational. Black Elk held out for a long time, and many Lakota never converted at all. Also, the early Native American revitalization movement of the 1930s described by Fools Crow never caused Black Elk to leave the church. This is best demonstrated through the witness of Fools Crow and Black Elk's son Ben. While both lived to see the full-scale Native American revitalization movements of the 1970s, they never accepted the American Indian Movement's critique of Christianity, and they never left the church.

A second reason proposed by those who dismiss Black Elk's Catholicism is that Black Elk saw the white man's religion as more powerful. They see this dynamic present in George Sword, one of J. R. Walker's informants on Lakota tradition and a deacon in the Episcopal church:

> When I served the Lakota *Wakan Tanka*, I did so with all my power. When I went on the warpath I always did all the ceremonies to gain the favor of the Lakota *Wakan Tanka*. But when the Lakotas fought with the white soldiers, the white people always won the victory. I went to Washington and to other large cities, and that showed me that the white people dug in the ground and built houses that could not be moved. Then I knew that when they came they could not be driven away. For this reason I took a new name, the name of Sword, because the leaders of the white soldiers wore swords. I determined to adopt the customs of the white people, and to persuade my people to do so.
>
> I became the first leader of the U.S. Indian Police among the Oglalas, and was their captain until the Oglalas ceased to think of fighting the white people. Then I became a deacon in the Christian church, and am so now, and will be until my death.[2]

Many academics argue that, like Sword, Black Elk was attracted to Christianity because the whites were stronger and thus their god must be stronger. However, while this may have been a factor in his conversion, it cannot be the foundational reason. According to Black Elk, during his two-year journey through the white world, he saw nothing good about the white world except some religious customs, which will be examined below. Black Elk did not give in, as Sword did, but fought in the aftermath of Wounded Knee. His conversion did not occur for another fifteen years. Most important, Black Elk's first involvement in Christianity was with the Ghost Dance, a Pan Indian movement based on the Christian narrative.

Perhaps the most popular argument is that Black Elk's primary motivation for conversion was significant economic gain.[3] Given the historical context out-

---

[2] James R. Walker, *Lakota Belief and Ritual*, ed. Raymond J. DeMaillie and Elaine A. Jahner (1980; repr., Lincoln: University of Nebraska Press, 1991), 74–75.

[3] This is interesting, given the lack of attention to economic considerations in the Black Elk–Neihardt collaboration.

lined in the previous chapter, it is likely that economic concerns played at least some role in Black Elk's Catholic life. From a Christian perspective, economic motivation is acceptable to a certain extent, because Christianity is supposed to be about communal economic sharing. If Black Elk saw the Catholic church as a source of stability in the early reservation period, it would be evidence that the church was living up to its call.

However, the evidence does not support the claim that Black Elk's conversion was first and foremost an economic decision. This is true for a number of reasons. First, Black Elk's conversion entailed a significant economic sacrifice from the start. When he converted, Black Elk gave up his *yuwipi* practice, which had been an important source of income during the early reservation period. In addition, the Jesuits did not offer catechist positions to non-Catholic Lakota in order to influence them to convert.[4] The Jesuits recruited Black Elk for the position of catechist because of his exemplary Catholic life. It seems that around three years passed between his conversion in 1904 and the start of his work as a catechist. During this time he acquired a thorough knowledge of scripture and the Catholic tradition. Thus, his dedication preceded his employment.

Black Elk also claims that initially he did not even want to be a catechist. He wrote in 1909: "When I was given this job I did not want it, but you people have encouraged me to take on this job. So that's why I'm doing this—for your own good."[5] Whether it was too much work, not enough compensation, or a lack of interest on his part, Black Elk did not want the catechist position. Because of the encouragement of the Lakota Catholic community, and for its benefit, he decided to accept the position.

However, this does not explain why Black Elk retired from his catechist position when he did. At this point the argument for Black Elk's economic motivation breaks down. Black Elk stopped working as a catechist in the early 1930s, precisely at the worst point of the Depression. If his motivation were the five or ten dollars a month he received as a catechist, he never would have left during the most difficult economic period of the reservation era.[6]

---

[4] Clyde Holler, who is sympathetic to Black Elk's Catholic life, still falls into this trap. He writes that "Black Elk clearly stood to benefit by accepting Christianity, since his income as a catechist was considerable. Since Black Elk subsequently made his living as a catechist, it could be said that the material benefits of his acceptance of Christianity point to the possibility of insincerity" (Clyde Holler, *Black Elk's Religion: The Sun Dance and Lakota Catholicism* [Syracuse, N.Y.: Syracuse University Press, 1995], 210).

[5] Black Elk, Letter, October 18, 1909, published in *Sinasapa Wocekiye Taeyanpaha,* St. Michael's Mission, Fr. Totten, North Dakota, date unknown. Translated from Lakota to English under Michael F. Steltenkamp, S.J., in Ivan M. Timonin, *Black Elk's Synthesis: Catholic Theology and Oglala Tradition in The Sacred Pipe,* dissertation proposal.

[6] Christopher Vescey points out that Black Elk never worked as a catechist after the Neihardt interviews, that his commitment to Catholicism was waning (see Christopher Vescey, "A Century of Lakota Catholicism at Pine Ridge," in *Religious Diversity and American Religious History: Studies in Traditions and Cultures,* ed. Walter H. Conser

This line of argument also imports colonial assumptions that damage both Black Elk and the Lakota. Implicit—and often explicit—in this argument for an economic motivation is the idea that Black Elk was deceiving the missionaries.[7] One may argue that if Black Elk had told his story the way Neihardt wanted to hear it, it is even more likely that he would have done the same thing with Catholicism; namely, Black Elk would have told the missionaries what they wanted to hear for the sake of material benefit.

This seems highly doubtful given the conclusions reached in Chapter 3. It is important to remember that Black Elk's audience during his Catholic life did not consist primarily of white missionaries; Black Elk spoke to and worked for the Lakota and other Native American tribes and gained over four hundred converts. If not a "true" Catholic, Black Elk would have had to deceive the Lakota, his own community and people. While it is possible that he may have deceived twenty or thirty Jesuits, it seems most unlikely that he could have deceived hundreds of Lakota and other Native Americans and motivated them to change their lives.[8] And if he had, his own community would have been the victims of his deceit. Ultimately, this argument turns Black Elk into an agent of colonialism, precisely the force he was combating.

---

Jr. and Sumner B. Twiss [Athens: University of Georgia Press, 1997], 273). Vescey does not consider the following facts in regard to Black Elk's retirement: (1) Black Elk was sixty-seven years old during the interviews; (2) he had progressive tuberculosis; and (3) he had been run over by a wagon and had almost died.

[7] Julian Rice suggests that "he may have 'lied.'" Rice also describes Black Elk's conversion as a "warrior reason." Lying to one's community over a forty-year period hardly seems to be a warrior's reason. See Julian Rice, *Black Elk's Story: Distinguishing Its Lakota Purpose* (Albuquerque: University of New Mexico Press, 1991), xii. Lakota do not tend to "lie" when ritual is involved. DeMallie describes the role that ritual plays in Lakota life: "For the Lakotas, belief and ritual were completely intertwined. Belief formed the intellectual and emotional underpinnings of religion, a system of knowledge representing mankind in relation to the universe. Belief made men's lives and the world in which men lived intelligible and acceptable, and it defined the moral structure for society. Ritual provided the means for actualizing religious power and for expressing belief. The Lakotas spoke of the purpose of ritual in terms of 'pleasing' the *wakan* beings, which they believed formed the structure and substance of their world. But ritual was no mere reflection of belief; it was also the means to further belief, for through ritual people came to expand their knowledge." DeMallie emphasizes that, for the Lakota, ritual is not a mechanical process separate from belief. Ritual and belief are a mutually reinforcing dialectic that defines the structure of the universe and increases belief. Consequently, Black Elk's and the Lakota's participation in Catholic rituals, such as the mass, could not be empty or duplicitous. In a Lakota context, Catholic rituals helped to define the world and reinforced and expanded belief (Raymond J. DeMallie, *The Sixth Grandfather: Black Elk's Teachings Given to John G. Neihardt* [Lincoln: University of Nebraska Press, 1984], 82).

[8] Black Elk was a godfather for at least 134 people (see William K. Powers, "When Black Elk Speaks, Everybody Listens," in *Religion and American Culture*, ed. David G. Hackett, 425–35 [New York: Routledge, 1995], 429).

## COLONIAL SOURCES OF THE ESSENTIALIST BLACK ELK

Although it seems that previous attempts to discredit the sincerity of Black Elk's Catholicism cannot be maintained, it is useful to determine why there is a need in the first place to show that Black Elk's Catholicism was not real or sincere. Why do scholars vehemently deny the possibility that Black Elk's conversion was sincere? One such attempt is Julian Rice's interpretation of Black Elk, written in 1991. Rice shrouds Black Elk in the image of the mythical Native American warrior fighting for cultural purity on all fronts. His conversion is viewed as a mere diversion to deceive outside observers. Black Elk "apparently compromise[s] his own beliefs" and "assume[s] a mantle of Christianity."[9] This mantle allows Black Elk to deceive observers but protects him from "compromising" what Rice assumes to be his unsaid intentions to protect an unchanging, pure Lakota tradition.

Defending his stance against a growing trend to interpret Black Elk's Catholicism as at least partially sincere, Rice writes again in 1998, staking out what amounts to a last stand:

> Just as missionaries used the Sioux to do the Lord's work, so a particular faction of the academic community now uses Native America culture to define itself favorably. Today "cosmopolitan" and "syncretic" describe the going, postmodern gospels. In the interest of social tolerance and intellectual complexity Native Americans have become brave denizens of the "liminal" divide. Black Elk, for example, cannot really be understood as a traditional Lakota because he had already been a Christian "for decades" when John Neihardt interviewed him in 1931.[10]

For Rice, any suggestion that Black Elk sincerely participated in Christianity sacrifices the purity of Native American culture. In opposition, Rice reasserts the "pure" Lakota Black Elk:

> The possibility that Black Elk could have distinctly remembered and perhaps wished to return to the spirituality he had exclusively lived until the age of thirty-seven is lost on these scholars. They make much of the collaborative nature of published writings and throw up their hands at the possibility of receiving an authentic Indian voice in any ethnographic text.[11]

Categorically dismissing Black Elk's exploration of Christianity in Europe, the Christian influence in the Ghost Dance, and over forty years of Catholic life, Rice conjectures a defiant warrior desperately and secretly clinging to a pure

---

[9]  Rice, *Black Elk's Story*, 104.

[10]  Julian Rice, *Before the Great Spirit: The Many Faces of Sioux Spirituality* (Albuquerque: University of New Mexico Press, 1998), 11.

[11]  Ibid.

spirituality. Rice creates the "authentic Indian," fighting to remain "pure" from impure outside cultural influences.[12]

Recent postcolonial scholarship, however, demonstrates that the desire to portray Black Elk's conversion as purely instrumental and thus insincere is itself a colonial phenomenon. As discussed in Chapter 1, the defiant warrior and his imagined cultural purity are creations of Western outsiders, a form of what Edward Said called Orientalism. Rice's "authentic" native depends on the *a priori* assumption that despite long histories of colonialism, natives should not change.

Philip J. Deloria, son of the famous Dakota writer Vine Deloria Jr., describes the construction of the authentic Native in an American context. In *Playing Indian*, Deloria argues that "Indian" identity is the cultural construction of the "other" in American colonialism:

> The quest for such an authentic Other is a characteristically modern phenomenon, one that has often been played out in the contradictions surrounding America's long and ambivalent engagement with Indianness.[13]

Deloria identifies the construction of the essentialized Native as a product of Western modernity rather than of traditional Native American cultures. He maintains that this search for the authentic has its roots in the West's insecurities:

> The authentic, as numerous scholars have pointed out, is a culturally constructed category created in opposition to a perceived state of inauthenticity. The authentic serves as a way to imagine and idealize the real, the traditional, and the organic in opposition to the less satisfying qualities of everyday life.[14]

As a result, the West searches for a replacement in the form of the unchanging authenticity of the cultural Other. R. S. Sugirtharajah illustrates this tendency with an article from the *Liverpool Post* of July 20, 1920:

> We of the West do not want from the East poetic edifices built upon a foundation of Yeats and Shelley and Walt Whitman. We want to hear the

---

[12] An interesting battle, since most Lakota in this era were primarily fighting to eat.

[13] Philip J. Deloria, *Playing Indian* (New Haven, Conn.: Yale University Press, 1998), 101.

[14] Ibid. Deloria argues that Native Americans used the West's expectation of authenticity to create the hybrid innovation of the "authentic Indian." By adopting American images of the essentialized Indian, Native Americans used the image for social and political advantage: "If being a survivor of the pure, primitive old days meant authenticity, and if that in turn meant cultural power that might be translated to social ends, it made sense for a Seneca man to put on a Plains headdress, white America's marker of that archaic brand of authority." According to Deloria, even an activity as ambiguous and potentially damaging as mimicking the noble savage provided a means of confronting colonialism. Ironically, "playing Indian" was a hybrid innovation for survival.

flute of Krishna as Radha heard of it, to fall under the spell of the blue God in the lotus-heart of dreams.[15]

A paraphrase of Rice's desperate plea for "authentic purity" voiced in 1998 is virtually identical to the passage from 1920: we of the West do not want visions built on a foundation of Christianity; we want to hear the whistle of the Sun Dancers as the Lakota who first ventured onto the Western plains heard it. In other words, the only value in different people is the "difference" they can provide for Western consumption. Like Deloria, Sugirtharajah describes this Western consumption as a product of Western cultural needs:

Such a search envisages the task of interpretation as establishment of an identity rather than as a process in which identity, context and texts constantly evolve in response to new demands. Rey Chow refers to those who yearn for the past as "root searchers" because roots signify a nostalgic return to the past so that the plurality of the present can be reduced to "a long-lost origin." Behind the post-imperial quest by Western interpreters for an authentic Thirdworldness there lurks a feeling of homesickness for traditional culture and values, which once they controlled and which now are not within their reach.[16]

Sugirtharajah, like Deloria, suggests that this quest for the pure native is a product of the emptiness of the modern West searching to replace its rootlessness.

As a result, the academy's attempt to deny Black Elk's Catholicism and to essentialize his Lakota identity is not a result of Lakota tradition but is a colonial endeavor. This should not be surprising. It has already been established (see Chapter 3) that the Lakota of Black Elk's generation raised in the Lakota language did not demonstrate the need to assert or create identity by denying cultural change. In other words, Rice's project imports a Western nostalgia to establish and protect a Lakota identity that did not exist in Black Elk's cultural context.[17]

In contrast to the West's search for the pure Native American, postcolonial writers emphasize that the changes natives made in colonial contexts were not

---

[15] R. S. Sugirtharajah, *The Bible and the Third World: Precolonial, Colonial and Postcolonial Encounters* (Cambridge: University of Cambridge Press, 2001), 279–80.

[16] Ibid.

[17] Postcolonialism also explains dynamics that contribute to tourist/seeker quests like Neihardt's. Edouard Glissant, a postcolonial writer from Martinique, writes: "We cannot underestimate the universal malaise that drives Europeans, dissatisfied with their world, toward those 'warm lands' that are deserted by unemployment as well as subjected to intolerable pressures of survival, to seek in the *Other's World* a temporary respite" (Edouard Glissant, "The Known, the Uncertain," in *Caribbean Discourse: Selected Essays*, trans. with introduction by J. Michael Dash, 13–95 [Charlottesville: University of Virginia Press, 1989], 23). Deloria describes this phenomenon also with hobbyist groups and New Age seekers (see Philip Deloria, *Playing Indian*).

corruptions but means for survival. This includes Native American involvement in Christianity. In this context Christianity is no longer interpreted as an exclusively destructive force but an area where both the colonized and the colonizer challenged the unmitigated forces of colonialism through the exercise of their agency. Irene S. Vernon argues that Native Americans, like colonized people throughout the world, often used the Christian narrative to challenge colonialism: "In Native Christian writings, and through the lens of postcoloniality, Christianity is presented as a means of survival and as a vehicle of adaptation, reflecting considerable choices which do not necessarily imply rejection of Native spirituality or 'Indianness.'"[18] Viewed from a postcolonial perspective, the use of the Christian narrative does not compromise identity but can be an exercise of native agency in confronting the systems of colonialism.

A postcolonial emphasis on native agents' appropriation of new thought and new cultural practices is not contrary to but in continuity with the fluid nature of Lakota culture in general and the role of the holy man in particular. O. Douglas Schwartz uses almost the exact same form as postcolonial writers to describe the agency that is inherent in the role of the Lakota holy man:

> The holy man has a "vision" of the world—its nature, its history and its destiny—and a sense of humanity's place within that scheme. Through that vision, the holy man can hope to solve problems for which the tradition offers no ready-made solutions. The *wicasa wakan* is then the theoretician—the theologian—of the Plains religion.[19]

The function of agency as described by postcolonialism was a central virtue embodied by the Lakota holy man: he brought innovation and reinterpretation of tradition in changing contexts.

The connection among the Lakota holy man, agency, and Christianity has already been made. In *Black Elk: Holy Man of the Oglala*, Michael Steltenkamp skillfully argues that Black Elk's conversion to Catholicism was an extension of his role as a holy man. Rather than being a rejection of Lakota tradition, Catholicism for Black Elk offered new access to *Wankan Tanka*. In other words, Christianity was a means of new power for Black Elk and other native agents in new contexts.

---

[18] Irene S. Vernon, "The Claiming of Christ: Native American Postcolonial Discourses," *Melus* (Summer 1999), 2, available online.

[19] O. Douglas Schwartz, cited in Clyde Holler, *Black Elk's Religion: The Sun Dance and Lakota Catholicism* (Syracuse, N.Y.: Syracuse University Press, 1995), 181. DeMallie elaborates on the role of the holy man in Lakota religion: "In Lakota culture, the quest for knowledge of the *wakan* was largely a personal enterprise, and it was predominately the work of men. . . . There was no standard theology, no dogmatic body of belief. Fundamental concepts were universally shared, but specific knowledge of the *wakan* beings was not shared beyond a small number of holy men. Through individual experience, every man had the opportunity to contribute to and resynthesize the general body of knowledge that constituted Lakota religion" (DeMallie, *The Sixth Grandfather*, 82).

It seems clear that not only is there no evidence that Black Elk's conversion was purely instrumental or an act, but the very desire to make this claim and deny Lakota claims to the contrary is a form of colonialism. Postcolonial theorists demonstrate that selective adoption of new thought and cultural practices—including Christianity—is a means of survival for colonized people. As noted above, this claim is in continuity with Lakota culture in general and the role of the holy man in particular. Finally, it has already been argued, and convincingly so, that Black Elk's conversion was an exercise of his role as a holy man to find new power in changing social and economic situations.

A final topic to be addressed is how in this new context—the new world created by Western colonialism—Catholicism might have been an advantage for Black Elk. In other words, what kind of power does Christianity provide for colonized people in general, and Black Elk in particular? How does Christianity in the hands of natives counter colonialism? Before addressing this question, a brief review is in order concerning the power the colonial West exerted on the world of colonized peoples.

Through colonialism the West reordered the world. In a systematic process the West appropriated the land of the peoples of the world through military force. Colonized peoples were reduced to poverty, and their villages became virtual prisons as their economies were disrupted and destroyed. The West justified this system through racism, relegating colonized people to subhuman status. The world was reordered by violence, greed, and the creation of myths of racial inferiority.

Given the strategy the West employed to reorder the world, I maintain that when colonized peoples "discovered Christianity," they often used it to counter the West. This is demonstrated by two recognized postcolonial Christian movements.

## THE RASTAFARI APPROPRIATION OF THE CHRISTIAN NARRATIVE

The first example of a postcolonial appropriation of the Christian narrative is the Rastafari movement of Jamaica. The context in which the Rastafari arose is not unlike the early Lakota Reservation period. According to Ennis Barrington Edmonds, the 1920s and 1930s brought renewed hardship for the colonized masses of Afro Jamaicans. The imperial strategies of American and British capitalists renewed the plantation system, reordering the land in the hands of powerful agribusinesses. This produced massive urbanization with resulting slums, unemployment, and poverty. Since Jamaica was still a colony of the British Crown, "the masses were excluded from the political process."[20] Racism was part of the colonial ideology that was firmly entrenched in Jamaican society. These conditions were exacerbated by the global Great Depression, which began in 1930.

---

[20] Ennis Barrington Edmonds, *Rastafari: From Outcast to Culture Bearers* (Oxford: Oxford University Press, 2003), 30.

In this context of intensifying colonial dominance, Black Nationalism preached the downfall of the colonial ordering of the world. Earlier, Jamaican Marcus Garvey had prophesied the crowning of a black king: "Look to Africa, when a black king shall be crowned, for the day of deliverance is near."[21] In 1930 the Ethiopian nobleman Ras Tafari was crowned emperor and took the name Haile Selassie. Patrick Taylor recounts the powerful effect this had on the Jamaican masses: "Many Jamaicans looked in awe at the photographs in the Kingston papers showing European leaders respectfully bowing down to this new African leader."[22] Many self-defined prophets began to preach the divinity of Ras Tafari and to proclaim that Christ had returned to redeem the African peoples. Now the white race would bow down to the black race. Taylor summarizes the prophets' message:

Europeans who called themselves Jews and Christians had distorted the biblical teachings and appropriated the place of God's chosen people, guardians of the Ark of the Covenant, the black race. The Messiah would come to redeem his people from the land of colonialism and slavery and lead them out of Babylon into the promised land, Ethiopia.[23]

According to Taylor, the Rastafari taught that Christ had returned to the colonized African peoples of the world. He would punish the colonizers who had been unfaithful to his message and had used their power to enslave the world. And Christ would redeem the colonized people and lead them to the Promised Land.

Scholars of Rastafari deny that this is some private religious experience or a form of Marxist opiate. According to the Jamaican scholar Rex Nettleford, the Rastafari "hijacking of the oppressor's God [was a] move that served to discommode the oppressor." The Rastafari use of the Christian narrative was the power to counter colonial ideology:

Such exercise of creative imagination and intellect remains, then, the most powerful weapon against all acts of inhumanity; and the Rastafarians have drawn on the tradition, which was nurtured [in the Caribbean] since the eighteenth century, to cope with and defy the harshness of twentieth-century indulgences. Wresting *the Christian message from the Messenger* as a strategy of demarginalization helped bring slave and free peasantry nearer a perceived mainstream as "children of God."[24]

---

[21] Patrick Taylor, "Sheba's Song: The Bible, the *Kebra Nagast*, and the *Rastafari*," in *Nation Dance: Religion, Identity, and Cultural Difference in the Caribbean*, ed. Patrick Taylor, 65–78 (Bloomington: Indiana University Press, 2001), 72.

[22] Ibid.

[23] Ibid.

[24] From Nathaniel S. Murrell, "Wresting the Message from the Messenger: The Rastafari as a Case Study in the Caribbean Indigenization of the Bible," in *African Americans and the Bible: Sacred Texts and Social Textures*, ed. Vincent L. Wimbush, 558–76 (New York: Continuum, 2000), 566.

This appropriation was embodied in communal life and had clear political implications. Nathaniel S. Murrell argues that the Rastafari use of scripture, reggae music, and distinctive cultural practices is a form of cultural dissonance that works to correct the ills of colonialism through peaceful means. According to Murrell, "Rastas believe that the expected liberation could come in the here and now if everyone joins in restructuring the political system and adopting the Rastafari social, economic, and political agenda spelled out in *The Rastafari Manifesto.*"[25] In other words, Rastafari apocalyticism is the *telos* for concrete political change.

While this is not a complete analysis of the Rastafari, it has a number of important themes for our study of Black Elk. Fundamentally, the Rastafari movement creates a larger narrative—or "outnarrates"—the West's colonial narrative with Christ at its center, the very figure claimed by the West. The story brought by the West condemns the West. Thus, by this creative imagination the Rastafari gain in two ways. First, Christianity provides a moral story that is greater than the West. Interpreted by the Rastafari, Christ provides a standard of ethical conduct used to judge colonialism. Second, under the higher power of Christ the West is judged and punished for the injustice of colonialism. A key characteristic of this postcolonial movement is the strict division between the two groups: the colonized are universally saved, and the colonizers are universally condemned. There is no redemption from the sin of colonialism.

## WILLIAM APESS'S APPROPRIATION
## OF THE CHRISTIAN NARRATIVE

William Apess (1798–1839) provides a significant example of a parallel postcolonial appropriation of the Christian narrative in a Native American context. Apess was a Pequot and a Methodist minister active in the political struggles of the Mashpee tribe of Massachusetts. In his *Eulogy on King Philip*, published in 1936, Apess delivers an excoriating rereading of the history of Native Americans in New England through the Christian narrative. The key figure is the Narragansett leader King Philip, who led a rebellion against the treacherous and violent expansion of the American colonies. Rather than retelling the entire story, I highlight here a few themes significant to the understanding of Black Elk.

Like the Rastafari, Apess benefited in several ways from his use of the Christian narrative. First, Apess recognizes Christ as the savior of all. Native Americans are "beings too that lie endeared to God as yourselves, his Son being their Savior as well as yours, and alike to all men."[26] For Apess, Christ is a standard bigger than the West.

---

[25]  Ibid., 571.

[26]  William Apess, "Eulogy on King Philip," in *On Our Own Ground: The Complete Writings of William Apess, a Pequot,* ed. Barry O'Connell (1936; repr., Amherst: University of Massachusetts Press, 1992), 286.

Apess uses this standard to measure the actions of the American colonists during the early history of New England. The expansion and war consistently initiated by the Pilgrims was not only bad for the Native Americans, but it blatantly contradicted the Christian narrative. Apess writes, "But it is certain that Pilgrims knew better than to break the commandments of their Lord and Master; they knew that it was written, 'Thou shall not kill.'"[27] Not only did the Pilgrims break the commandments of God, but they invented justifications that they called the will of God:

> How they could go to work to enslave a free people and call it religion is beyond the power of imagination and outstrips the revelation of God's word. O thou pretended hypocritical Christian, whoever thou art, to say it was the design of God that we should murder and slay one another because we have the power.[28]

Despite the Pilgrims' colonial theology, Apess is not deceived about the true nature of the gospel or the hypocrisy of Christian Pilgrims. "Although the Gospel is said to be glad tidings for all people, yet we poor Indians never have found those who brought it as messengers of mercy."[29] Instead of mercy, the whites brought rum, powder, guns, and disease.[30] After the great atrocities of the war, the whites gathered on the Sabbath and used the book that says that "'he [who] loves God and hates his brother is a liar, and the truth is not in him'—and at the same time they hating and selling their fellow men in bondage."[31]

According to Apess, if the Pilgrims were hypocrites then it cannot be the Christian narrative that produced colonialism. Rather, the source is nothing more than greed and the usurpation of power, and "we find no excuse in the Bible for Christians conducting [themselves] toward us as they do."[32] The Pilgrims acted for reasons contrary to the gospel, and for that reason, whites were the real savages.[33]

Ironically, for Apess, history shows that Native Americans were more faithful to Christian teachings than whites. According to Apess, the Pilgrims would not have survived their first year in New England in 1622. The same people condemned as savages and subhuman gave them venison, beans, and corn to survive the first winter. "Had it not been for this humane act of the Indians, every white man would have been swept from the New England colonies. In their sickness, too, the Indians were as tender to them as their own children; and for all this, they were denounced as savages by those who had received all the acts of kindness they possibly could show them."[34]

---

[27] Ibid., 289.
[28] Ibid., 279.
[29] Ibid., 286.
[30] Ibid.
[31] Ibid., 301.
[32] Ibid., 308.
[33] Ibid., 309.
[34] Ibid., 280.

Yet the Christian standard that Apess uses to measure the West is the very standard they proclaim to hold:

> It is with shame, I acknowledge, that I have to notice so much corruption of a people calling themselves Christians. If they were like my people, professing no purity at all, then their crimes would not appear to have such magnitude. But while they appear to be by profession more virtuous, their crimes still blacken. It makes them truly to appear to be like mountains filled with smoke, and thick darkness covering them all around.[35]

According to Apess, the Pilgrims condemned themselves.

The Christian narrative is used by Apess to reread the history of New England. It also clearly identifies God as the power who will judge and punish the injustice of colonialism. Apess writes, "Remember that their wall of prejudice was built with untempered mortar, contrary to God's command; and be assured, it will fall upon their children."[36] God will punish the West, and bring redemption to the colonized. "Let them [people of color] rather fast and pray to the great Spirit, the Indian's God, who deals out mercy to his red children, and not destruction."[37] God will be true to his promises and will redeem his children.

Like the Rastafari, Apess's apocalypticism was embodied in the community, and it had political implications. In 1834 the Mashpee tribe under the leadership of Apess staged the peaceful and successful Mashpee Revolt. As a result the Mashpee gained the same rights of township self-governance as all the citizens of Massachusetts, as well as control over church leadership.[38] According to Barry O'Connell, "It is not fanciful to see him as one of the earliest indigenous leaders of an Indian rights movement."[39]

In addition to making use of the ethical standard of Christ and God's judgment on the colonialists, Apess called for an end to colonialism. Through the Christian narrative as a Methodist minister, Apess not only condemned whites but he also called them to repentance, conversion, and salvation. What Apess calls the "national sin" of colonialism could be ended:[40]

> A fire, a canker, created by the pilgrims from across the Atlantic, to burn and destroy my poor unfortunate brethren, and it cannot be denied. What then shall we do? Shall we cease crying and say it is all wrong, or shall we bury the hatchet and those unjust laws and Plymouth Rock together and become friends? And will the sons of the Pilgrim aid in putting out the fire and destroying the canker that will ruin all that their fathers left behind them to destroy? . . . Let us have principles that will give everyone his

---

[35]  Ibid., 300.
[36]  Ibid., 288.
[37]  Ibid., 286.
[38]  Barry O'Connell, in Apess, *On Our Own Ground,* xxxvii.
[39]  Ibid., 163.
[40]  Apess, "The Increase of the Kingdom of Christ," in *On Our Own Ground,* 107.

due; and then shall wars cease, and the weary find rest. Give the Indian his rights, and you may be assured war will cease.[41]

For Apess, even friendship and peace were possible:

You and I have to rejoice that we have not to answer for our fathers' crimes; neither shall we do right to charge them one to another. We can only regret it, and flee from it; and from henceforth, let peace and righteousness be written upon our hearts and hands forever, is the wish of a poor Indian.[42]

Judgment and punishment were not the final hopes of Apess. Justice for Native Americans could lead to reconciliation and peace for all. The West could be saved. This should not be surprising, as it was justice, hope, and love for all peoples that first called Apess to Christ. In his autobiography, *Son of the Forest*, Apess describes his conversion:

I felt convinced that Christ died for all mankind—that age, sect, color, country, or situation made no difference. I felt an assurance that I was included in the plan of redemption with all my brethren. No one can conceive with what joy I hailed this *new* doctrine, as it was called . . . my soul was filled with love—love to God, and love to all mankind. Oh, how my poor heart swelled with joy—and I could cry from my very soul, Glory to God in the highest!!! There was not only a change in my heart but in everything around me. The scene was entirely altered. The works of God praised him, and I saw him in everything that he made. My love now embraced the whole human family.[43]

Apess's postcolonial appropriation of the Christian narrative is similar to that of the Rastafari, yet his apocalyptic vision offers hope. For Apess, Christ does not just judge the West and redeem the colonized; Christ heals all of creation. Christ redeems the West from absolute judgment, allowing for the possibility of the West's redemption. Apess sees in the Christian narrative the possibility for repentance and for reconciliation between colonized and colonizer. Thus, Christ is not only greater than the West but bigger than the sin of colonialism. Christ offers the possibility of healing the sin of the world.

## BLACK ELK, CATHOLICISM, AND COLONIALISM

Christianity offered the Rastafari and William Apess a moral story far greater than the West's colonial story; it had the power to judge and condemn the West. Christianity offered Apess another power, the possible redemption of the West,

---

[41]   Apess, "Eulogy on King Philip," 306, 307.
[42]   Ibid., 310.
[43]   Apess, "Son of the Forest," in *On Our Own Ground*, 19, 21.

and the healing of all of creation. This vision was also at the center of Black Elk's Christian life.

One factor in Black Elk's decision to join Buffalo Bill's Wild West Show was his search as a holy man for new power. He wanted to study and evaluate the white man's ways to determine if his people should adopt them. As we saw in Chapters 4 and 5, he concluded that the only worthwhile custom is what he calls "trust in God." This inspired Black Elk to investigate Jesus further and to adopt the Christian trust in God.

### PARALLELS BETWEEN THE RASTAFARI MOVEMENT AND THE GHOST DANCE

When Black Elk returned to Pine Ridge, he found that news of the Messiah had spread among the Lakota and all of Native America. Black Elk later told Neihardt about the Lakota who had visited Wovoka, the Paiute Messiah:

> These people told me that these men had actually seen the Messiah and that he had given them these things. They should put this paint on and have a ghost dance, and in doing this they would save themselves, that there is another world coming—a world just for Indians, that in time the world would come and crush out all the whites.[44]

Among the Lakota, hope grew that *Wankan Tanka* would assert his great power and destroy the West. After cautious investigation and despite the fact he could not go to the land of the Messiah in America or the Holy Land, Black Elk joined the Ghost Dance.

The parallels between the Rastafari movement and the Lakota Ghost Dance are striking. A far-off prophet inspired a Pan Indian/African movement that taught of the messianic restoration of a colonized people. The adherents embodied a distinct community and way of life in the form of an apocalyptic political movement. In other words, the Ghost Dance incorporated the Christian narrative in a way similar to that of the Rastafari; the standard of God's justice became the moral framework within which Western colonialism was measured,[45] and the figure of the Messiah would judge and condemn the West in an apocalyptic intervention of history.

---

[44] DeMallie, *The Sixth Grandfather*, 257.

[45] Steltenkamp describes the Christian source of the Ghost Dance: "Theologically, the Ghost Dance was a non-mainstream version of Christianity that joined Lakota tradition. Its Christian content was so apparent that one of the priests [Father Craft] who visited ghost dancers at the peak of their activity was of the opinion it was 'quite Catholic, and even edifying'" (Michael F. Steltenkamp, S.J., "Contemporary American Indian Religious Thinking and Its Relationship to the Christianity of Black Elk, Holy Man of the Oglala," in *American Catholic Traditions: Resources for Renewal*, ed. Sandra Yocum Mize and William Portier, 29–52 [Maryknoll, N.Y.: Orbis Books, 1997], 40). Powers emphasizes that, according to informants, Black Elk's preaching of the Ghost Dance was "decidedly Christian" (Powers, "When Black Elk Speaks, Everybody Listens," 427).

Black Elk incorporated the power of the Ghost Dance into his understanding of Christian trust in God. He told Neihardt in 1931 that Native Americans loved the West (meaning the colonists) as their neighbor and the West did not love them in turn. As a result, Black Elk had faith that God would intervene:

> Today I feel sorry—I could just cry—to see my people in a muddy water, dirty with the bad acts of the white people. . . . Now, when I look ahead, we are nothing but prisoners of war, but the Great Spirit has protected us so far, and this Great Spirit takes care of us. . . . I think there will be a great punishment for the whites in the future as a result of this. . . . It is up to the Great Spirit to look upon the white man and they will be sorry.[46]

Like the Rastafari, Apess, and the Ghost Dance, Black Elk holds the West to the standard of God's justice and invokes God's judgment. Fools Crow demonstrates these same beliefs when he confronts colonialism in the 1970s:

> To avoid more tragic times than those that already beset us today, and to avoid economic disaster in the United States and the world, the government must purify its conscience by recognizing the 1868 treaty that was made with us in the name of God. Its provisions must be met. And there are incredibly bad times coming upon us, coming fast like an angry charging buffalo, because they have not been met, and because far too many people do not believe in God. Therefore, people do not understand that treaties made in His name are not to be violated. . . . If the white leaders do not follow the pathway set forth by God and that leads to Him, and if they do not chose to honor their promises, then the godly people will soon disappear, and the entire earth will need to be purified by a great catastrophe.[47]

Like Black Elk, Fools Crow bases his anti-colonial discourse on the real presence of the Christianized *Wakan Tanka*. God is greater then the power of Western colonialism and will judge its lies and destruction. The only way to avoid this judgment is repentance and restitution so that all may live in love as brothers and sisters under God.

## BLACK ELK'S VISION AND THE SALVATION OF ALL PEOPLE

Like the Rastafari, the Ghost Dance, and William Apess, both Black Elk and Fools Crow use the Christian narrative to provide an ethical framework to engulf and judge colonialism. The West will not escape the judgment and punishment of God. Black Elk claims even more. Not only did God have power over the West, God had given the power to Black Elk to administer his justice and

---

[46] DeMallie, *The Sixth Grandfather*, 289.

[47] Mails, *Fools Crow* (1979), 195. For Fools Crow's discussion of justice and his understanding of the apocalypse, see 195–97.

destroy the West. Not only would whites disappear, but Black Elk would be the destroyer. But given the power to destroy the West, Black Elk would not use it. Why did Black Elk spare the West, if he had the power to do exactly what the ghost dancers and colonized peoples across the world had been hoping for?

Black Elk experienced the defeat of the Lakota and their confinement to the reservation system. But Black Elk knew the West not only as an invading force, but also from being a part of it as he traveled for two years throughout America and Europe. He saw its vastness, and the incredible horrors of the Industrial Revolution. Black Elk described the new world in a letter from England: "Many of the ways the white men follow are hard to endure. Whoever has no country will die in the wilderness. And although the country is large it is always full of white men. Here the country is different; the days are all dark. It is always smoky so we never see the sun clearly."[48] So Black Elk knew not only the West's external shell of power, but he also saw the vulnerability and weakness that permeated the West and the millions of whites who also suffered at the hands of the West.

Because of his extensive travel, Black Elk's change in worldview led to a new recognition of the human condition. The Lakota were not the only ones who suffered at the hands of the West. Suffering was an immense reality that encompassed the West itself. In a letter in the *Catholic Herald,* July 15, 1909, Black Elk writes about his travels:

> I have seen a number of different people—the ordinary people living on this earth—the Arapaho, the Shoshone, the Omaha, the tribe living in California and Florida, the Rosebud, the Cheyenne River Sioux tribe, the Standing Rock, and our own, the Oglalas. The white men living in all these places—I have said prayers for their tribe. I'm really moved that I was able to travel to these places and meet people that are very friendly. In all these, good things come from God because of your faith. The United States—all the people—should have faith in God. We all suffer on this land. But let me tell you, God has a special place for us when our time has come.[49]

Black Elk's understanding of white men and Native Americans in this context is similar. They are friendly, and he has prayed for them. Most important, all people should have faith in God, because *all* suffer:

> Those of us here on earth who are suffering should help one another and have pity. We belong to one family and we have only one faith. Therefore, those who are suffering, my relatives, we should look toward them and

---

    [48]   Black Elk, Letter to *Iapi Oaye* (Santee Agency, Nebraska), 17/3 (March 1888), 9, trans. Raymond J. DeMallie in collaboration with Vine V. Deloria Sr., cited in DeMallie, *The Sixth Grandfather,* 9.
    [49]   Steltenkamp, *Black Elk,* 69.

pray for them, because our Savior came on this earth and helped all poor people.[50]

Suffering is not associated just with the defeat of the Lakota but is inherent to the human condition; all are united in their suffering, and all who suffer are the recipients of the Savior's help. In a letter to Lakota Catholics, a community still influenced by the theology of the Ghost Dance, Black Elk emphasizes the universal nature of suffering. He writes: "God did not come to the rich, but he came to the poor people. Not only Indians, but all of the poor people."[51] So according to Black Elk, Jesus came for all people, even the whites.

As noted in Chapter 5, love of neighbor was a biblical theme found in all of the Black Elk's sources as well as a theme he used to critique colonialism. The Great Spirit would judge the white man, because he did not return the love the Lakota showed for him. According to his daughter, Lucy, Black Elk used this theme in a speech to a white crowd to challenge colonialism. Christian love gave Black Elk the means to challenge the white world on its own terms, using its own language.

As it had for William Apess, love, for Black Elk, developed to include more than just a challenge to colonialism by providing a standard for holding the white world accountable to God's judgment. It provided Black Elk with the ability to recognize the humanity and equality of the white world. Trust in God provided Black Elk with the power to understand the new suffering world. It was a vision that not only applied to the Lakota but to all nations and the suffering that all people experience.

Black Elk's vision makes this clear. There are two points in his vision where white people are present. The first is the beginning of the third ascent, when conditions start to worsen for the nation. Black Elk says that despite the bad acts of the whites, the Great Spirit will judge them and hold them accountable for their actions. Immediately after, Christ comes and the church is established. After the final war of the fourth ascent, creation is renewed and all people are happy. Among the millions of faces, even whites appear.

So Jesus Christ makes room for the Lakota world in the chaos of the white world *and* makes room for the suffering white world in the Lakota story. Fools Crow supports this reading of Black Elk's understanding of Lakota tradition and Christianity:

[Black Elk thought] that we could pick up some of the Christian ways and teachings, and just work them in with our own, so in the end both would

---

[50] DeMallie, *The Sixth Grandfather,* 19. Part of a letter written by Black Elk to the *Catholic Herald* in July 1908.

[51] Black Elk, letter to friends and relatives written at Pine Ridge Reservation, Manderson, South Dakota, April 21, 1907, published in *Sinasapa Wocekiye Taeyanpaha,* June 15, 1907. Translated from Lakota to English under Michael F. Steltenkamp, S.J., in Timonin, *Black Elk's Synthesis*.

be better. Like myself, Black Elk prayed constantly that all people would live as one and would cooperate with one another. We have both loved the non-Indian races, and we do not turn our backs on them to please even those of our own people who do not agree.[52]

According to Fools Crow, it is the Christian teaching of universal love that was the new teaching Black Elk incorporated into Lakota tradition. And like Black Elk, Fools Crow believed that there was still hope for the West: "Although the 1868 treaty has been ruthlessly violated, many of the current and future problems of this country could be solved if the federal government made things right with us today, and made it possible at last for us to live as brothers under God."[53]

Black Elk fulfilled his role as a leader like the holy man in Leslie Marmon Silko's novel *Ceremony*. Black Elk did what Old Betonie told Tayo to do in a world dominated by colonialism: change in order to survive in a changing world. He was no different from the African Christians that Sanneh describes:

The old religions provided the rules, rewarding good conduct and punishing wrong, but they had only a limited ethical range: the family, the clan, the village, the tribe. . . . Christianity answered this historical challenge by a reorientation of the worldview so that the old moral framework was reconfigured without being overthrown. It was not that the old spells, turning benign from overuse, had dulled the appetite, but that, under challenge, their spent potency sparked a clamor for a valiant God. People sensed in their hearts that Jesus did not mock their respect for the sacred or their clamor for an invincible Savior, and so they beat their sacred drums for him until the stars skipped and danced in the skies. After that dance the stars weren't little anymore. Christianity helped Africans to become renewed Africans, not remade Europeans.[54]

## THE LAKOTA WORLD AND THE CHRISTIAN NARRATIVE

When asked why he joined a white church, Black Elk thought for a moment and replied: "Because my children have to live in this world."[55] This statement has been interpreted as a pragmatic response to the realities of reservation life; the "white church" provided a source of income and helped the Lakota to understand the white world. While this cannot be denied, it has also been interpreted to support the theory that Black Elk was not sincere or did not really believe Christianity. Despite evidence to the contrary, this interpretation presupposes

---

[52] Mails, *Fools Crow* (1979), 45.

[53] Ibid., 195.

[54] Lamin Sanneh, *Whose Religion Is Christianity? The Gospel beyond the West* (Grand Rapids, Mich.: Eerdmans, 2003), 43.

[55] Neihardt and Wise, "Black Elk and John G. Neihardt," 95.

that Black Elk was a passive subject, a member of a static culture, a "pure" Native American "other" who could not possibly be attracted to any new cultural influence.

But if he did in fact live like the fictional Old Betonie as an active agent of a dynamic culture, fighting for survival, the evidence indicates that Black Elk accepted that the West and colonialism were real and here to stay. Participation in the church was not a show but rather provided him as a holy man with new power to help the Lakota live in the new world. Although the colonizing West reordered the world through violence, greed, and the creation of myths of racial inferiority, it was precisely Black Elk's Catholic innovations to Lakota tradition that allowed him, in turn, to reorder the West. The powers of the all-powerful Christian *Wankan Tanka* would judge and punish the West, and the powers of the Messiah's universal love and forgiveness for all of the suffering world would overcome the West's story of violence, greed, and racism.

If, among the spectrum of white responses to American colonialism, missionaries, and most particularly the Jesuits, were most able to transcend white prejudice, interact with the Lakota on an equal basis, vocally challenge American colonialism, and mitigate the physical suffering inflicted by American colonialism, it was because these same anti-colonial themes demonstrated by the Rastafarians and William Apess were at least partially embodied in the church. More than any other group, the church offered principles of economic sharing and nonviolence. It offered a story of equality between colonized and colonizer and relationships that suggested equality and even love. And most surprising, it created the opportunity for cultural pluralism in practices built on unique Lakota cultural patterns.

There were also tragic aspects of the missionary presence. Its inability to relinquish power over theological interpretation, its inability to escape completely its relationship with colonialism, and its continuing participation in educational programs that eroded a functioning Lakota language and contributed to the advancing American secular culture —all of these prevented an integral Lakota Catholic Church.

Postcolonial interpretations give modern interpreters a new lens with which to see why Black Elk remained an active Catholic and a participant in Lakota ceremonial life despite the shortcomings of the church. Lakota ceremonies did not cease to be relevant to the sacred hoop of his people. Black Elk realized that the new world was here to stay, but the Lakota still had meaning as a people. Lakota religion still interceded with *Wakan Tanka* and helped the Lakota get back into the sacred hoop. Black Elk's long formation in Lakota tradition validated its power. Like Sword, Black Elk embraced the Christian *Wankan Tanka* because he was stronger. *Wanka Tanka* was not stronger because the Christian *Wankan Tanka* defeated the Lakota *Wankan Tanka* in battle. It was the same *Wakan Tanka*, transformed and stronger than the West.

This postcolonialist interpretation also helps us understand Black Elk's vision. It explains why he broke with Lakota tradition and told his vision to an outsider from the West: Black Elk felt it was the West that needed to hear of his vision of the Lakota Christ, teaching the world the oneness of all people and the beauty of the Lakota place in it.

> Then the LORD answered me and said:
>    Write down the vision
> Clearly upon the tablets,
>    so that one can read it readily.
> For the vision still has its time,
>    presses on to fulfillment, and will not disappoint.
>                                      (Hb 2:2–3)

The vision of mine ought to go out, I feel, but somehow I couldn't get anyone to do it. I would think about it and get sad. I wanted the world to know about it. It seems that your ghostly brother has sent you here to do this for me. You are here and have the vision just the way I wanted, and then the tree will bloom again and the people will know the true facts. We want the tree to bloom again in the world of true that doesn't judge.[56]

Like the prophet Habakkuk and the visionary John, Black Elk declared that the sacred vision would go out, so that the tree would bloom in a world of truth, justice, and love.

---

[56] DeMallie, *The Sixth Grandfather*, 43.

# Conclusion

This book has focused on the central question of the Black Elk debate: which was the real Black Elk—the essentialist Black Elk or the Lakota Catholic Black Elk? Members of the Lakota community have long described the Lakota Catholic Black Elk as the real Black Elk, and this book has laid out the conceptual categories involved in this portrayal and the framework that supports them. In addition, it is relatively easy to understand why an essentialist Black Elk came into being and why it is an inaccurate portrayal. But in establishing those points, it is important not to let the story end there, because the content of Black Elk's Catholicism is the most powerful aspect of the debate.

After all, something much greater than historical accuracy is at stake in the Black Elk story. As the preceding chapters have demonstrated, Black Elk's Catholicism was more than just a matter of personal religion: indeed, it was a profound response to the brutality of colonialism. In other words, this small story from a seemingly insignificant corner of the world is part of the very big story of Western colonialism and its impact on the world.

By the time John G. Neihardt arrived in South Dakota, the nations of the West had conquered the entire world through the use of violence. The Lakota were only one of hundreds of nations whose economies were destroyed and whose cultural patterns were disrupted by Western greed. And, of course, the violence of poverty and disease continued long after the actual wars had ended. By 1930 the Western nations had reordered the Lakota and many other nations, becoming the conquerors of the world.

However, as a Lakota Catholic, Black Elk challenged this story. As Chapter 7 demonstrated, faced with the West's reordering of the Lakota and the apparent failure of the church to live out the teachings of the gospel of Jesus, Black Elk did not remain a passive victim of the colonial world. He became an active agent against it as a holy man in continuity with Lakota traditions, but one who embraced new ways in order to adapt to new situations. The form of his agency was his conversion to Catholicism. Through his Catholicism, Black Elk countered the influence of the Western conquest. Like the Rastafari of Jamaica and participants in the Ghost Dance, Black Elk used a much bigger moral story to accuse the West. Jesus Christ, king of the universe, he maintained, would judge the West for its sins of colonialism and redeem the Lakota. Black Elk called the West to repentance, as did the Pequot William Apess, extending the salvation of Christ to all peoples, even the colonizers, for the redemption of all creation.

179

This would not have been possible for an essentialist Black Elk. If Black Elk had not been influenced by Catholicism, he would not have had the resources to address the West's reordering of the Lakota world. By protecting Lakota cultural purity, a concept imagined by the outsider, an essentialist Black Elk would have been left with nothing more than the tragedy of a colonial victory. Black Elk would have been remembered as a tragic figure to be mourned, a solitary old victim alone on a mountaintop, lamenting his powerlessness and the death of his people.

Ironically, Black Elk turned the debate on its head. Having taken on the Western story of the Messiah, Black Elk issued a challenge to the West. Black Elk and the conquered nations of the world judged the cultural purity of the West and the sincerity of its Christianity by its implementation of the gospel message. The Lakota Catholic Black Elk clearly found Western Christianity wanting. According to Black Elk, the West had rejected love in its rush for colonial expansion: "Christ himself preached that we love our neighbor as ourself. . . . You came to this country, which was ours in the first place. . . . But you're not doing what you're supposed to."[1] The narrative of his youth is one long account of the violence of American expansion, culminating in the massacre of Wounded Knee. According to Black Elk, "The white man has taken our world from us."[2] Colonialism was theft, and this sin was nothing less than satanic: "The whites think we have the power from the devil, but I'll say that they probably have that themselves."[3] For Black Elk, the story of the colonized world was not merely a lamentable tragedy, but it was also the tragedy of the West's rejection of the Messiah.

Even though Jesuit missionaries working with the Lakota challenged the story of colonialism, Western Christianity did not escape complicity. In the words of Lamin Sanneh, "The Modern West has demanded a retreat from any real and meaningful adherence to the central claims of historic Christianity."[4] Western Christianity had domesticated the Messiah to accommodate colonialism. Through his vision Black Elk called Western Christianity back to central claims of the gospel—nonviolence, the rejection of greed, and the equality of all human persons—and the rejection of colonialism. The Lakota Catholic Black Elk preached the newly incarnated Christ to a church that had forgotten the difficult message of the Messiah.

Even now the bigger story of colonialism continues. Today the Lakota continue to live in the same poverty as other colonized peoples of the Third World.[5]

---

[1] Michael F. Steltenkamp, *Black Elk: Holy Man of the Oglala* (Norman: University of Oklahoma Press, 1993), 67–68.

[2] Raymond J. DeMallie, *The Sixth Grandfather: Black Elk's Teachings Given to John G. Neihardt* (Lincoln: University of Nebraska Press, 1984), 265.

[3] Ibid., 289.

[4] Lamin Sanneh, "Vincent Donovan's Discovery of Post-Western Christianity," in Vincent J. Donovan, *Christianity Rediscovered,* 25th anniv. ed. (Maryknoll, N.Y.: Orbis Books, 2003), 155.

[5] Pine Ridge Reservation has an unemployment rate of 85 percent, and the life expectancy for males is 57.2 years and for females 61.9 years. In the general U.S. population

The rejection of Christianity by many contemporary Native Americans is far from unwarranted, for they live in a world created by those who have emptied the gospel of its meaning. As Black Elk taught, the reservations and broken economic systems of contemporary Native America are nothing more than the embodiment of the ongoing rejection of fundamental Christian teachings by those who claim to be Christian. Consequently, those formerly Christian Native Americans who have given up on the gospel have done so at least in part because they have learned that the Christian West has not truly heard the gospel message.

Black Elk's explicit condemnation of the West and of the failure of Western Christianity leaves challenges unmet and questions unanswered. But for Black Elk, condemnation was not the final word. Black Elk preached a love that called him to chastise his conquerors while he embraced them as sisters and brothers. He told the Lakota that "God did not come to the rich, but he came to the poor people. Not only Indians, but all poor people."[6] He told Neihardt that while at first he was not sure, he did see white people in the promised land of his vision. Despite the West's rejection of Christ and the brokenness of the world, Black Elk was confident in God's salvation, and he taught this hope to all people. Fellow Lakota catechist John Lone Goose remembered that Black Elk "taught the name of Christ to Indians who didn't know it. The old people, the young people, the mixed blood, even the white men."[7] For Black Elk, no one was beyond the mercy of Christ, The One Who Makes Live. To the end, Black Elk called the West away from the power of the devil, back to the life given by the Messiah. This is why Black Elk wanted to go to Harney Peak to preach his vision of the Lakota Christ to the world. Black Elk explained:

I am telling you this, Mr. Neihardt. You know how I felt and what I really wanted to do is for us to make the tree bloom. On this tree we shall prosper. Therefore my children and yours are relative-like and therefore we shall go back in the hoop and here we'll cooperate and stand as one. This is why I want to go to Harney Peak, because here I shall send the voices to the six grandfathers and maybe it will be that Mr. Neihardt['s] and my family will be the happy faces. Our families will multiply and prosper after we get this tree blooming.[8]

---

the unemployment rate in 2002 was 5.8 percent; life expectancy for males is 75 years and for females 80 years. The country with the highest rate of unemployment in the world is Zimbabwe, with 70 percent unemployment (see the Red Cloud School website and the *CIA World Factbook* [December 2003], both available online).

[6] Black Elk, letter to friends and relatives written at Pine Ridge Reservation, Manderson, South Dakota, April 21, 1907, published in *Sinasapa Wocekiye Taeyanpaha,* June 15, 1907. Translated from Lakota to English under Michael F. Steltenkamp, S.J., in Ivan M. Timonin, *Black Elk's Synthesis: Catholic Theology and Oglala Tradition in The Sacred Pipe,* dissertation proposal.

[7] Steltenkamp, *Black Elk*, 54.

[8] DeMallie, *The Sixth Grandfather*, 294.

On Harney Peak, Black Elk taught Neihardt the message of the Lakota Christ and prayed that all peoples in colonial America, "all who suffer in this land," would live in peace and prosperity in communion, in hope of *Wakan Tanka*'s mercy. He felt there was still time for the West to provide new evidence of the sincerity of its Christian heritage.

Even today Black Elk's vision has a message that needs to be heard. Black Elk teaches us that the problem of Western expansion was not in bringing the gospel to the Lakota; instead, the problem was not hearing the gospel. The focus on nonviolence, equality, and the rejection of greed—the firm rejection of colonialism—is the witness that Black Elk's vision preached and still preaches to Western Christianity, to the church, and to the broken world. Despite the tragedy of Western colonialism, there is still hope, there is still time to hear and respond to the gospel. Black Elk, a great saint of the colonial era, still calls all people through his vision and the witness of his life to hear the Lakota Christ: colonialism must end so the sacred tree may one day bloom for all people.

# Bibliography

Apess, William. "Eulogy on King Philip." In *On Our Own Ground: The Complete Writings of William Apess, A Pequot,* edited by Barry O'Connell. 1936. Reprint, Amherst: University of Massachusetts Press, 1992.

———. "The Increase of the Kingdom of Christ." Originally published in 1931. In *On Our Own Ground: The Complete Writings of William Apess, A Pequot,* edited by Barry O'Connell, 101-12. Amherst: University of Massachusetts Press, 1992.

———. *On Our Own Ground: The Complete Writings of William Apess, a Pequot.* Edited by Barry O'Connell. Amherst: University of Massachusetts Press, 1992. Originally published in 1829.

———. "A Son of the Forest: The Experience of William Apess, a Native of the Forest." In *On Our Own Ground: The Complete Writings of William Apess, A Pequot,* edited by Barry O'Connell, 3-97. Amherst: University of Massachusetts Press, 1992.

Archambault, Marie Therese, ed. "Ben Black Bear, Jr.: A Lakota Deacon and a 'Radical Catholic' Tells His Own Story." *U.S. Catholic Historian* 16/2: 90-106.

Archambault, Marie Therese, Mark G. Thiel, and Christopher Vecsey, eds. *The Crossing of Two Roads: Being Catholic and Native in the United States.* Maryknoll, N.Y.: Orbis Books, 2003.

Bataillie, Gretchen M., ed. *Native American Representations: First Encounters, Distorted Images, and Literary Appropriations.* Lincoln: University of Nebraska Press, 2001.

Born, David O. "Black Elk and the Duhamel Sioux Indian Pageant." *North Dakota History* 61 (1994): 22-29.

Briggs, Charles L., and Richard Bauman. "'The Foundation of All Future Researches': Franz Boas, George Hunt, Native American Texts, and the Construction of Modernity." *American Quarterly* 51/3 (September 1999): 479-528.

Brown, Joseph Epes. *The Sacred Pipe: Black Elk's Account of the Seven Rites of the Oglala Sioux.* 1953. Reprint, Norman: University of Oklahoma Press, 1989.

Buechel, Eugene, S.J. *A Dictionary of the Teton Sioux Language.* Edited by Paul Manhart, S.J. Pine Ridge, S.D.: Red Cloud Indian School, 1970.

———. *Wowapi Wakan, Wicowoyake Yeptecelapi: Bible History in the Language of the Teton Sioux Indians.* Edited by Paul Manhart. New York: Benzinger Brothers, 1924.

Deloria, Philip J. *Playing Indian.* New Haven, Conn.: Yale University Press, 1998.

Deloria, Vine, Jr. "Introduction." In *Black Elk Speaks,* edited by John G. Neihardt. Lincoln: University of Nebraska Press, 1979.

Deloria, Vine, Jr., ed. *A Sender of Words: Essays in Memory of John G. Neihardt.* Salt Lake City, Utah: Howe Brothers, 1984.

DeMallie, Raymond J. "John G. Neihardt's Lakota Legacy." In *A Sender of Words: Essays in Memory of John G. Neihardt*, edited by Vine Deloria Jr. Salt Lake City, Utah: Howe Brothers, 1984.

———. "Pine Ridge Economy: Cultural and Historical Perspectives." In *American Indian Economic Development*, edited by Sam Stanley, 237-312. Paris: Mouton Publishers, 1978.

DeMallie, Raymond J., ed. *The Sixth Grandfather: Black Elk's Teachings Given to John G. Neihardt*. Lincoln: University of Nebraska Press, 1984.

DeSersa, Esther Black Elk, and Olivia Black Elk Pourier. *Black Elk Lives: Conversations with the Black Elk Family*. Edited by Hilda Neihardt and Lori Utecht. Lincoln: University of Nebraska Press, 2000.

Diamond, Jared. *Guns, Germs, and Steel: The Fates of Human Societies*. New York, W. W. Norton & Company, 1999, 1997.

Duratschek, Sister Mary Claudia, O.S.B. *Crusading along Sioux Trails*. St. Meinrad, Ind.: The Grail Press, 1947.

Edmonds, Ennis Barrington. *Rastafari: From Outcast to Culture Bearers*. Oxford: Oxford University Press, 2003.

Edmunds, R. David, ed. *The New Warriors: Native American Leaders since 1900*. Lincoln: University of Nebraska Press, 2001.

Enochs, Ross Alexander. "Black Elk and the Jesuits." In *The Black Elk Reader*, edited by Clyde Holler, 282-301. Syracuse, N.Y.: Syracuse University Press, 2000.

———. *The Jesuit Mission to the Lakota Sioux: Pastoral Theology and Ministry, 1886-1945*. Kansas City, Mo.: Sheed & Ward, 1996.

Feraca, Stephen E. *Wakinyan: Lakota Religion in the Twentieth Century*. Lincoln: University of Nebraska Press, 1998.

Foley, Thomas W. *Father Francis M. Craft: Missionary to the Sioux*. Lincoln: University of Nebraska Press, 2002.

Frazier, Ian. *On the Rez*. New York: Farrar, Straus & Giroux, 2000.

Gans, Herbert J. "Symbolic Ethnicity: The Future of Ethnic Groups and Cultures in America." In *Theories of Ethnicity: A Classical Reader*, edited by Werner Sollors. New York: New York University Press, 1996.

Garroutte, Eva Garroutte. *Real Indians: Identity and the Survival of Native America*. Berkeley and Los Angeles: University of California Press, 2003.

Glissant, Edouard. "The Known, the Uncertain." In *Caribbean Discourse: Selected Essays,* translated by J. Michael Dash, 13-95. Charlottesville: University of Virginia Press, 1989.

Grobsmith, Elizabeth S. *Lakota of the Rosebud: A Contemporary Ethnography*. New York: Holt, Rinehart & Winston, 1981.

Handler, Richard. "Boasian Anthropology and the Critique of American Culture. *American Quarterly* 42/2 (June 1990): 252-73.

Hirschfelder, Arlene, and Paulette Mouline, eds. *Encyclopedia of Native American Religions*. New York: Facts on File, Inc., 2000.

Holler, Clyde. "Black Elk's Relationship to Christianity." *American Indian Quarterly* 8/1 (Winter 1984): 37-49.

———. *Black Elk's Religion: The Sun Dance and Lakota Catholicism*. Syracuse, N.Y.: Syracuse University Press, 1995.

Holler, Clyde, ed. *The Black Elk Reader*. Syracuse, N.Y.: Syracuse University Press, 2000.

Holloway, Brian. *Interpreting the Legacy: John Neihardt and Black Elk Speaks*. Boulder: University of Colorado Press, 2003.

Hoxie, Frederick E., ed. "Black Elk," *Encyclopedia of North American Indians*. New York: Houghton Mifflin, 1996.

Kaye, Frances W. "Just What Is Cultural Appropriation, Anyway?" In *The Black Elk Reader*, edited by Clyde Holler, 147-68. Syracuse, N.Y.: Syracuse University Press, 2000.

Killoren, John J., S.J., *"Come Blackrobe": De Smet and the Indian Tragedy*. Norman: University of Oklahoma, 1994.

MacCannell, Dean. "Reconstructed Ethnicity: Tourism and Cultural Identity in Third World Communities." *Annals of Tourism Research* 11 (1980): 375-91.

MacGregor, Gordon. *Warriors without Weapons*. Chicago: University of Chicago Press, 1946.

Mails, Thomas E. *Fools Crow*. With Dallas Chief Eagle. New York: Doubleday, 1979.

———. *Fools Crow: Wisdom and Power*. Tulsa, Okla.: Council Oak Books, 1991.

———. *Sundancing at Rosebud and Pine Ridge*. Sioux Falls, S.D.: Center for Western Studies, 1978.

Means, Russell. "For the World to Live, 'Europe' Must Die." *Mother Jones*. September 1980.

Means, Russell, with Marvin J. Wolf. *Where White Men Fear to Tread: The Autobiography of Russell Means*. New York: St. Martin's Press, 1995.

Medicine, Bea. "Native American Resistance to Integration: Contemporary Confrontations and Religious Revitalization." *Plains Anthropologist* 26 (1981): 277-86.

Matthiessen, Peter. *In the Spirit of Crazy Horse*. New York: Viking Press, 1983.

Murrell, Nathaniel S. "Wresting the Message from the Messenger: The Rastafari as a Case Study in the Caribbean Indigenization of the Bible." In *African Americans and the Bible: Sacred Texts and Social Textures*, edited by Vincent L. Wimbush, 558-76. New York: Continuum, 2000.

Neihardt, Hilda. *Black Elk and Flaming Rainbow: Personal Memories of the Lakota Holy Man and John Neihardt*. Lincoln: University of Nebraska Press, 1995.

Neihardt, Hilda, and R. Todd Wise. "Black Elk and John G. Neihardt." In *The Black Elk Reader*, edited by Clyde Holler, 87-103. Syracuse, N.Y.: Syracuse University Press, 2000.

Neihardt, John G. *Black Elk Speaks: Being the Life Story of a Holy Man of the Oglala Sioux / as Told to John G. Neihardt (Flaming Rainbow)*. Illustrated by Standing Bear. 1932. Reprint, Lincoln: University of Nebraska Press, 1979, 2000.

———. *A Cycle of the West: The Song of Three Friends, the Song of Hugh Glass, the Song of Jed Smith, the Song of the Indian Wars, the Song of the Messiah*. Fiftieth anniv. ed. Lincoln: University of Nebraska Press, 2002.

O'Connell, Barry, ed. *On Our Own Ground: The Complete Writings of William Apess, A Pequot*. Amherst, Mass.: University of Massachusetts Press, 1992.

Ong, Walter J., S.J. *Orality and Literacy: The Technologizing of the Word*. New York: Methuen, 1982.

Owens, Louis. "As If an Indian Were Really an Indian: Native American Voices and Postcolonial Theory." In *Native American Representations: First Encounters, Distorted Images, and Literary Appropriations*, edited by Gretchen M. Bataille, 11-24. Lincoln: University of Nebraska Press, 2001.

Paper, Jordan D. "The Sacred Pipe: The Historical Context of Contemporary Pan-Indian Religion." *Journal of the American Academy of Religion* 56, 4 (xx): 643-65.

Philip, Kenneth R. *John Collier's Crusade for Indian Reform, 1920-1954*. Tucson: University of Arizona Press, 1977.

Pickering, Kathleen Ann. *Lakota Culture, World Economy*. Lincoln: University of Ne-
	braska Press, 2000.
Porterfield, Amanda. "Black Elk's Significance in American Culture." In *The Black Elk
	Reader*, edited by Clyde Holler, 39-58. Syracuse, N.Y.: Syracuse University
	Press, 2000.
Powers, William K. *Beyond the Vision: Essays on American Indian Culture*. Norman:
	University of Oklahoma Press, 1987.
———. "Dual Religious Participation: Stratagems of Conversion among the Lakota."
	In *Beyond the Vision: Essays on American Indian Culture*, edited by William
	K. Powers. Norman: University of Oklahoma Press, 1987.
———. *Oglala Religion*. Lincoln: University of Nebraska Press, 1977.
———. *Sacred Language: The Nature of Supernatural Discourse in Lakota*. Norman:
	University of Oklahoma Press, 1986.
———. "When Black Elk Speaks, Everybody Listens." In *Religion and American Cul-
	ture*, edited by David G. Hackett, 425-35. New York: Routledge, 1995.
Rice, Julian. *Before the Great Spirit: The Many Faces of Sioux Spirituality*. Albuquer-
	que: University of New Mexico Press, 1998.
———. *Black Elk's Story: Distinguishing Its Lakota Purpose*. Albuquerque: University
	of New Mexico Press, 1991.
Riggs, Stephen R. *A Dakota-English Dictionary*. Edited by James Owen Dorsey. St.
	Paul: Minnesota Historical Society Press, 1992.
Sanneh, Lamin. *Encountering the West: Christianity and the Global Cultural Process*.
	Maryknoll, N.Y.: Orbis Books, 1993.
———. *Translating the Message: The Missionary Impact on Culture*. Maryknoll, N.Y.:
	Orbis Books, 1989.
———. "Vincent Donovan's Discovery of Post-Western Christianity." In Vincent J.
	Donovan, *Christianity Rediscovered*. Twenty-fifth anniv. ed. Maryknoll, N.Y.:
	Orbis Books, 2003.
———. *Whose Religion Is Christianity? The Gospel beyond the West*. Grand Rapids,
	Mich.: Eerdmans, 2003.
Silko, Leslie Marmon. *Ceremony*. New York: Penguin Books, 1977.
Spider, Emerson, Sr. "The Native American Church of Jesus Christ." In *Sioux Indian
	Religion: Tradition and Innovation*, ed. Raymond J. DeMallie and Douglas R.
	Parks, 189-209. Norman: University of Oklahoma Press, 1987.
Starn, O. "Missing the Revolution: Anthropologists and the War in Peru." In *Rereading
	Cultural Anthropology*, edited by G. E. Marcus, 152-80. Durham: Duke Uni-
	versity Press, 1992.
Steinmetz, Paul B., S.J. *Pipe, Bible, and Peyote among the Oglala Lakota: A Study in
	Religious Identity*. Rev. ed. Knoxville: University of Tennessee Press, 1990.
Steltenkamp, Michael F., S.J. *Black Elk: Holy Man of the Oglala*. Norman: University
	of Oklahoma Press, 1993.
———. "Contemporary American Indian Religious Thinking and Its Relationship to
	the Christianity of Black Elk, Holy Man of the Oglala." In *American Catholic
	Traditions: Resources for Renewal*, edited by Sandra Yocum Mize and Will-
	iam Portier, 29-52. Maryknoll, N.Y.: Orbis Books, 1997.
———. "A Retrospective on Black Elk: Holy Man of the Oglala." In *The Black Elk
	Reader*, edited by Clyde Holler, 104-26. Syracuse: Syracuse University Press,
	2000.
Stolzman, William, S.J. *The Pipe and Christ: A Christian-Sioux Dialogue*. Chamber-
	lain, S.D.: Tipi Press, 1995.

Stover, Dale. "A Post Colonial Reading of Black Elk." In *The Black Elk Reader*, edited by Clyde Holler, 127-46. Syracuse, N.Y.: Syracuse University Press, 2000.

Sugirtharajah, R.S. *The Bible and the Third World: Precolonial, Colonial and Postcolonial Encounters*. Cambridge: University of Cambridge Press, 2001.

———. *Postcolonial Criticism and Biblical Interpretation*. Oxford, New York: Oxford University Press, 2002.

Taylor, Patrick. "Sheba's Song: The Bible, the *Kebra Nagast*, and the *Rastafari*." In *Nation Dance: Religion, Identity, and Cultural Difference in the Caribbean*, edited by Patrick Taylor, 65-78. Bloomington: Indiana University Press, 2001.

Thiel, Mark G. "Catholic Sodalities among the Sioux, 1882-1910." *U.S. Catholic Historian* 16, no. 2 (Spring 1998): 56-77.

Timonin, Ivan M. *Black Elk's Synthesis: Catholic Theology and Oglala Tradition in The Sacred Pipe*. Dissertation proposal.

Tinker, George E. *Missionary Conquest: The Gospel and Native American Cultural Genocide*. Minneapolis: Fortress Press, 1993.

Vecsey, Christopher. "A Century of Lakota Sioux Catholicism at Pine Ridge." In *Religious Diversity and American Religious History: Studies in Traditions and Cultures*, edited by Walter H. Conser Jr. and Sumner B. Twiss, 262-95. Athens: University of Georgia Press, 1997.

———. *The Paths of Kateri's Kindred*. Notre Dame, Ind.: University of Notre Dame Press, 1997.

Vernon, Irene S. "The Claiming of Christ: Native American Postcolonial Discourses," *Melus* (Summer 1999): 1-13. Available online.

Walker, James R. *Lakota Belief and Ritual*. Edited by Raymond J. DeMallie and Elaine A. Jahner. 1980. Reprint, Lincoln: University of Nebraska Press, 1991.

———. *Lakota Myth*. Edited by Elaine A. Jahner. 1983. Reprint, Lincoln: University of Nebraska Press, 1989.

Williamson, Tomas S., and Stephen R. Riggs, trans. *Dakota Wowapi Wakan: The Holy Bible in the Language of the Dakotas*. New York: American Bible Society, 1880.

Wilson, Raymond. "Russell Means: Lakota." In *The New Warriors: Native American Leaders since 1900*, edited by R. David Edmunds. Lincoln: University of Nebraska Press, 2001.

# Index

# Also in the Faith and Cultures Series

*Of Related Interest*

## The Crossing of Two Roads
*Being Catholic and Native in the United States*
Marie Therese Archambault, Mark G. Thiel, and
Christopher Vecsey, editors
ISBN 1-57075-352-0

"Scholars and interested readers will find this readable collection
invaluable for its presentation of diverse Native, clerical, and informed
voices on a range of topics...."
—*John A. Grim, Bucknell University*

## Translating the Message
*The Missionary Impact on Culture*
Lamin Sanneh
"This daring and far-reaching book marks a turning point.... It shifts
the whole focus away from what the missionaries themselves were
doing and places the true agency where it belongs—among the
receivers who not only heard but transformed and deepened the
message in ways that often surprised and shocked the missionaries."
—*Harvey Cox, Harvard Divinity School*

Please support your local bookstore or call 1-800-258-5838.
For a free catalog, please write us at
Orbis Books, Box 308
Maryknoll, NY 10545-0308
or visit our website at www.orbisbooks.com

Thank you for reading *Black Elk: Colonialism and Lakota Catholicism*.
We hope you profited from it.